# The Streets of Liverpool

By
James Stonehouse

The City of Liverpool

First published 1869

This edition specially produced by
Cedric Chivers Limited, Bristol
for the publisher
Liverpool Libraries and Information Services
William Brown Street, Liverpool L3 8EW
2002

ISBN 0 902990 21 7

Printed in Great Britain by Antony Rowe Ltd.
Chippenham, Wilts.

# FOREWORD

I am very pleased that Liverpool Libraries and Information Services has reproduced this book on the history of Liverpool. It is the second in a series of reprints in the build-up to the 800$^{th}$ anniversary of Liverpool in 2007.

James Stonehouse wrote this book which was published in 1869. He came to Liverpool from London in 1832. He was a keen local antiquarian and contributed articles to *The Liverpool Courier*, the *Liverpool Standard* and *The Chester Chronicle.* He was an original member of the Historic Society of Lancashire and Cheshire, appearing in the first list of members dated 23 November 1848. He read papers before the Society and these were printed in the *Transactions of the Historic Society of Lancashire and Cheshire.* He prepared a paper on Joseph Williamson, but did not deliver it because of a threat of legal action by the artist Cornelius Henderson, who had married Williamson's housekeeper. The paper finally appeared in Volume 68 for 1916 in an article by Charles Hand on "The King of Edge Hill."

He wrote the text of a guidebook entitled *Stranger in Liverpool* (1845 edition). As well as writing *The Streets of Liverpool,* he wrote *Recollections of Old Liverpool by a Nonagenarian.* This first appeared in the *Liverpool Compass* and was subsequently published in book form in 1863. As an article on Stonehouse in the *Evening Express* of 26 September 1921 stated the two books "throw on to a reader's mental screen a graphic film of Liverpool as it was, and focus his verbal pictures fascinatingly."

James Stonehouse died at Neston on 8 May 1890. His obituary in *The Liverpool Courier* on 9 May 1890 describes him as "filling the role of a local oracle, and gladly giving reminiscences of old Liverpool and old Wirral too, for the entertainment of interested listeners." He had made his living since 1843 as an employee of Liverpool Corporation. He was for a long time Manager of St John's Market. He also wrote poems, stories, plays and operas, such as *Mr Trotshaw's troubles: a boarding house story, Telemachus: a burlesque*, and *Nestonian Lyrics.*

The papers of James Stonehouse are held at Liverpool Record Office in Liverpool Central Library, William Brown Street (collection reference 942 STO). They include correspondence, notes, lectures, stories, plays and poems.

Illustrations have been added to the original edition from the extensive collections of Liverpool Record Office and Local Studies.

An index has been compiled by Eve Cant, a member of the Society of Indexers.

I would like to thank all of the staff of Liverpool Record Office for their hard work in seeing this reprint through and in particular David Stoker, Manager, Kay Parrott, Team Leader, and Janice Utting, Library and Information Assistant, for their research, administration, marketing and promotion. Thanks are also due to Eileen Organ, a former member of staff, for her picture research and help with proof-reading.

I am sure that you will enjoy this book and find the information useful.

Councillor Warren Bradley
Executive Member for Leisure, Culture and Tourism

October 2002

## Illustrations added to the 2002 edition

Front cover: Port of Liverpool. View from George's Dock Basin. Coloured lithograph by F. Courtin after Chapuy. c.1854.
Binns Collection C131A.

### Colour illustrations

1. Goree Piazzas and George's Dock Quay. 1860.
   Watercolour by J. Barter.
   Barter Collection 50.

2. Mason Street, Edge Hill, west side showing the entrance to excavations made by Joseph Williamson. 1858.
   Watercolour by W. Herdman.
   Herdman Collection 486.

3. River Mersey, showing the hulks off Rock Ferry. 1840.
   Watercolour by A. Hunt.
   Hunt Collection 13.

4. London Road, showing Windmill Inn. 1865.
   Watercolour by J. McGahey.
   Herdman Collection 1387.

5. Alexandra Theatre, Lime Street, later the first Empire Theatre, demolished in 1924. 1870.
   Watercolour W. Herdman.
   Herdman Collection B1115.

### Black and white illustrations

1. Map of Liverpool in 1859, produced for British Medical Association meeting July 1859.
   Photographs and Small Prints Collection.

2. Chapel Street, south side from the Old Sessions House (demolished 1865) to St. Nicholas Church. 1865.
Watercolour by W. Herdman.
Herdman Collection 1186.

3. Water Street, looking eastwards from Prison Weint. 1860.
Watercolour by W. Herdman.
Herdman Collection 895.

4. Oldhall Street, east side showing Albany Buildings, between George Street and Ormond Street. 1866.
Watercolour by W. Herdman.
Herdman Collection 496.

5. Tithebarn Street, north side from Silkhouse Lane westwards, showing part of the south side of Chapel Street. 1856.
Watercolour by W. Herdman.
Herdman Collection 348.

6. Dale Street, general view from the Town Hall. 1790.
Watercolour by J.I. and W. Herdman.
Herdman Collection 1113.

7. Dale Street, south side from Davies Street eastwards, showing the Municipal Buildings under construction. 1865.
Watercolour by W. Herdman.
Herdman Collection 1152.

8. Scotland Road, east side from Rose Place looking towards Scotland Place. 1869.
Watercolour by W. Herdman.
Herdman Collection 105.

9. Castle Street, east side between Union Street and St. George's Crescent. 1862.
Watercolour by W. Herdman.
Herdman Collection 704.

10. Castle Street, looking towards the Town Hall and showing the widening of the street on the west side. 1786.
Watercolour by W. Herdman.
Herdman Collection B1267.

11. Lord Street, north side from Doran's Lane to Whitechapel. 1867.
Watercolour by J. Innes Herdman.
Herdman Collection 1296.

12. Lord Street, south side, showing some of the seventeenth and eighteenth century houses. 1810.
Watercolour by W. Herdman.
Herdman Collection 580.

13. Church Street, south side showing St. Peter's Church and portion between Church Lane and Paradise Street. 1867.
Watercolour by W. Herdman.
Herdman Collection 1295.

14. Bold Street, north east side. 1856.
Watercolour by W. Herdman.
Herdman Collection 1265.

15. Ranelagh Street, south side from Lawton Street to Ranelagh Place, showing construction of Central Station. 1872.
Watercolour by W. Herdman.
Herdman Collection 1148.

16. Lime Street, west side, showing St. John's Church in c.1835.
Watercolour by E. Beattie. 1878.
Beattie Collection 335.

17. London Road, showing Gallows Mill in 1733.
Watercolour by S.Herdman.
Herdman Collection 1331.

18. Shaw's Brow (later William Brown Street), north side from Mill Place to Mill Lane. 1854.
Sepia painting by W. P. Herdman.
Herdman Collection 660.

19. William Brown Street and Byrom Street, east side showing St.Stephen's Church, high level plateau, Wellington Monument and part of St.George's Hall. 1870.
Watercolour by J. Innes Herdman.
Herdman Collection 1142.

20. Brunswick Road, from Greenside to Shaw Street. 1869.
Watercolour by W. Herdman.
Herdman Collection 344.

21. West Derby Road at junction with Low Hill, Brunswick Road and Everton Road, showing the entrance to the Necropolis Cemetery. 1867.
Watercolour by W. Herdman.
Herdman Collection 15.

22. Pembroke Place, between Gill Street and Pembroke Street. 1862.
Watercolour by W. Herdman.
Herdman Collection 169.

23. Seymour Street looking west from London Road, showing St. Vincent Street. 1870.
Watercolour by W. Herdman.
Herdman Collection 891.

24. Judge's House at the corner of St. Anne Street and Mansfield Street. Undated.
Watercolour by W. Herdman.
Herdman Collection 19.

25. St.Thomas' Church, Park Lane, south view. 1855.
Watercolour by W. Herdman.
Herdman Collection 498.

26. Liverpool from the slipway of Birkenhead Ferry, showing (from the left) the dome of St. Paul's Church, St. Nicholas' Church, the Pier Head Baths, the Town Hall and the spire of St. George's Church, Derby Square. c.1830.
Lithograph by Crane, after R. Barrow.
Photographs and Small Prints Collection.

27. Everton Village. 1828.
Hand coloured lithograph by W.G.Herdman.
Local Illustrations Collection 74.

28. Everton Brow, north side looking west towards Everton Crescent. 1860.
Watercolour by W.Herdman.
Herdman Collection 418.

# THE

# STREETS

OF

# LIVERPOOL.

BY

JAMES STONEHOUSE,

AUTHOR OF 'YE LEGEND OF YE PREHISTORIC MANNE,' 'RECOLLECTIONS OF A NONOGENARIAN,' 'LACEY'S HANDBOOK,' ETC., ETC.

[ENTERED AT STATIONERS' HALL.]

PRICE 3/6.

LIVERPOOL: HIME AND SON, CHURCH STREET,

AND ALL BOOKSELLERS.

# PREFACE.

The following account of the "Streets of Liverpool" originally appeared in the columns of the *Liverpool Journal.*

The information contained in these pages has been gathered from a variety of sources: From the *Gentleman's Magazine* and other serials of a bye-gone time. From Smithers', Troughton's, Enfield's, Aikens', Baines', and Brooke's Histories. From Herdman's "Ancient Liverpool; and from Syers' (especially relating to Everton); From Mr. Mayer's papers in the "Historic Society's" proceedings, and from those by Mr. Ecroyd Smith, Mr. Picton, Mr. Joseph Boult, Dr. Hume, Dr. Thom, and other local authorites.

The author has to acknowledge gratefully many valuable communications from unknown correspondents, as well as near friends and aged acquaintances, who lived "when George the Third was king," whose memories of the good old town are still green.

With but little time he could presume to call his own, the author hopes he has not uselessly spent it, in picking out from here and there, and arranging in their appropriate places, anecdotes of the "Streets of Liverpool," that might otherwise have been forgotten and lost.

# INDEX.

PAGE

Chapel Street - - - - - - 5
Water Street - - - - - - 10
Oldhall Street - - - - - - 20
Tithebarn Street - - - - - - 27
Dale Street - - - - - - 33
Byrom Street - - - - - - 39
Scotland Road - - - - - - 44
Castle Streets - - - - - - 52
Lord Street - - - - - - 64
Church Street - - - - - - 69
Bold Street - - - - - - 76
Ranelagh Street - - - - - - 79
Lime Street - - - - - - 85
London Road - - - - - - 91
William Brown Street and Islington - - 99
Brunswick Road - - - - - - 105
West Derby Road - - - - - - 113
Pembroke Place - - - - - - 123
Mason Street, Edge Hill - - - - 130
Rodney Street - - - - - - 147
Clarence, Russell, and Seymour Streets - - 154
St. Anne Street - - - - - - 160
The Park - - - - - - - 168
„ Southward - - - - - - 174
„ Westward - - - - - - 182
The Silent Highway - - - - - 189
Everton—Northward - - - - - 205
„ Central - - - - - 214
Southward - - - - - 219

# The Streets of Liverpool.

## CHAPEL STREET.

Chapel Street, at the close of the last century, consisted of houses of the second and third series of erections, some half timbered, with porches, while the others were of modern construction. In Chapel street lived many of the leading merchants of their day, who had their counting-houses and warehouses attached to their dwelling-houses. Mr. William Hesketh, who was Mayor in 1783, dwelt in it, as did also Mr. Lawrence Spencer, who was Mayor in 1759. Dr. Houlston, a physician of some eminence, who discovered or brought into notice in 1773 the mineral spring in the Quarry, had a house in Chapel street. Dr. Houlston, in 1775, was the originator of the Liverpool Humane Society. The first mention of Chapel street is found in a mortgage dated the Wednesday before the feast of St. Mary Magdalen, in the forty-third year of Edward III., in which John de Formeby confirms, in mortgage to John Amoryson, of Wygan, the half of a burgage, with its appurtenances, in the town of Lyverpool, lying in "le Chapel strete," clearly contained within its marks and bounds, to be held until seventeen pounds of silver, to the said John Amoryson, are paid. In the reign of Elizabeth, at the top of the street was the White Cross Market. The Cross stood opposite the end of Old Hall street. It was a stone cross. Round the base and pedestal of the pillar were five stone steps. The market people clustered round the cross, amongst whom the potato growers of Formby were conspicuous, their potatoes being at that time of such high repute that they were even sent to a distance as presents to friends. At the bottom of Chapel street was the Mordyke House, which at one time was used as a poor-house, and afterwards as a prison. The Mordyke Fort stood a little to the north of it and was one of the defences of the town during the siege. On the top of a warehouse near New Quay, the machinery being in the uppermost story, previous to its removal to Tower-buildings, was the Liverpool telegraph, which communicated with Holyhead, Voel Nant, Voryd, Llysfaen, Great Ormshead, Puffin Island, Point Lynas, and Cefn-du. The line was 72 miles in length, 8½ miles intervening between each station. The first proposals for a telegraph were made by Mr. Boaz (who was doubtless a good mason), in 1802. His plan was to have lines of telegraph between Hull and towns intervening, and Liverpool, also with Manchester, Leeds, Birmingham, and other important localities. He estimated the cost of these lines to be about £15,000, and the profit at three to four hundred per cent. The telegraph above described, though proposed in 1826, was not established till 26th October, 1827.

The Church of St. Nicholas, one of the parish churches, has many interesting records connected with it, exhibiting at various periods the manners of the time. Although not mentioned in "Domesday Book," the original chapel of "St. Nicholas and Our Lady" was, without doubt, in existence, and had been so long before that book was compiled. The first mention we find of it was at the date of 1050. For some centuries the chapel of "St. Nicholas"—the patron saint of sailors—was the chapel of Ease to Walton, and it was not severed from it until 1699, when Liverpool was constituted a separate parish. In 1360 the chapel was taken down and a larger building erected. In 1361 the Bishop of Coventry and Lichfield issued a licence to bury the dead in the chapel cemetery, to save them being taken to Walton. The deaths were then very frequent from Sweating Sickness—the "*Sudor Anglicanus*" as it was called. Those attacked would die on their way home, and in the night time so suddenly as to be almost instantly beyond aid or relief. At the dissolution of the Monasteries, in 1533, it was found that there were four chantries attached to the "Chapell of St. Nicholas." First, the high altar, of the foundation of Henry Duke of Lancaster, about 1346 or 1352. This was held by Ralph Howard, aged 59, who had yearly £5 19s 10d in lands and tenements, besides his living, value £10. Secondly, the chantry of St. Nicholas, of the foundation of John O'Gaunt, Duke of Lancaster, established about 1380. The incumbent was Thomas Frodsham, aged 80, whose salary was £5 14s 7d, besides his living, £40. Thirdly, the altar of St. John, of the foundation of John Crosse, of Liverpool. The incumbent was Joshua Hurd, whose income was £5 6s 3d, and his living £37. The ornaments of the chantry of St. John were estimated by the commissioners as worth 40s, besides eight ounces of plate in the chalice. Fourthly, the altar of St. Catherine, of the foundation of John Crosse, of Liverpool. The incumbent was Humphrey Crosse, aged 50, whose salary was £6 2s 10d, besides his living of £2. The ornaments of the chapel were worth 3d, besides twelve ounces of plate. In 1718 the outer aisle of St. Nicholas' Church was added, at the cost of the Corporation, Mr. Thomas Johnson, and Madame Waters. In 1725 a new peal of bells was put up, cast at Bristol. They arrived by sea, the old bells being sent thither by the same route. The cost, exceeding the amount allowed for the old bells, which weighed 29cwt. 1qr. 26lbs., being £257 1s, a levy of 8d in the pound, on houses and lands in Liverpool, was laid to meet this amount and other charges. In 1749 the churchyard was enlarged westward. The new ground is much lower than the other portion. Hereon, in 1759, a battery of fourteen 18-pounders was raised, in expectation of Mons. Thurot's visiting the port. In 1765 a new organ was put up in the church, the old one being given to the Blue Coat School. In 1810 the steeple of this church fell, by which calamity twenty-four of the children of the Moorfields School, who were proceeding up the middle aisle, were killed, as were also three adults who were seated in their pews preparatory to the commencement of the service. The Rev. Rector Roughsedge, and the curate, Rev. R. L. Pugh, were entering the church at the time the steeple fell, and, had it not been that they were drawn back by a bystander, they would have been overwhelmed with the rest. The accident arose from the perversity of the ringers, who "would set the bells going," although they were warned that the belfry and steeple were unsafe. The ringers being on the ground floor, successfully made their exeunt, having been warned of the coming catastrophe by the falling of a large stone on one of the bells, which prevented its swing. The dead children were laid out in a row in the churchyard, to be picked out by their parents. It is said to have been a harrowing sight by those now living who witnessed the scene. Immediately after the accident occurred, hundreds of persons flocked to the churchyard, and gave assistance in clearing away the ruins. In 1558 the stipend of the minister of St. Nicholas' was £4 17s 6d. In 1700, it was £110 per annum; in 1764, £150; in 1826, £200; in 1831, £350; and at present over £850. On the eastern side of the churchyard, at one time, were some picturesque half-timbered houses, of considerable antiquity, being probably the dwellings of the second series. A celebrated tavern stood at the corner of the alley, called the "Old Style House." At the south-west corner of the churchyard was an octagon building that was considered a great nuisance, as standing in the way. It may be seen in old drawings and prints of the churchyard. In the churchyard, at the north-west corner, was a public-house much in vogue at the time, called "Hindes," approached by steps in the west wall of the churchyard. The abbots and monks of St. Peter and St. Paul, at Shrewsbury, originally held Walton, the advowson of which they sold to the Molyneux family. In 1747 Sir William Heathcote bought it for £2,500; and Sefton at the same period for £1,600. The Leighs bought the advowson of Walton and hold it still. In the churchyard are some quaint epitaphs on the tombstones, but they are only such as are found in seaboard cemeteries, slightly varied in their phraseology, to suit the locality. Here is one to the memory of Mr. Richard Bloore, who died 1789:—

> This town's a corporation full of crooked streets,
> Death's in the market place where people meets;
> If life like merchandise that men could buy,
> The rich would always live, the poor would always die.

Here is another on James Scanlion, who died 1786:—

> In the morning I rose up all right
> And pursued my business until night,
> When going to my Vessel's Stock,
> Death plunged me in the Salthouse Dock.

There is also a plain slab to the memory of Col. Broadneaux, dated 1727. He died at the age of 109. For 26 years he slept in the same room as his coffin was placed in, which at the age of 80, he had made for him in anticipation of his death. The coffin was rubbed and cleaned with the rest of his household furniture. Lancelot's hey was part of Sir Edward Moore's property, and was called after Lancelot, "an idyll drunken fellow."

In Lancelot's hey once resided Mr. Williamson, an eminent brewer. His house was said to be the handsomest furnished in Liverpool, and the rooms in it of the largest size. His dining room was so wide and lofty as to require columns to keep up the floor above. His mansion was destroyed in the great fire in Lancelot's hey of 1833, when about £168,000 worth of property was destroyed, of which £38,000 only was insured. Another fire broke out in this street in 1834, when Birkett's warehouses were destroyed; and in 1854 Molyneux's warehouses were burnt down, when £150,000 worth of merchandize was sacrificed.

Opposite St. Nicholas' Church, in Chapel street, about fifty years ago, there stood a public-house, called "The Salmon," kept by a man named Dugdale, a carrier. Over the door was the picture of a man standing in a cart laden with fish, holding up what was intended for a salmon in his right hand. Below were these lines—

> This salmon has got a tail,
> It's very like a whale;
> It's a fish that's very merry,
> They say it's catch'd at Derry;
> It's a fish that's got a heart,
> And it's put in Dugdale's cart.

This sign was afterwards changed to "The Fishing Smack," and the following lines were added, on Dugdale's widow marrying a man named Shafter, who was a Torbay fisherman—

> The cart and salmon has stray'd away,
> And left the fishing boat to stay;
> When boisterous winds do drive you back,
> Come in and drink at the "Fishing Smack."

At the bottom of Chapel street, adjoining the church-yard, in 1675, the fish market was held. It consisted of stalls, under arches. Adjoining were stables for the accommodation of the fishermen's wives, who came to it from Formby on horses, ponies and asses. These women were called "Formby Trotters"—they came in strings of sixteen at a time. In 1756 the fish-stalls were destroyed by a mob in a riot amongst the fish people. In 1764 the fish stones were removed to the top of Redcross street; in 1786 they were taken down to the Goree, near the end of Moor street; in 1822 to St. John's Market, where they were located at the Roe street end; and to the Fish Market, erected specially for the trade, in 1837.

At the "New Quay," which locality still retains the name, vessels used to unload and take in cargo. It was considered a great convenience at the time. The Prince's Dock, which occupies the area in front of New Quay and Bath street, was opened in 1821, the first stone being laid in 1816. The act for it was obtained in 1799, which empowered the authorities to widen George's Dock and construct Clarence Dock, which was opened 1830.

---

## WATER STREET.

WATER STREET was originally called "Bonke street," that is "Bank street."

Bonke street is first mentioned in a deed bearing date of "Sunday after the Feast of the Invention of the Holy Cross, in the 43rd year of the reign of Edward III."—that is to say, 1355—wherein "Adam le Clerk, of Leverpull, grants to William, the son of Adam, of Leverpull, a piece of land 20 feet by 17, in Bonke street, between the tenements of St. Nicholas (the chapel), and that of John de Stanley, or Staney."

Water street is one of the oldest of the old streets of the town, being the main approach to it from the river, on the shore of which, at its foot, landed the travellers from the south and west, by way of Chester. The ferry-boats in the time of Edward II. were owned by the monks of Birkhed, (Byrkheid or Byrkheved, as it was then written). They had the privilege, under permission of the King, to erect houses to shelter the passengers they ferried, or were about to ferry over; but in the reign of Edward III. they obtained a charter which confirmed the former grant and privileges, and also empowered them to levy a toll of ferriage. The charge was high enough:—For a man and horse, it was 2d., or 2s. 6d. of our money; for a footman, ¼d, or 4d. of the present rate of currency. On market day (Saturday), the charge for "a man and his goods"—that is, his produce, was 1d., or 1s. 3d. One of the houses of the Birkhed monks stood in Water street, and was long known as "Jonathan Hunter's Hoose." It was standing in the 17th century, just below Drury lane. In this house the unsold grain of the monks was stored, and doubtless their passengers were accommodated in it when detained by stress of weather.

Near the top of Water street, previous to 1832, was one of the old inns of the town—on the site of the Bank of Liverpool. This was "The Talbot," a famous coaching-house. The stables were in Fenwick street, and the entrance to the yard was under an arch in Water street. The Town-hall stood in Water street previous to the erection of the present edifice. Behind it were the butchers' shambles and passages leading therefrom. Pemberton's alley opened upon Tithebarn street. Clayton's alley had its entrance from Water street. These alleys consisted of wretched houses, of which more than one traveller, recording his experience of Liverpool, complains. High street was then to the east of the Town-hall, and was the junction between Castle street and Tithebarn street, and lineable with Oldhall street. High street was formerly called Jugglar street. The first mention of it was in a deed dated 18th August, 16th Henry VI, in which John Gregory, chaplain, gives to William Gaythread, of Leverpull, merchant, a piece of ground near the Cross, below Dale street and Jugglar street.

The houses in Water street, at the commencement of this century, were of the same ordinary character as others in the town at the time, and such as still may be met with in some of the older parts. The merchants then dwelt over their "counting-houses," as they were then called, and had their warehouses on the same premises. There was then no starting out to West Derby, or Aigburth, or other shady retreats, in the outskirts of Liverpool, to be reached in handsome traps, waggonettes, and well-appointed carriages. The merchants of that day would have reckoned that man a false prophet who told dreams of people going to the *domus et placens uxor* at the close of business hours, at Southport, Chester, Hoylake, and other places equally distant from the town. In Water street some very leading people resided at one time; amongst them was a lady, a Mrs. R. H——, who stood high amongst the fashionable. This lady, on one occasion, returning home, beheld a crowd gathered outside of her dwelling, and was astonished to see things flying in the air in front of it. On approaching her domicile she discovered that her monkey was amusing himself with casting out of her bed-room window all the loose pieces of dress and linen he could lay his hands upon.

The present magnificent suites of offices in Water street are the marvel and admiration of all strangers. Emanating from the taste and skill of a Picton, and other well-known architects, Liverpool is much indebted to these eminent men for truly noble and beautiful commercial buildings, where elegance of design is mingled with convenience and comfort. The sewering of Water street commenced in 1831.

The passing away of the Tower of Liverpool, in 1820, severed almost the last of the very few links that held together the modern days with the old days. The Tower of Liverpool stood at the bottom of Water street, on the site of the present Tower buildings, which superseded the iron warehouses of Messrs. Bailey Brothers.

The first stone of these noble buildings, of which Mr. Picton was the architect, was laid by Mr. Bailey, M.P., 4th December, 1846. In excavating the foundations of these offices, traces of the old tower were found, but the major part of them had been removed when the first series of buildings were erected on the site by Messrs. Bailey, about 1822.

The Tower of Liverpool "in its time played many parts." In 1252 it was a dwelling-place only, about which date it was supposed to have been erected. In 1360 it is recorded as being the property of Sir Thomas Lathom, of Lathom, with other "burgage houses and lands." In 1404, in the reign of Henry IV., Sir John Stanley, into whose possession the Tower had passed, made an application to be allowed "to fortify his house at Leverpull." In 1413, it is said to have been rebuilt by "John the Irischman." From that period it became a place of strength, and so it continued for three hundred years, as a point of embarcation to, and communication for the Stanley's with, their lordship of the Isle of Man (granted to them after the Battle of Shrewsbury,) which they held with the patronage of its bishopric, doing suit and service at the King's coronation by presenting two falcons. It is a curious circumstance, and by no means a common one, to find that two powerful families should have, within arrow-flight almost of each other, fortified strongholds in such an insignificant little town as Liverpool was, and continued to be for centuries after. It seems clear that between the two houses hot blood was sometimes engendered, for in 1424 (reign of Henry VI.,) we find that a quarrel arose between them. Thomas Stanley, the younger, afterwards Lord Stanley, mustered in Liverpool 2,000 men at arms, while Sir Richard Molyneux, of Sefton, was preparing to march with 1,500 men from West Derby, to give him battle in the immediate neighbourhood of the town. The cause of the quarrel is not stated, but it appears the neighbouring Justices of the Peace, having heard "great rumours of congregations of routes," accompanied by the Sheriff of Lancashire, Sir Richard Radcliffe, proceeded to the Tower of Liverpool, the house of Sir John Stanley, where they found Thomas Stanley with his men waiting to sally forth to receive Sir Richard Molyneux. The Sheriff arrested both the noble delinquents. Thomas Stanley he packed off to Kenilworth, and Sir Richard Molyneux to Windsor. Whatever was the cause of the quarrel, it was soon made up, for we find the two houses shortly afterwards became connected by marriage, and taking the same side in the bloody Wars of the Roses. Fancy Lord Stanley in the present day, attended by the Knowsley tenants, marching to meet Lord Sefton and the Croxteth tenants, with the intention of fighting out their differences of opinion—say about Messrs. Turner and Cross, and Messrs. Gladstone and Grenfell!

In 1532 Lord Derby maintained 250 Liverpool residents, fed 60 old people daily, and entertained guests in the tower, three times weekly. In the king's rent roll of the 8th October, 1539, 23rd reign of Henry VIII., Lord Derby paid 19s. 8d. for tower lands. Leland, who visited Liverpool about this time, speaks of the tower in Water street as "the Earl of Derby's stonehouse." On one Good Friday about this date he feasted a thousand persons. In those days great state was kept up, and it seems that the Derbys then and on other occasions took a warm interest in Liverpool affairs. In 1561 his lordship forbade grazing cattle in Toxteth park. The cause of offence was this: The spoil of all vessels stranded on the coast was anciently esteemed an important advantage to the lord of the neighbouring shore. In 1561 "a stranger shippe" was wrecked on the Lancaster shore, within the boundaries of his lordship's estates, in attempting to gain the harbour of Liverpool. The Earl laid claim to the vessel, which the towns-people resolutely resisted, thus creating much ill-feeling between them. In retaliation Lord Derby withheld pasture from the people of Liverpool and their cattle in Toxteth Park, in consequence of which they were obliged to humble themselves under his lordship's displeasure, entreating a restoration of his favour. The burgesses made a most abject submission, showing the white feather on the occasion, but the restriction was doubtless withdrawn and the offence forgiven; for in 1563 we find a record of a present of a buck to the Corporation.

In 1574 there is a charge made in the town expenses for four banquets at divers times to the Earl of Derby, amounting to 14s. 6d., and for charges spent upon my lord's venison given to the town 8s. In 1577 the Corporation sumptuously entertained Lord Derby on St. George's Day. This banquet cost 24s. In 1581 the Secretary Walsingham addresses Lord Derby as "the chief person in, and patron of, the poor town of Leverpole," on the subject of the monopoly of the Company of Chester merchants, who by a grant of Queen Mary had obtained it for trading from Chester and Liverpool with Spain and Portugal, through which the gold of Mexico and Peru, and the sugar from the Brazils, were then obtained. Lord Derby had been applied to by the Liverpool merchants to help them to get rid of the obnoxious impost of 25 per cent. on all goods of persons trading with these kingdoms. Liverpool was then subject to Chester for custom-house purposes. Through the good offices of the Secretary of State, the Earl obtained for his neighbours a withdrawal of the monopoly. The question, however, had to be settled by the Lord Chief Justice of England and the Master of the Rolls, who decided "that if retailers of such poor cities and towns where small trade and navigation is used, should be put from their trade and shipping, it would be a great decay to the same poor cities and towns." It was in the reign of Elizabeth that the Mayor of Liverpool, Ralph Seckerston, petitioned the Queen on behalf of the "poor and decayed town" over which he presided.

In 1626, James Strange, Lord Stanley, was the first mayor of Liverpool, under the charter of Charles II.

During the siege of Liverpool, in 1644, the Tower was used as the head-quarters of the Parliamentarians. Although from its position it was of no use to repel the onslaught on the town, it was necessarily of some importance. After the surrender of the town, Prince Rupert divided his forces between the Castle and the Tower, in both of which, and St. Nicholas' Church, he imprisoned the principal inhabitants and others found in arms against him. In 1648, Colonel Birch was Governor of the Tower, and retaliated on Lord Derby for the indignity he had undergone at his lordship's hands, of being dragged at a cart's tail through Manchester. Birch seized the daughters of his lordship, at Knowsley, and imprisoned them in the Tower of Liverpool, where he kept them in close confinement for some months. These two young ladies were so badly supplied with food and raiment, that had they not been secretly attended to by some friends in the town they must have perished from cold and hunger.

In 1667 Lord Derby presented a silver mace to the Corporation. In 1734-5 James, Earl of Derby, was mayor of Liverpool, and kept up great state and show of hospitality. It is to be regretted that the history of this interesting fortress is not more ample, as there must have been stirring incidents taking place constantly within and without its walls.

In 1737 the Tower passed out of the hands of the Stanleys and became the property of the Liverpool Corporation, by whom it was converted into a gaol. It must have been a very picturesque object from the river. Including its gardens, it occupied an area of 3,700 square yards. The Tower was constructed of red sandstone, in the Norman style. It was at one time battlemented, but afterwards creneted. Between the Tower and the river at one time there was a passage which led into the churchyard. As the frontage of the town began to be pushed out this passage became a street, and is now Prison Weint. Two houses then skirted the river side —one of which was a tavern, called the "Ferry House." In the Tower gardens, "the common garden," the inhabitants of the town used to walk and show off the finery of their day. For years after the Tower became a gaol the utmost disorder took place in it. Scenes of the grossest depravity were frequent. Prisoners of war were incarcerated in it. From the lax discipline carried out, these prisoners frequently made their escape. In 1759 several got away at one time. Many of these, however, came back to the Tower of their own accord, while others were captured in a state of starvation. In 1774, Howard, the great philanthropist, visited the Liverpool Tower Gaol. He gives a deplorable account of it. There was no classification of prisoners. The debtors mingled with the criminals,—the place was insufferably dirty, grimy, and wretched. There were two large yards, in one of which poultry was kept, and in the middle of it was a great dung-heap. The cells were seven in number, 6 ft. 7 in. in length, 5 ft. 9 in. in breadth, and 6 ft. high. In each cell three persons were locked up nightly. There was a large dungeon, looking on the street, in which as many as twenty and thirty prisoners were confined at a time. There was no infirmary, nor accommodation for the sick. The women debtors were lodged over the Pilot-office in Water street, and were somewhat better cared-for than the rest of the inmates. Although Mr. Howard made strong representations to the authorities of the disgraceful state of the prison, nothing seems to have been done to improve it, except some whitewashing and cleaning. Mr. Howard received the freedom of the borough, and was highly complimented for his investigations, and was the lion of his day.

On the 12th March, 1796, died Mrs. Lyons, wife of the keeper of the Boro' Gaol, in Water street On the following day Mr. Lyons died. The two were conveyed to the church-yard of St. Peter, in two hearses abreast, then followed one mourning coach, next two coaches abreast, and then two more coaches abreast. Thousands of persons gathered in the streets to witness the unusual procession. The cause of death in these persons was said to have been gaol fever.

Mr. Howard made five visits to Liverpool,—the last was in 1787. When Mr. Neild went over the same ground, in 1803, he found the gaol, if anything, in a worse state than it was in Mr. Howard's time. Mr. Neild found 109 prisoners—of whom 39 were felons, and 70 debtors—mingled together. The prison allowance for each prisoner was a threepenny loaf, of nineteen ounces, daily. The Corporation found firing. The poorer debtors were allowed straw to lie upon. Beds were provided by the gaoler at one shilling per week. Detaining creditors had to pay fourpence per day to maintain their debtors. In one room were three beds, and in another was a single bed. In one of the towers there were seven rooms for the accommodation of debtors. In the cells below there were apertures over the doorways to admit light and air. The dirt in some of the passages was three to four inches thick.

Spirits and malt liquors were freely circulated through the prison, without restriction. A low typhoid fever was constantly prevalent among the prisoners. The most shameless extortion and robbery also prevailed, the strong overcoming and tyrannizing over the weak. The debtors, whose rooms overlooked Prison Weint, used to hang out bags or gloves by a string, with a label attached, "Pity the poor debtors;" when any money was placed in the bag it was drawn up and spent in drink. In the large hall, used as a chapel in 1755, the town assemblies were held, and it is said that on these occasions the sounds of the music were so plainly heard throughout the building that the prisoners used to jig it as well as the free merry-makers. Great improvements subsequently took place. The sick were cared for, and service was performed in the chapel, at which the inmates of the gaol were compelled to attend.

The Tower has also been the scene of an execution, for, in 1789, two men, named Sylvester Dowling and Patrick Burns, were hung on the top of it for a desperate robbery in the house of Mrs. Graham, on Rose-hill, then quite out of the town. These men with two others entered the house about seven o'clock in the morning of December 23rd, 1788. One of them stayed below while the others ransacked the rooms. With knives in their hands they threatened the inmates with frightful violence if resistance was offered. In two of the apartments they tied the persons found in them to their beds. They carried off 19 guineas, a bill for £30, another for £10, several other bills of exchange for sums from £100 to £300, besides many other articles of value. Dowling and Burns were soon after arrested at Bristol, in consequence of an anonymous letter received by the Mayor. These men were embarking for Dublin, and had bank post bills for £1,100 in their possession, with other property belonging to Mrs. Graham, which they had in packages on board the vessel. Dowling would have escaped but for a dog belonging to one of the police-officers seizing him and holding him by the leg. In that year 82 persons were hung in different parts of England for offences, from sheep-stealing to murder. The beautiful arch between the Tower and the opposite building at the entrance of Tower Garden was taken down in 1820, when the materials of the Tower and an adjoining house were sold (Dec., 1819) for £200. In the Derby Museum there is a remnant of one of the old doors of the Tower. The wall of the coal-yard skirting Dutton street is constructed of the Tower stones, as was also a wall which bounded Chaffer's stone-yard near the Northern Hospital. Some of these had the Lancastrian rose sculptured on them, with other devices.

It may not be irrelevant to mention here that the passage or tunnel which was lately discovered under the south wing of the New Exchange building has been known to have been in existence since 1803. It was met with in excavating the foundations of the first Exchange. It was then explored for a considerable distance, and was found to tend, after running a short distance in a southerly direction, down towards the river, and it was at that time stated that it was a communication between the Tower and an old house near the White Cross. The side passages then met with quite tally with the present descriptions, were open, and did not penetrate far. They were considered to be receptacles for valuables in troublous times, and places of refuge on perilous occasions. These secret passages were very prevalent in connection with fortified houses. They provided a means of ingress and egress to and from the fortresses for the chieftain and his family when they wished to leave them without remark. They usually terminated at the house of some trusty retainer residing in the surrounding town. G. P. R. James, in his story of "Heidelburg," gives a graphic description of one of these subterranean places, and the incidents which took place therein connected with his narrative.

The Goree warehouses, erected in 1780, were destroyed by fire in 1802. It was a tremendous conflagration: the fire was in existence for weeks. De Quincey, who then resided in Liverpool, says that the sparks flew in clouds as far as Warrington, filling the hearts of men and beasts with terror when first perceived. The clouds of smoke that arose were marvellous, in consequence of the inflammable nature of the contents of the warehouses. The cotton floated away ignited for miles. There was a westerly wind blowing at the time, or great damage would have been done to the shipping in the port. The amount of loss was estimated at £323,000. The consequence of this fire was the breaking up of the first insurance company established in Liverpool. It was entitled the "St. George's Insurance Company." The merchandize in the Goree was heavily insured in it. It is said that some thousands of pounds worth of property were sold, the proceeds of which were paid into a Liverpool bank, where the amount still remains unclaimed to this day. In 1846 two warehouses were burnt in Back Goree, the loss being £65,000. It was intended at one time to have continued the Goree piazzas and warehouses along the line of Strand street, to the end of Brunswick Dock. In Wapping, portions of the projected buildings were commenced, but abandoned unfinished. The object of this description of building was to have had a continuous covered walk along the dock sides.

## OLDHALL STREET.

THIS street was originally called "Milne street," and previously to that "Peppard street," which name was formerly that of the Blundells of Ince, who obtained a right to change it by Act of Parliament, April, 1772. Like the other leading original streets of Liverpool, Oldhall street, in the last century, was narrow and shabby. The houses, for the most part, were little better than cottages. There were very few shops in the street, and these were of the most ordinary description. The descendant of one of the shopkeepers of the last century still pursues in it the avocation of his relative. When the widening of the street took place, about 1825, the houses on the west side were removed, the line on that side being thrown back. The houses on the east side gradually assumed a better appearance by being new fronted. When any of these houses are taken down it will be noticed how venerable are their interiors.

It was along Oldhall street that the victorious Royalists, in 1644, made their entry into the town, when access had been made for them by some traitor throwing over a part of the Woolpack ramparts into the ditch that skirted the north side. Rupert's followers committed great excesses on their way to the High Cross, although the inhabitants threw down their weapons and cried quarter. The Old Hall of the Moores did not escape their plundering propensity, for the barns and outhouses were burnt, while the hall itself was ransacked for portable valuables. The hall stood on the site of the handsome suite of offices erected by Mr. John Briscoe, who carried on, previous to his retirement from business, nearly opposite, an extensive drapery establishment. These offices are called "Briscoe's buildings." The site was previously occupied by the offices of Messrs. Barton, Irlam, and Higginson, at the back of whose premises a portion of the old hall might at one time have been seen. There was a curious fatality attendant upon the shipping owned by this once eminent firm, for every vessel of theirs called after the members of it, was lost in succession.

When the Old Hall was in its prime the gardens attached to it went down to the shore, and were said to be most abundantly productive. There are many still living who can remember the view of the Mersey being uninterrupted from the ends of Union street and Queen street. Sir Edward Moore in his rental shows how much property he held hereabouts. He describes his tenants on it, and advises his son in the management of his possessions with a selfishness and shrewdness that showed him to be a narrow-minded old fellow, who did not seem to care for anybody but himself and his belongings. He roundly abuses the Mayor in 1665, Mr. Alderman Thomas Ayndoe, who then occupied the Old Hall, which he was obliged to let to him, in consequence of the difficulties into which he had been plunged by his father's incurring heavy debts during the Parliamentary Wars.

When the road to Bootle was cut through, and before it was covered with houses, the noise made by the frogs thereabouts at night was astounding. These animals were called "Bootle organs."

In consequence of the want of accommodation for their friends in the Tower, in Water street, the Stanleys purchased, about 1700, the Old Hall, and converted it into a "guest house." It was a long, low building. It was for some time occupied by the widow of the rector of Winwick. In Union street there are some excellent houses. They were erected by the leading merchants of their time. At the north end of Oldhall street was the "Ladies' Walk," a fashionable place of public resort in the last century. The "Ladies' Walk" at the end of Oldhall street is said to have been an exceedingly pleasant promenade, commanding an uninterrupted view of the Mersey estuary, and the fine open country to the north, which was laid out in fields, orchards, and gardens. One of the entrances to the "walk" was from Oldhall street, through a swing gate which stood on the site of the coal yard, on the left of the present canal bridge. The approach at the west end was from Bath street up a broad flight of steps. Like the Duke street walk, there were four rows of trees, with a centre and side promenades. On fine days throughout the year, and on Sundays especially, these walks used to be thronged with the townsfolk, who sported their bravery in broad-skirted coats, satin breeches, gold-laced waistcoats, silk stockings, square-toed large-buckled shoes, and three-cornered hats; while the ladies exhibited high toupées, hooped dresses, and high-heeled shoes. The dandies of the time wore swords, and it is said that not unfrequently the hot young bloods were sometimes too ready to take offence at trifles, in spite of the presence of the ladies. The destruction of the "Ladies' Walk" was a source of deep regret to all classes. The opening of the Leeds canal, in 1774, was of more importance than all the "Ladies' Walks" in the world, and, therefore, the weak, as usual, gave way to the strong. Portions of the Ladies' Walk remained as late as 1816. Mr. Clarke, Mr. Roscoe's partner, used part of it for storing his coal from the Wigan mines. The Liverpool Baths faced the foot of the steps leading to the walk. They were erected originally by Mr. Wright, a boat-builder, about the middle of the last century. They contained hot and cold water baths, while outside was an open area, 33 feet by 30, enclosed in a pallisading, which admitted the sea-water direct, to enable persons to bathe therein in preference to the baths in the interior of the building. In 1794 the Corporation purchased these baths, and greatly improved them. They were swept away in 1817 to make room for the Prince's Dock. There was another public bath, at one time, called "Dwerryhouse's Bath," at the river end of Parliament street. It was a mere tank or immense tub, into which the water from the river was pumped. Near the northern baths, on the shore, were a few fishermen's cottages, where, from a flight of steps leading out of Bath street (which there was lost in the sand-hills,) people used to take their plunge, leaving their clothes with little urchins, who made a livelihood by taking charge of them. At that time, and for a great many years later, the shore was all open (beyond the Clarence Dock and the fort,) where people used to bathe from machines, and from the shore also. There was a man named Sommerton, who afterwards kept a public-house in James' street, who at one time owned two large stationary caravans capable of holding forty or fifty people, wherein as many have been known to undress at one time. On the shore was the "Wishing Gate" public-house, where the friends of outward-bound vessels were wont to assemble, to see the last of the good ship that bore away their relatives or companions, and to drink to their "God speed, a prosperous voyage, and *wishing* a speedy and safe return." In 1802, during a dreadful storm, a small vessel belonging to Greenock, was driven on the rocks near the Wishing Gate, within fifty yards of the shore. In consequence of the violence of the waves no assistance could be rendered to the crew, one out of thirteen only being saved. At the close of the last century, and the beginning of the present, the disgraceful conduct of the "dowkers," as the bathers were called, was such as to call forth the strenuous interference of the authorities. Men and women might have been seen bathing at one time, indiscriminately, from the north shore, without the least regard for decency, while their acquaintances and strangers, looked on from the strand, with the utmost complacency, at the gambols taking place in the water.

Beyond the Ladies' Walk was all open gardens and fields, which extended towards the river until met by the sandhills. Great Howard street, called after the great philanthropist, was projected through the Common heys, along Mile lane. Mile lane was a continuation of Oldhall street. It ran through the fields already mentioned to the "Mile House," which stood on the shore on this side of Beacon's gutter. It may be here mentioned that, when the docks opposite this portion of the shore were in progress, immense quantities of woodland *debris* were discovered in hazel and oak trees, and abundance of nuts and acorns. A thick wood must have stood here at one time, through which the Beacon's gutter (then a stream rising at Everton) abundantly flowed. In Great Howard street stood the Borough Gaol, which superseded the Tower as a prison. This building was also called the French Prison, from the number of prisoners of war that were at one time incarcerated in it. These people improved their condition by the exercise of their ingenuity in manufacturing various nicknacks, as well as useful things, models of ships and houses. Some of the ships they constructed were of exceeding beauty, and were sold or raffled for at high prices in the town. The writer once saw an exquisite model of a frigate made by one of these captives, which was constructed of some hundreds of pieces of ivory, rivetted with brass nails, the cordage being manufactured by the prisoner's wife from her own hair. When the French prisoners were discharged it was said that they had damaged the building to the amount of £2,000. Among the prisoners confined in this prison was once a man named Domeri, who possessed a marvellous appetite. This person was known to have eaten in one day 14lbs. of *raw* beef, 2lbs. of candles, and drank twelve bottles of porter. He could eat grass weighing 4lbs. and 5lbs. at a time. Cats, dogs, and rats went but small way with him. The prisoners used to get up French plays, and as much as £50 have been taken at one representation.

Mr. Edward Falkner, of Fairfield, resided at one time in Oldhall street. He was high sheriff in 1788. Falkner square and surrounding streets take their names from the Falkners. After Falkner terrace had been commenced, it stood so long in a skeleton state, and was considered so far out of town that it was called "Falkner's Folly."

In Edmund street, on the site of the present beautiful and spacious Chapel of St. Mary, stood at one time an ancient chapel, which was destroyed by fire in 1745. This chapel was succeeded by a plain building, which was demolished in the disgraceful riots which took place in 1759.

The improvements in Oldhall street, in 1828, cost £2,043; Great Howard street, £15,303; Lancelot's Hey, £3,049; and Bevington hill, £3,000.

Of the value of property in Oldhall street there has been of late years great changes—all of an upward tendency. Thirty years ago land could be got in it for £2 10s. the square yard. Some of the property in the vicinity of the canal was at that time sold for £3, which now would fetch four or five times that amount, while land nearer the Exchange has been sold at prices ranging from £25 to £30 per yard.

In 1767 the Leeds Canal was projected. The engineer was a Mr. Longbotham. In December, 1768, he called a meeting of gentlemen favourable to the proposal, when it was agreed to obtain an Act of Parliament to carry out the scheme. In 1770 this act was obtained, and the first turf was cut at Halsall in December of that year. About thirty-five miles of canal were opened at the Leeds and also at the Liverpool terminus, but the middle portion was not opened for years afterwards. The canal occupied in completion forty-five years. Its length is 198 miles, from Liverpool to Leeds. The fall from the central level on the Lancashire side is 525 feet, and on the Yorkshire side 446 feet.

At one time it was proposed to supply Liverpool with water from the overflow of the canal. Castle street top is six feet below the canal level; Scotland road 13 feet; bottom of Shaw's brow 22 feet 5 inches; bottom of Duke street 35 feet, and of Mersey street 37 feet; Old Dock Sill 56 feet 7 inches. The waste water from the canal bank would flow 40 yards up Richmond Row, and 100 yards up Shaw's brow.

At the corner of Virginia street and Paul's square, in 1770, was born the Rev. Leigh Richmond, the son of a physician of great eminence in Liverpool. He was grandson or great-grandson of the Rev. H. Richmond, rector of Liverpool in 1700. Rev. Leigh Richmond was the author of the graceful little tract, the "Dairyman's Daughter," which has been circulated throughout the length and breadth of the land, and is familiar to all. He wrote several other very pleasing compositions of this description, such as "Little Jane." This excellent clergyman was rector of Turvey, in Bedfordshire. He died and was buried there in 1825. In Edmund street resided at one time a remarkable man, the Rev. John Newton, who was in 1752 and 1753 captain of an African slaver, owned by Mr. John Manesty, an eminent African merchant, after whom Manesty lane takes its name. Through the influence of Mr. Manesty, Mr. Newton was appointed in 1755 one of the tide surveyors of the port of Liverpool. In 1764 Mr. Newton entered the Church and became curate of Olney, in Buckinghamshire, where he continued till 1779. While there, in conjunction with Cowper, the poet, he published the "Olney Hymns." He afterwards became rector of St. Mary's, Woolnoth, in the city of London.

At the corner of Plumbe street and Leeds street, about forty years ago, where there is now a flag-yard, stood a Wesleyan chapel, with its graveyard surrounding. It was built in 1798. On the removal of the chapel the dead were reverently interred elsewhere. St. Paul's Church was erected in 1762. The square was open to "Maiden's Green" for some years. The first incumbent of St. Paul's was a Mr. Henderson, who had seceded from the Dissenters occupying Benn's-gardens Chapel. His curate was the learned Gilbert Wakefield, who, oddly enough, seceded from the Church to join the Dissenters, quitting Liverpool to become one of the tutors at the once famous Warrington Academy, with which it will be recollected Aiken, Barbauld, Enfield, Priestley, and others of literary and scholastic eminence, were connected. Gilbert Wakefield gives a wretched account of the inhospitality of the Liverpool clergy. He states in his memoirs that during the whole time of his stay in Liverpool he remained unnoticed, and had only one invitation—to drink tea with a brother clergyman. He lodged in Duke street, near the bottom.

Opposite the eastern end of the Ladies' Walk was a lane skirted on each side by trees, called "Maiden's Green." Leeds street occupies its site. Its memory is perpetuated in a small street or passage of the same name in the neighbourhood. "Maiden's Green" was a favourite lover's walk of the time. It ran to Pinfold lane, now Vauxhall road.

In 1760, in *Williamson's Advertizer*, Feb. 15, a large house is announced "to be let in Oldhall street, containing four rooms on a floor, with a counting-house, two stalled stable, and a warehouse wherein may be laid 70 hogsheads of sugar on a floor, and a large commodious yard with a coach or cookhouse to it."

## TITHEBARN STREET.

Tithebarn street, or Tithebarn lane, as it was called at one time, was originally known as Moor street, either named after the Moore family (who had much property in its vicinity), or from the "Moor Land" through which it ran. The first mention of it as Moore street is in a deed dated the day of St. Gregory the Pope, 12th March, 1304, wherein we find that Adam, son of Ranulf, of Letherpull, gives to Richard of Mapelduram two bovates of land ( a bovate was as much land as an ox could plough in a day), lying in the field which is called Dalefield, near the Royal road, (*id est*, the King's highway), and the lands of Robert le Mercer; and there is also an assignment in the same deed of a burgage which lies in the Moore street, between the tenement of Roger, son of Elkinwald, and the tenement of John de Mora. It may not be uninteresting to know that at that time beer was selling in Liverpool at one halfpenny per gallon, or 7½d of our money. In country places the price was 1½d per gallon. Barley was selling for 2s, or 30s of our money per quarter. Land was then very unproductive in Lancashire. In Essex the average produce of wheat was only 6 bushels per acre, barley 12 bushels, oats 5 bushels. In the fifteenth of Henry VIII., 1524, the Mayor and burgesses granted a few roods of waste land situated in Moore green to Sir William Molyneux, to enable him to build thereon an office or tithe-barn, wherein to store the tithes of that part of Walton parish, which then comprised the town of Liverpool and village of Kirkdale. The actual Barn which gave the name to the street has been a source of much debate, some supposing it to be a barn which stood on the north side of the lane on the way to Bevington hill; while others have believed it to have been a large building which stood at the end of Tempest hey and extended to Stephen's weint or lane. This barn is in the recollection of many living. The end fronted Tithebarn street. One part of the barn in its latter days was occupied as a shippon and dairy, the entrance to which was from Tempest Hey. In the middle was a blacksmith's forge, and at the other end was a school. Tithebarn street, at the close of the last century, and the commencement of the present, was a very narrow, crooked thoroughfare. Vast sums of money have been spent in rendering it convenient, but its ungainly condition has never been much amended. The houses were all of a very humble description, the shops being small and of little repute. The class of houses of which it consisted may still be seen in Leather lane and other small streets running out of the main road. In Hackins-hey ("Hey" from Haie, Fr., meadow), there was at one time a Quakers' meeting-house, with a school and cemetery. The meeting-house was erected about 1700, and was licensed in 1709. Many of the leading members of the Society of "Friends" have preached in it. In the cemetery, the gift of Penelope Rathbone in 1752 (the Rathbones then as now practising good and kindly deeds in Liverpool)—many eminent Quakers have been interred. The last interment took place in 1791. The school was in Quaker's alley, under the direction of a Miss Farrer. Sir Edward Moore in his rental advises his son concerning Hacking's-hey, "That he has amongst his tenants (in Tithe Barn street) John Hacking, 'a very honest man.'" Sir Edward had a high opinion of all who thought as he did, gave him his own way, and voted for him at the elections. He says further—"When his house, barn, and ground fall out, then doth likewise fall out of lease a house called 'Hacking's-house,' in the Dale street—through the lower end of which house, I charge you, with God's permission, to make a street which will run directly north, through the croft belonging to the house and barn, and it will be a most convenient passage for a street from the Dale street to Tithe Barn street." This street was thus projected by Sir Edward Moore, and carried out by his son according to his suggestions. It is a specimen of the old Liverpool thoroughfares.

Tempest-hey was called after the Tempests, who held land thereabout. Riley's gardens were actually at one time gardens, occupied by Mr. Riley, a gentleman whose house stood in them. In 1730, within the area of Moorfields, Dale street, Dig lane, and Tithebarn street, it was all open ground. In 1768 we find it laid out in Bachelor's Weint (now Bachelor street), Glasshouse Weint, Vernon street, Cunliffe street, and Hockinhall alley. Messrs. Macfie's sugar house swept away a number of little houses and shops in Bachelor's Weint. These refineries were burnt down in 1846, when £50,000 damages were done. In Glasshouse Weint was a glass work. There was also in this lane an extensive Tennis-court. Hockinhall alley was called after the Hockinhalls, an old Cheshire family. The present Cheapside is the Dig lane above mentioned. It was originally called "Dog and Duck Lane," from a celebrated tavern that stood at the corner of it. Hatton garden takes its name from Mr. Hatton whose gardens occupied a part of the site of the present paint-works. At the top end of the site of Hatton garden there was in the latter end of the last century a large pond called The Flashes, which was afterwards known as the "Watering Pond." Attached to it were gardens which skirted Moorfields. St. Patrick's Cross stood opposite, at the junction of the three cross-roads.

St. Patrick's Cross is mentioned in the Act of Parliament of George I. 1771, which granted powers to repair the road from it "to the town of Preston," and it was at this spot tradition has it that St. Patrick preached Christianity on his way to Ireland. This cross was standing in 1775. At the angle of Pinfold lane and the lane to Bevington hill were the house and gardens of Mrs. James. In Pinfold lane stood the town pound. This was in use in 1784, for in this year there was an entry in the Corporate accounts of the sum of 50s being paid to Richard Marsh, as an annual wage for "taking care of it." The present Vauxhall bridewell stands on its site. Marybone is a perversion of *Marie bon* or *bona*, which name was given to the new street, then a mere country lane, having cabbage gardens on each side, by the request of some of the Catholic inhabitants of the neighbourhood, who began to occupy the houses that were being erected in it. It was known only formerly as "the way to Ormskirk."

In 1815 a man named Thomas Cosgrove, residing in Cheapside, killed his wife and afterwards poisoned himself. He was buried at the top of Hatton garden, where the four roads meet. The remains of this man were discovered on sewering Tithebarn street about 1854, and were re-interred. Johnson street, North street, Trueman street, and Fontenoy street, running out of Dale street, had their northern ends all open to Mr. Cross's fields. At one time, near the top of Marybone and Vauxhall road was a cotton factory, which was given up, after some years' trial, not proving profitable. In 1807 the streets in Scotland road were laid out, and some of them built upon; but those in Vauxhall road or Pinfold lane, and Marybone, were not then even projected.

On each side of Vauxhall road were fields, owned by several proprietors, such as Lord Derby, Mr. Foster Cunliffe, Mr. Sergeant Aspinall, Mr. Almond, Mrs. James, Mr. Williamson, Miss Blackstock, and others. In the memory of many living, Vauxhall road was a narrow lane, having fields on each side, in which the town roughs used to play. The road was then considerably lower than it is at present, being in fact on a level with the fields. The "Pumpfields" were so called from the town pipes and pumps, which were made of wood, being manufactured in them. These ducts were of ash or birch, bored hollow, and had iron rings on their ends. The writer has been told by an old resident in town that Vauxhall-road, in his young days, was very unsafe to travel along, especially at night time. When he went courting his present wife, he said he used to go along the road in fear and trembling, so lawless then were the inhabitants of the neighbourhood. There was a family of the name of Moore that was a terror to every one. The elder Moore kept a public-house called the Bull, at Warbrick moor. His two sons were blacksmiths; one lived in Maguire street and the other in Eldon place. After committing a variety of crimes, and perpetrating endless robberies, two of them, the father and one son, were either hung at Lancaster or transported for life. There was also a family of the name of Mulvey, who lived in Marybone, or one of the streets out of it, that about five and thirty years ago was constantly committing highway robberies in the outskirts of the town. This gang also consisted of a father and two sons, who waylaid travellers after dark in the then thinly populated suburbs of Liverpool. However, on one occasion, in Breck road, near the "Odd House," they accosted a musical traveller who proved too much for them, for he actually captured the two sons, and so *scored* the father as to make him readily identified on the following day, when the police officers were sent in search of him. These three desperados were all transported. The gallant captor of the Mulveys still stands six feet two in his stockings, and possesses as much pluck, if not strength, as would incite him to make a similar capture if occasion required.

Bixteth street was named after the Bixteth family. Alderman Bixteth was bailiff in 1629, and mayor in 1635 and 1642. It is said that "he paved the street in front of his house with his own hands, for which he was highly complimented by the corporation."

When Tithebarn street was widened the improvements extended as far as Key street. A grocer's shop, kept by a Mr. Bates, who held also a small shop adjoining, had to be removed. In exchange for these premises Mr. Bates got a strip of land in front of Key street and Lumber street, now occupied as the Lancashire and Yorkshire Railway Company's premises. In front of the land given to Mr. Bates were some small shops and a public-house. In one of these houses were found, on its being taken down, several ingeniously contrived little rooms, of which even its late inmates were unaware. In one of them was found a small parcel of tobacco. It was supposed that these rooms had been constructed for the purpose of carrying on the contraband trade, and for hiding smuggled goods. In the last century smuggling and wrecking were practiced to a great extent on the Lancashire and Cheshire seaboards. The fishermen of Hoylake on the one side and the fishermen of Formby on the other were always ready to board either inbound or outbound vessels, from which they could obtain excisable articles for the purpose of "running" them. It was said that at one time on either coast a man could get a drop of brandy and a supply of tobacco at any cottage on the seaboard line *if he only knew how to ask for it.* The Lancashire and Yorkshire Railway was the cause of the removal of at least 2,000 people from this vicinity. This caused much injury to the trade of the neighbourhood at the time, especially to Pownall square Market. Pownall square was laid out about the middle of the last century. It was named after Mr. William Pownall, whose death took place in May, 1768, during his Mayoralty. He was called up one night in the month of March of that year, to suppress an alarming riot which had arisen in a place called the "Devil's Acre," near the corner of the Salt-house Dock. From the lawless character of the inhabitants of this quarter, the fact of appearing among the rioters was no small act of courage, but Mr. Pownall so greatly and gallantly exerted himself to restore order that he took a severe cold from which he never rallied. There is extant an excellent portrait of this gentleman attired in his robes. He was highly esteemed by all his fellow-townsmen, and his death was much lamented. Pownall square Market, after being closed for some years, was re-opened in 1836. In Cockspur street, out of Pownall square, there was once a Dissenters' Chapel which occupied the site of a cockpit. The history of it is curious. The cockpit was closed between 1788 and 1790, in consequence of the scenes of depravity. violence, and robbery that took place therein. In 1792 the building became a chapel, and was first occupied by a Scotch congregation, who removed to Oldham street. Next it was taken by a congregation of Independents in 1800. Dr. Shepherd, speaking of Young Spencer, then in the dawning of his fame, so unfortunately cut short by his early accidental death by drowning, 15th August, 1811, near the Dingle, said of him, alluding to the old cockpit, "that he was the best cock the Dissenters ever had to pit against the Devil." The chapel was let in 1812 to a body of Kilhamites, who took their name from Mr. Alexander Kilham, who formed a new connection of Methodists. In 1815 the Swedenborgians had possession of the little building, they keeping it till 1819. The Independents then once again occupied it. In 1820 the Baptists rented it. In 1824 the Primitive Methodists met in it, and finally a sect of Methodists calling themselves the "Christian Society," closed its curious and changeful career. It was then pulled down, and houses were erected on its site. Near Vauxhall road, on the left hand side of Cockspur street, its memory is perpetuated by a stone tablet over the entrance to a court bearing the inscription, "Chapel Place, 1839."

---

## DALE STREET.

Dale street was originally called Dele street from the Saxon "Dele or Dale," a Valley. It was one of the four leading streets of the town, proceeding from the High Cross, which stood on the site of the Exchange. The first mention of Dale street appears in a deed bearing date, 15th April, 3rd of Edward III., in which Cecilia Utting "in her pure widowhood," gave to Richard de Walton the half of a burgage in the town of Lyverpoll "in le Dele street," to be sold, &c., rendering to Alexander, son of Matthew de Walley, eighteen pence.

When Dale street was widened in 1808 it was thought to be broad enough for all purposes. Previous to that period it was about the width of Cable street. It was again widened in 1819, and again in 1828, at the latter date the cost of improvement was about £800. If it were now twice its present width, it would be only sufficient for its traffic. The houses that were removed at the top of the street on the south side were of considerable antiquity. There are two or three old tenements yet remaining near Sir Thomas's buildings. It was astonishing the amount of opposition the authorities had to encounter from some of the inhabitants in their attempt to improve this thoroughfare. There was one man, a cobbler, in particular, who occupied a house to the west of Hockenhall alley, who cared neither for his Worship the Mayor, the Aldermen, nor the burgesses, and set everybody at defiance. He stuck to his old house until it was entirely isolated, and the street went past him on either side. Threats he laughed at, cajoling he despised, and ridicule went for nothing. The cobbler stuck to his stall, until at length public opinion, and the nuisance of the man's dwelling, which stood so obnoxiously in the way of improvement, compelled the authorities to turn out this sturdy son of Crispin without further ceremony. A barber also, who occupied a shop at the corner of Temple lane some thirty years ago, was as recalcitrant as the cobbler, and was driven from floor to floor till he was obliged to scamper out of his house to escape from the timber falling above his head. For days this man and his house were objects of public interest and wonderment. Until 1720 there were no houses to the southward of Dale street, that side being all open fields to Frog lane. About 1683 there was a ferry over the Pool-river, at the bottom of Sir Thomas Johnson's field. While excavating for the sewers during the present year in this vicinity, there was found a fine specimen of a wild boar's skull, with tusks beautifully marked. Sir Thomas's "buildings" were erected at the top of the fields on the left hand side from Dale street. Liverpool owes its first start in prosperity to Sir Thomas Johnson. He was knighted by Queen Anne on the presentation of an address, March 10th, 1707. His father was Mayor in 1695.

In Cumberland street, called after "The Butcher of Culloden," stood the first Jewish synagogue. It was a square brick building, with the front to the south. It was surrounded by a yard. On the removal of the Jewish congregation to Frederick street this chapel was occupied by Sandemanians or Glassites. Skeletons and parts of coffins have frequently been disinterred in digging foundations of warehouses in this vicinity. About sixty years ago a great excitement was caused by the discovery of human remains, and as late as the present year (1869) bones have been found in excavating the foundations of some new warehouses. Whether these bones were those of Jews or Gentiles has not been so far clearly made out. Might they not have been the remains of some of Liverpool's gallant defenders who fell during the seige?

The houses in Sir Thomas's buildings were of the same description as we see in Hockenhall alley, Cumberland street and Stanley street. In 1786 there was a house in Dale street, the front wall of which was only six feet high: it was covered with thatch. Near Sir Thomas's buildings, in Dale street, there are some old houses partly modernized. Many of the leading merchants of the time had houses in Dale street.

Opposite Sir Thomas's buildings, in 1766, were erected, in Dale street, meat shambles, "which were thought very convenient for the inhabitants of this part of the town." At that period there were only a few houses beyond Dig lane, now Cheapside, facing the street. The backs of these houses had gardens, and were close to the fields.

The little chapel in Sir Thomas's Buildings was erected about 1785 or 1790, and was occupied originally by Roman Catholics. In 1818 it was held by the Baptists, and afterwards by the Independents. These were followed by a congregation of Christian Israelites. From 1836 to 1841 the Church of England Service was conducted in it, by the Rev. J. R. Conor, M.A., when it was called St. Simon's. On the removal of Mr. Conor and his congregation to the Old Scotch Secession Meeting House in Gloucester street, the little edifice became tenanted by a body of Protestant Germans, who still worship in it.

The Crosses, one of the leading families of the olden time, had a handsome mansion in Dale street, somewhere about the present site of the Public Offices. Their gardens extended to the Pool. When Blome visited Liverpool in 1673, he described the Crosses as "living in a fine mansion called the "'Crosse Hall,' in Dale street, where divers worthy gentlemer "had lived of the name for many generations."

In 1552 Mr. Crosse founded a free grammar school for children, especially those of the same name as himself. This was the first free grammar school in the town. In 1571 Sir John Crosse obtained leave to erect a wall to prevent the encroachment of the Pool river. Probably this wall ran along the site of the Old Haymarket to the middle of the present Whitechapel, to which their lands and gardens extended. The Crosses held land also on the west side of Byrom street. Sir Edward Moore had a windmill in Dale street. He and Mr. Crosse, of Crosse Hall, held the exclusive right of grinding all the corn in the borough. This privilege they had purchased from the ancient Lords of Liverpool. They took one bushel in twenty for dues. Sir Edward states that at one time he got 20 measures a week, for two years together, when malt sold at 5s. the Winchester measure. This was when there was trade between Lochaber, in Scotland, and Liverpool. In the time of Sir Edward's grandfather the allowance to his household was 16 measures of malt a week, and 16 measures of bread corn, all of which were received as toll for grinding. On the Dale street fields batteries were erected to reply to Prince Rupert's on the Great Heath.

At one time there were some handsome mansions in Dale street. The Bull Hotel was erected by Mr. Houghton as a mansion about 1800. Mr. Shaw, the eminent potter, after whom Shaw's-brow was called, dwelt at the east corner of Fontenoy street. His works were behind his residence. His house is even now little changed in outward appearance. Near Hatton garden, where are the Police offices and Fire station, on the site of premises once occupied by the Gas Company, was "Wyke's court," built by Mr. Wyke, who introduced in 1758, into Liverpool, watchmaking to a great extent. Mr. Wyke came from Prescot, which has always been a celebrated locality for the manufacture of watch tools and works. "Wyke's Court" was erected in 1764. It contained, besides a spacious dwelling, workshops, warehouses, out-houses, and stables. The entrance was under an archway. There was a large garden behind, extending nearly to Tithebarn street. Mr. Wyke was one of the founders of the "Academy of Art." In 1769, rooms in John street were taken for the use of students, but for want of encouragement the undertaking languished until in 1770. Mr. Wyke succeeded in establishing a dispensary, which was opened in John street and Prince's street. Roscoe drew up Mr. Wyke's will, in which considerable bequests were made to Liverpool charities. He died 1787, and was buried under an altar tomb in Prescot churchyard that he had erected in memory of his parents. It stands near the north-west corner of the tower.

In *Williamson's Advertiser*, 8th September, 1758, a house, with garden 180 yards long, in Dale street, is advertised to be sold. Fancy the value now of a garden 180 yards long in Dale street!

Dale street has always been a thoroughfare of great importance—perhaps more so than either of the other three original streets, as it constituted the old way, by Ormskirk and Preston, to the north. From its two inns, the "Golden Lion" and the "Fleece," issued forth at one time strings of pack-horses, consisting of fifty and sixty quadrupeds laden with goods for the interior, each horse's burthen weighing on an average three cwt.; or they might have been seen returning with produce for consumption or exportation—the drivers herding together for safety on the unprotected roads. From these inns afterwards, when the roads became passable, went out the cumbrous waggons drawn by their eight horses, on the harness of which jingled merry bells, giving warning on dark nights of their approach. In these waggons passengers were wont to occupy any vacant space; and we may gather pretty well what the scenes were that took place in them, if we read "Roderick Random," "Tom Jones," "Joseph Andrews," or any such works of the time.

Previous to 1757 there was not a single public conveyance out of Liverpool. To reach the metropolis, it was necessary to take horse to Warrington, whence, from the Red Lion, a coach started every Monday and Thursday, arriving in London in three days. The fare was two guineas, one guinea being paid in advance. Fourteen pounds weight of luggage were allowed each passenger. In 1766 there were two coaches to the metropolis, which started from the Golden Fleece, Dale street, on Tuesday and Friday mornings, making the journey in two days in summer, and three in winter. The passengers generally went armed, to be prepared for highwaymen, who at that time frequented the roads, especially the heaths and commons round the metropolis.

In Gore's Directory of 1774, we find "that John Hesketh comes to the Old Angel in Dale street with his waggon every Monday, and goes out on Tuesday to York," and that "J. and J. Parkinson go to the Mill Stone and Castle, Dale street, once a week, days uncertain;" "while from the same inn and from the Cross Keys, goods are taken to Ormskirk every Wednesday and Saturday."

The principal inns in Dale street at that time, beside the above mentioned, were "The Golden Lion," "The Fleece," "The Angel and Crown," "The Bull and Punch Bowl," "The Wool Pack," and the "Red Lion." All these houses have disappeared.

The Saracen's Head, which stood on part of the site of the Public Offices, was a celebrated establishment some thirty years ago whence coaches departed to almost all parts of the kingdom. Under the old archway, many of us are still alive who have ducked our heads to avoid a concussion when outside passengers of the "Tally-ho," "The Rob Roy," or some other of the famous fast coaches of their day. The George, in Dale street, was another favourite Inn, which stood on the site of Rigby's Buildings, where the beauty of the barmaids, at all times, proved a great attraction to the "snobs" of the time.

Dale street has in it many beautiful buildings, such as the Temple, the Queen Insurance Buildings, the offices of the Liverpool Fire and Life, the Royal Bank Buildings, the

North Western Bank, Rigby's Buildings, and the Royal Insurance Offices. Doubtless, in the course of time, many of the shops and smaller properties will be converted into spacious and handsome offices, to embellish and enrich the architecture of the great Liverpool thoroughfare, Dale street.

---

## BYROM STREET.

Byrom street up to the middle of the last century was called Townsend lane. A mansion stood at the south-eastern corner of it, which was known as "Townsend House." Byrom street takes its name from Mr. Octavius Byrom, who was church-warden about 1800. In 1636, near the entrance to Townsend lane, were floodgates, which were erected to keep back "the brook" that flowed on its western side on or about the line of Fontenoy street, which will be still noticed as having the appearance of rising from the hollow way of Byrom street. In 1644, at the time of the siege, as this part of the town was subject to frequent attacks, and vigorously defended, the sluices were broken down.

After the siege the Townsend bridge was built that crossed the Pool river, making a continuous roadway up "Shaw's-brow," as it was afterwards called. Previous to this bridge being built, carts and horses went through the stream, while doubtless there were stepping-stones for foot travellers. In 1654 a bridge of stone succeeded the one of wood to improve the way to Prescot over "the Great Heath." In 1664 the bridge was ordered to be repaired, and in 1667 the water was kept up by flood-gates. These flood-gates were to restrain the Pool waters, which rose and fell with the tide. It is a singular circumstance that we have few records of the siege, and scarcely any accounts have been discovered relative to the bridges over the Pool. There is a record, however, of a bridge with sluices being constructed in 1635, across the Pool near the site of the present Cooper's Row. About 1690 the brook was carried or run under ground, the present street being then formed.

At the bottom of Dale street the "cuck stool" was erected for the chastisement of scolds. We find, in 1656, a "*new one* was ordered to be set up." This cruel punishment was in use until comparatively a recent period. Howard found it in operation in the Tower prison, as did also Mr. Neild when he visited the House of Correction, which stood at the back of the present fever hospital. On his second visit, in 1803, it had been discontinued. In Cheshire the "cuck stool" was a common village punishment; and doubtless if this engine were still in use there would be crowds of gaping spectators to witness an exhibition of human suffering and mental torture. We are not a whit more civilised or less ferocious in many things than were the men of the "good old times."

The cuck stool apparatus consisted of an upright post to which a long beam was fixed by means of a pivot or hinge. At one end of the beam a chair was fastened, in which the unhappy culprit was seated and bound. To the other end of the lever or beam, ropes were attached, by which means the chair could be directed any way, and lowered or raised as occasion might require, and the punishment of the culprit meted, according to the enormity of her transgressions. Truly might such an one exclaim with Queen Catherine—"Do with me what you will, for any change must better my condition." Death from cold and rough usage not unfrequently ensued amongst the victims of this cruel punishment. On the south east corner of Byrom street was a field which at one time was called the "Gorsey," or "Gorse field," and also the "Gallows field," the rent of which was one of the sources of revenue by which the haven was kept in repair. Townsend lane was a mere country way, with hedges, the "brook" supplying the tanneries which were in operation about the site of the back of Cook and Townshend's shops and Fontenoy street. In the barn of Townsend House, in 1722, the Baptists met to worship, having converted it into a chapel, coming thereto from

Low hill. When the original chapel in Byrom street was opened it was complained of, as being too far out of the town to be convenient; but, nevertheless, the congregation every year increased to such an extent that it was obliged to be enlarged in 1773. In 1789, the members of the Baptist community still gaining strength, it was determined to erect a larger and more commodious building, which was accordingly done, the chapel at the foot of Gerard street being the result of that resolution. The original chapel was converted into a Church of England, and became, as it is at present, "St. Stephen's." It was currently reported at the time that the celebrated Dr. Shepherd, the Presbyterian minister at Gateacre, a man eminent for his preaching, scholarship, and ready wit, was for some years proprietor of St. Stephen's, and held the advowson. During the Baptists' occupation several famous ministers of that sect occupied the pulpit. The Rev. Mr. Johnson, in 1741, was one. He was a descendant from Sir Thomas Johnson, who may be said to have given Liverpool its first start towards prosperity. Another was the well-known and highly esteemed Rev. Samuel Medley, who, from 1772, attracted large congregations to hear him. He devoted much of his time to addressing the sailors and the working-classes. Mr. Medley was exceedingly popular in Liverpool. He was originally a midshipman in the Royal Navy, and afterwards served as master's mate. He was in the smart action off Cape Lagos in 1759, where he was so severely wounded as to oblige him to quit the sea and take to school-keeping. Mr. Medley died in the 61st year of his age, on the 17th July, 1799. The congregation in Gerard street chapel still rapidly increased. In 1825, when Mr. Fisher was pastor, it was proposed to relieve him of part of his duty, to which he objected, on the plea of losing his sole authority, for, said he, "If two men ride on horseback, one must sit behind." In connection with the chapel in Gerard street a droll occurrence took place about 1836 or 1837. One Sunday, in January, the weather had been exceedingly mild in the morning part of the day, towards sunset a thick, drizzling rain began to fall, when between seven and eight o'clock an extraordinary change took place, for an intense frost then set in, which in a very short time covered the whole of the streets in the town with hard sheets of ice. On the conclusion of the service at the chapel referred to, those who first issued from the door fell down, while those following tumbled over them. An alarm was raised by those pressing forward on seeing those before them so mysteriously "floored," When the reason for persons thus falling was ascertained, arrangements were made for others to get into the street in safety. To climb up Gerard street, however, was next to impossible, while to reach Byrom street was a matter of no small difficulty. First one and then another person dropped amidst shouts of laughter and no few cries of pain. At length strings of ladies and gentlemen were formed to sustain each other, but, like autumn leaves, many of these human ropes came to grief. The scene, as described by an eye witness and sufferer, was ludicrous in the extreme. Somewhat similar occurrences on the same night took place in front of other places of worship. In the quiet and little-frequented streets numbers of young men availed themselves of the opportunity of enjoying the pleasure of skating up and down the parapets as deftly as if they had been on canals or deep waters.

The Crosse family held large plots of ground in and about Liverpool. In Byrom street they possessed a considerable portion of it. The land from Dale street corner to Addison street belonged to Mr. Crosse, and it was through his field (about 1801) that the "New Crossehall street" was formed, since entitled "Great Crosshall street." Milton street, Sawney Pope street, and Addison street were projected about the same period. Addison street occupied the site of a country lane, running to Bevington lane; this locality, in the time of Elizabeth, was called "Sick Man's lane," from the fact that when a virulent plague was raging, numbers of persons were accommodated in temporary receptacles erected therein, and who were buried in the vicinity if they fell victims to those dreadful visitations, the nature of which we are now quite ignorant of, whether epidemic or endemic. The lane was also called "Deadman's lane." In making some excavations of late years for the sewers, quantities of human bones were discovered by the navvies, who sold them by the bushel to the marine store dealers, until stopped by the authorities.

As late as 1802 there were no houses erected in Byrom street, on the west side, as far as nearly opposite Hunter street. In Scotland place there was, previous to the opening of St. Martin's Market in 1831, a market held, which was called "Richmond Row Market." It was not a legitimate market, but a mere assemblage of hucksters; it was well supported however, by the Everton people. In the area enclosed by Richmond row, Comus street, and Gay street, was a large porter brewery, which at one time carried on an extensive trade. The site of it is covered with houses. The Scotland road front is now occupied by shops and large spirit vaults. At the south corner of Richmond row were the dog kennels of the "Liverpool Hunt Club." The brook ran through this establishment. "The harriers" were liberally at one time supported by the leading gentlemen of equestrian proclivities in the town and neighbourhood. These kennels were afterwards removed to the North Shore. The Corporation, in 1775, subscribed £5 5s. towards their support. The brook, previous to passing through the kennel, ran down the "Dingle," a part of the site of which is now Downe street. The Liverpool harriers were kept up for many years.

Previous to 1819 there was a custom in Liverpool of taking what were called ingate and outgate tolls. One of the toll-houses stood at the end of Byrom street. A man named Joliffe, the father of a once well-known Liverpool musician some years ago, was the last of the toll-takers. These tolls were levied on all produce coming into or going out of the town at the various main street ends. There were collectors stationed at the pierhead, at the end of St. James's street, and other approaches. In consequence of the increasing difficulties that arose in collecting these ingate and outgate tolls, and circumventing "the dodges" that were constantly put in process to evade them, an act was obtained on the 23rd of March, 1819 (59 Geo. III.) to enable the authorities to levy rents and standing-room charges in the markets instead of in the streets. This act did not interfere with the Altcar people or the inhabitants of the town of Prescot, or the freemen of Liverpool, who had been free from toll from custom and by prescription.

Mr. Joshua Rose, after whom Rose hill, Rose place, and Rose vale were called, it is said, gave the names of the poets to the streets in this quarter of the town, as we find exemplified: in Ben Jonson, Chaucer, Virgil, Dryden, Milton, Addison, Juvenal, and Sawney Pope streets. It is a matter for wonder that the latter should have been allowed to have been so designated, considering the genius of the man whose name has been made use of. Although the denizens of Sawney (Alexander) Pope street are antithetical to poetry, it is not too late to do away with the soubriquet bestowed by Mr. Rose. "Pope street" would be more seemly to be used than with its prefix.

Although from Richmond row end to the turning into Bevington Bush the street is called Scotland road, it ought to have been called Byrom street, for Scotland "New" Road, as the thoroughfare was at first called, actually commences only at Bevington lane end. In the lane leading to Bevington Bush will be seen one or two old houses, which give us a good idea of the Liverpool dwellings of the second series. These houses at one time had gardens behind them, and that part of the lane which is skirted by Addison street, Scotland road, Marybone, and Bevingtou hill, was, in 1807, an open field.

## SCOTLAND ROAD.

At the close of the last century, to afford greater facilities to enter the town, it was found expedient to avoid the circuitous route of Bevington-hill, by making a short cut between Byrom street and the Kirkdale road. This new thoroughfare was called "New Scotland road,"—the whole line being so entitled from Richmond row end to Kirkdale. An act to widen and repair the road "from Patrick's Cross, in the town of Liverpool, to Preston," had been obtained in 1771, causing it to become one of the two turnpike roads out of Liverpool. This new cut was considered a great improvement to the north end of the town, but houses did not spring up in its vicinity so quickly as it was expected. Even as late as 1827, Dryden street was the limit of the buildings on the east side of the road, while Great Oxford street was only then projected. Beyond Westmorland-place there were no houses between it and Kirkdale. Where St. Martin's Market stands there was originally a field, in which was a large stone quarry. The streets hereabouts, as was the fashion of the beginning of the century, were called after celebrated men, who provided the names for all the new streets in the various towns throughout the kingdom, especially in Liverpool. In Scotland road we have "Wellington," "Ellenboro'," "Horatio" (Nelson's Christian name), "Great Nelson," "Collingwood," &c., streets. The first houses in Scotland road were erected for private dwellings, and it was only within the last thirty years that shops have superseded them. Where the new cut met Kirkdale road it was called "St. Anthony's place," and "Mile-end," being one mile exactly from the Exchange. The "Mile House," opposite Virgil street, was kept by one Kitty Eccleston, who was famous in her time for making meat pies. It was at one time quite a country jaunt for holiday people to go out to eat Kitty's pies, and spend the afternoon on Bevington Hill and Summer Seat, to enjoy the fine prospect obtainable therefrom. From the gardens in that vicinity were uninterrupted views of the river, the Cheshire coasts, and the open sea. Mr. Gildart had thereabout a garden and summer-house, on the site of "Gildart's Gardens."

Limekiln lane was called Back lane originally, and was only an occupation road terminating about Great Oxford street. When the lime works were erected the name of Limekiln lane was adopted. In this lane in 1801 dwelt a man who obtained a livelihood by spinning catgut. He used to boast that in his youth he was Madam Clayton's footboy, and that he stood behind that lady's carriage when she and her father passed over the drawbridge of the George's Dock gut or passage, being the first private vehicle that had done so. This drawbridge was constructed after the Dutch fashion, the flaps being raised by means of beams elevated on posts. In Virgil street, about 1835, a curious discovery was made of a gang, or rather a family, of coiners, who had been issuing base coin, principally in five-shilling pieces, to a very great extent. These coins were so beautifully got up and contained such a quantity of real standard metal that they were valued at from three shillings and tenpence to four shillings each. These crown pieces had long been met with by the Mint authorities, and had puzzled them exceedingly, being quite in the dark as to what part of the kingdom they had their origin. It was clear to the Mint that whoever fabricated them possessed a good capital to work with, great skill in manipulation, and machinery of no common order. It was at length conjectured that the makers of the money must be receivers also of stolen plate, as they could not carry on their work profitably at the market price of silver if they had to purchase it fairly. An extensive plate robbery in the neighbourhood of Liverpool having attracted much attention, active inquiries were set on foot, which put the Mint authorities on the scent. After no end of watching, and great vigilance, the stolen property was traced to the house of a family named Harnett, the elder of whom kept a small chandler's shop in Richmond row. The Harnetts dwelt in one of the still to be seen good houses, on the south side of Virgil street, and were regarded in the neighbourhood as very quiet, respectable, well-to-do people. Julia Harnett, the daughter, was a particularly attractive and handsome-looking girl, and was much noticed for her ladylike appearance. For a considerable time no progress was made towards the capture of the delinquents. Two then well-known active and intelligent police officers were engaged to watch the Harnetts' house, into which they had repeatedly endeavoured to get admission. At length one of them, dressing himself up in a postman's uniform, knocked one morning at the door, with the usual "double," when, on the door being answered by Miss Harnett, the detective pushed in, followed by his comrade, and the citadel was won. A great quantity of stolen plate was found in the house, with a large amount of spurious coin, and some very costly machinery, with powerful presses. On taking the Harnetts (brother and sister) into custody—for the father was not implicated in the affair—they said, "their money could do no poor man harm." The house was handsomely-furnished. As Julia Harnett passed the piano, she said to the detective, "I'll have one tune, at any rate, before I go," whereupon she sat down to the instrument and played in good style "Over the Water to Charley." The Harnetts were convicted and transported. A year or two after Miss Harnett's arrival in Sydney she wrote to Mr. Powell, the then solicitor to the Mint, to tell him that she at first cursed him in her heart for the steps he had taken to secure her conviction, but that at the time of writing to him, she remembered him in her prayers, and would be grateful to him all her future life, for being the cause of her leaving England, as she had married a gentleman in Sydney of large fortune, and rode in her carriage!

For many years the fields on the east side of Scotland road, beyond Dryden street, were used as brick-fields. In them were many deep pits of water in which several persons were found who had been thrown, or fallen in accidentally,—for crossing these fields after nightfall was rather a dangerous exploit, from the lawless character of the tenants of the huts that had been erected on them. These people kept pigs and poultry, and formed quite a colony at one time. In latter years, mountebanks, showmen, roundabouts, and swing proprietors congregated on these fields, so that occasionally their aspect presented quite a *fair-y* scene on a small scale. In 1827, opposite Bostock street, there were the ruins of an ancient cross. Adjoining the yard of St. Anthony's Chapel there is a little tavern called the "Throstle Nest." At one time it was kept by a man of the name of Falvey, who made himself of some note in the town by speaking at public meetings and elections. In the great Ewart and Denison contest, in 1830, he was particularly conspicuous by his addresses on the Liberal side. Falvey was at one time a "teacher of languages." He entered into a public discussion, in 1830, on the subject of "Romanism," with a clergyman of the Church of England, the Rev. William Dalton, M.A., incumbent of St. Jude's Church, and Mr. Finch, a layman. The discussion occupied twelve days. Falvey once brought out a publication called the *Comet*, which, although short-lived, exhibited a considerable amount of talent. When Falvey, occupied the "Throstle's Nest" he used to treat his customers occasionally to a Latin oration. He was a fluent speaker, and an excellent Latin and Greek scholar. A rather curious circumstance connected with the "Throstle's Nest" took place shortly after, or during Falvey's occupation of it. A poor, little Italian boy, accompanied by his dog, mice, and monkey, was sheltered under its roof one frightfully inclement winter night; they remained next day in consequence of the lad being taken ill. Through the sufferings he had undergone he died at the "Throstle's Nest." He was interred in St. Anthony's burial-ground, adjoining, where the dog and monkey, whenever they could make their escape, were sure to be found by their master's grave.

The view of Everton Hill from Scotland road was at one time exceedingly pleasing, especially when lit up by an afternoon or evening sun. In 1829, Great Homer street only ran as far as Rose Vale. The whole of the hill side was then a range of corn-fields and pastures. When the sunlight was reflected from the windows of the mansions on the brow of the hill, it was as if a brilliant illumination was taking place.

St. Matthew's Church was originally erected as a Kirk of Scotland. After a considerable amount of litigation connected with it had taken place, with the heartburnings incidental, it was bought by the Lancashire and Yorkshire Railway Company, and given to the Rev. Dr. Hillcoat, in lieu of St. Matthew's Church, in Plumbe street, that the company was obliged to take down to make way for their station in Tithebarn street.

St. Martin's Church was commenced in 1828 and consecrated in 1829. In the great storm of 1841, when St. Michael's Church steeple was stricken by lightning, St.

Martin's also received considerable damage. The bolt seemed to shoot over the town, striking the two church spires, and were simultaneously, as witnessed by the writer of these sketches. The altitude of the steeple, compared with surrounding objects, may not prove uninteresting. The top is on a level with the battlements on the body of Everton Church. It is three feet above the battlements of the tower of St. Mary, Edge Hill, and sixteen feet above the base of Bidstone Lighthouse. The sill of the belfry window is five feet below the sandhills, at the Rock Point. The clock face is level with the ridge of the Governor's house of Kirkdale Prison. The footwalk round the base of the tower is twenty-eight feet above the level of the canal, and sixty-six feet above the level of the river at high water at spring tides.

Before quitting this neighbourhood, a few memoranda connected with some of the streets in it may prove interesting. At the close of the last century Rose place was not cut through to Scotland road, or Byrom street, as it was then called. There was a row of hedges on the one side of it. St. Anne's Church was the limit of the town northward. Cazneau street was projected by Mr. B. B. Cazneau, who resided at the bottom of Islington. Cazneau street was, some forty years ago, a very pretty street, the houses on the west side having very nice gardens in front of them. They are now covered with cottage property and court houses. Crossing the site of this street, running east and west, in 1795, was the archery ground of the Mersey Bowmen. Their club-house is, or was lately in existence. It stood on the West side of the street, being used as a workshop. It had devices in stone, of cross-arrows, surmounded by a wreath with "M.B," let into the west wall. Over the window was a bugle-horn in a tablet.

The Roman Catholic Chapel of St. Joseph, in Grosvenor street, occupies the site of a tennis-court and racket ground. This game, requiring considerable skill and activity of frame, was in the last century a favourite pastime. It seems unaccountably to have gone out of fashion. There were at one time several tennis-courts in and about Liverpool. On the erection of Christ's Church by Mr. Houghton, it was expected that he would have given it to the Rev. R. Banister, a clergyman who had won for himself many friends. Upon Mr. Houghton making up his mind adverse to Mr. Banister, that gentleman's friends got up a subscription and built a church for him on the site of the Tennis-court, calling it "All Saints." The pulpit of it was occupied by Mr. Banister till his death, when the church got into the hands of the Rev. Henry Turner. Mr. Banister held very liberal views on church matters, and allowed Dissenters to address his congregation. Amongst others, on one occasion, was the Rev. John Gadsby, of Manchester. In 1827 Mr. Turner became connected with Montgomery West, or "Bishop West," as he was called, who will be mentioned as consecrating the little church or chapel in Russell street. West was an Irishman, and came to England accredited as chaplain to the Rev. Philander Chase, Bishop of Ohio, to raise subscriptions for the enlargement of Kenyon College, Gambier. West was an admirable speaker, and contrived to get patronised by several of the bishops, English and Irish, and picked up a large sum in furtherance of his object. On his return to America he and his bishop fell out upon money matters, when West returned a "consecrated bishop" himself, and in this capacity, on joining Mr. Turner, had All Saints "consecrated" by Dr. Mathews, who had been "consecrated" a bishop by West. After this West and Turner failing to agree, a regular row took place one evening at All Saints, which ended in West's friends quitting the church, and eventually purchasing a piece of land in Soho street whereon to erect a church for their pastor. This land was opposite Queen Anne street. The first stone of the building was laid with much ceremony by West himself. His supporters and friends, until the building was completed, assembled to worship in the Music-hall, Bold street. But "Bishop" West and his people did not long agree; consequently the new church was never finished, and was eventually sold to the Baptists, who now occupy it. In Nov., 1833, All Saints' was licensed by the then Bishop of Chester, and continued as a place of worship of the Church of England until it was sold to the Catholic body in 1846 or

1847. The Rev. John Lyons was the first minister after it was licensed; the last was the Rev. Andrew M'Conkey, M.A., who became incumbent of St. James's, West Derby, until his death in August, 1868. The Rev. Andrew M'Conkey was a remarkable man, and many droll stories are current about him. He was a great favourite with his congregations, and often told them some home truths. Just previous to quitting All Saints' Mr. M'Conkey was at a meeting of the clergy of this diocese, at which the then Bishop of Chester was present. Addressing Mr. M'Conkey, his lordship remarked that he was surprised that he had not received his resignation of All Saints', as he understood he was to have the then newly-erected Church of St. James, West Derby. "My lord," said Mr. M'Conkey, "were you ever in a Zoological Garden, and did you ever look at the monkeys?" "Yes," replied his lordship, smiling, "I have." "Well, my lord, did you ever take notice that, when a monkey was climbing up the tree, he never let go of the lower bough until he had got firm grip of the upper one?" "Yes, I have," replied the Bishop. "Well, then, my lord," added Mr. M'Conkey, "I'm the monkey." The rev. gentleman's rich brogue and quaint mode of expression convulsed his clerical brethren with laughter, in which the Bishop heartily joined. Another characteristic anecdote of this worthy clergyman may be told, as showing his aptness and readiness to "improve an occasion." One Sunday, soon after his appointment to St. James's, Mr. M'Conkey's sexton told him that a certain great gun amongst the Liverpool clergy was present. "Indeed!" said Mr. M'Conkey, in a very significant way. On entering the pulpit to preach his sermon the rev. gentleman looked round his church, until, fixing his eye upon the unexpected visitor, he announced his text from Genesis xlii. 9.—"Ye are spies; to see the nakedness of the land are ye come."

Out of Rose place runs Meadow street, named after a Mr. William Meadows, who resided in it. He was blessed with six wives. His first wife lived two years. He remained a widower one year, when a Miss Peggy Robinson became his next venture. She lived twenty years, and bore him nine children. After her death he remained a widower only one month, marrying a lady who only lived with him two years. After continuing single seven weeks he met with his fourth spouse, who lived with him eighteen years. At her death he continued a disconsolate widower nine months, when he took to himself a fifth wife. She lived with him eight years. After mourning for her six weeks he took to himself his sixth "venture," a Miss Mary Lowe, of Preston street. They were married at Walton on the 18th June, 1807, he being then 75 years of age. He was born in 1732, and married his first wife in 1755. A man, who was blessed with a rather shrewish wife, on being told about Meadows' wives, remarked—"What an extraordinary run of luck some men have!"

---

## CASTLE STREETS.

THE principal streets of Liverpool in the last century were so inconveniently narrow that it was with difficulty two vehicles could pass each other—indeed there were so few carriages in it at that period that such a predicament rarely occurred, in fact, it was necessary to mount up the steps of a house to get out of the way of waggons and carts. The streets were badly paved, and worse lighted, while the dwellings in them were of the most ordinary character. The people were ill-dressed, and the manners of the time were of the sea—salty. Liverpool was a sort of a "Wapping" Town. The man who walked down Castle street then, attired in a broad-skirted coat, knee-breeches, cotton or silk stockings, and a three-cornered hat, would not have been believed as a true prophet had he told his young son that by the time he (the boy) was eighty years old, he would inhabit a town full of wide handsome streets, with fine shops in them, palatial-looking suites of offices and noble public buildings. If we want to realize in our minds what Castle street was like of old, we need only step into Atherton street, or Cable street, or Stanley street, and there we see it standing before us. Castle street is replete with interesting memories. It has witnessed the assembling of the retainers of two lordly houses, ripe for bloodshedding; it has seen rollicking savage cavaliers, cutting and maiming all they met in revenge for the sturdy resistance they encountered during the siege; it has witnessed gangs of infuriated sailors clamouring for an increase of pay or redress of wrongs; it has been scoured by press-gangs, and has been the scene of contested elections, that cost fabulous sums of money, engendering, in the lavishing of them, venality, intemperance and immorality. The history of Castle-street, if fully told, would occupy ten-fold more space than is here allotted to it.

The present Town-hall was completed in 1797. In the Town-hall royalty has been regally entertained. The greatest and most eminent men of their time, of this and other nations, have been guests within its walls and partakers of its lavish hospitalities. Princes, eminent statesmen, gallant soldiers, brave sailors, acute lawyers, and pious divines have assembled at its table; while, outside of it, George Canning, William Huskisson, and Henry Brougham have rung out stirring appeals to the swaying crowds that gathered in its front. The Town-hall, so to speak, has seen several generations. It has been an often renewed building. The first Hall was probably a very primitive structure, and was used for many purposes. While the old chapel of St. Nicholas was being rebuilt, about 1355, the Town-hall was called "Domus beatœ Marie," or "Lady Marie Haule," from its being most likely used as a place of worship during the repairs or rebuilding of the sacred edifice, as the case might have been. Close to the windows of the Town-hall, by Dale street, are, or were at one time, marks of the cannon balls fired by the riotous sailors in 1775.

The chartered fairs of Liverpool were held on the 25th of July and 11th November, each commencing ten days before and continuing ten days after those dates. They were held on the site of the present Exchange-buildings, in High street, and Castle street, when the Mayor and Aldermen and Bailiffs walked the limits of the fair, attended by a band of music, afterwards partaking of a collation at the Town-hall at the Mayor's expense. These fairs do not seem to have been of any importance, as they gradually dwindled away when the necessity for such meetings decreased. The memory of them till lately was kept up, by the exhibition of a hand or glove in front of the Town-hall, to indicate "protection" during fair time from arrest, to any person, by warrant issued from the local court. The limits of the fair ground were indicated by boundary stones; one of these is or was to be seen opposite the shop of Messrs. Mander and Allender, in Castle street. Another reminder of the Liverpool fairs is to be found in the charge of double toll for agricultural produce taken into the Hay Market at those periods of the year. The Town-hall has been used as a court-house, a gaol, a custom-house, and an assembly-room where "dauncings" have taken place, when the hire of it was "sixteen pence." In 1674 the Town-hall was rebuilt in High street, superseding the old structure. This edifice was erected on arches, whereunder the merchants congregated. It was embattled at the top; it had a square lantern tower in the centre, and a belfry with a fire bell at one corner. This building was taken down in 1747. In 1748 the foundation stone of the present edifice was laid by the Mayor, Mr. Glegg. When completed it was said at the time "that the arrangements of the interior were laid out in a novel and very ingenious manner." On Sunday, January 18th, 1795, the interior was destroyed by fire—the progress of the flames being expedited in consequence of the want of water from the frost, and the inflammable nature of the wood of which the building was constructed. While the Town-hall was in course of renewal a house was run up in Brunswick street, next to the Union Bank, for the use of the Corporate officials. The Mayor's stables were adjoining in Lower Castle street, where they continued many years. The dome and figure of Britannia

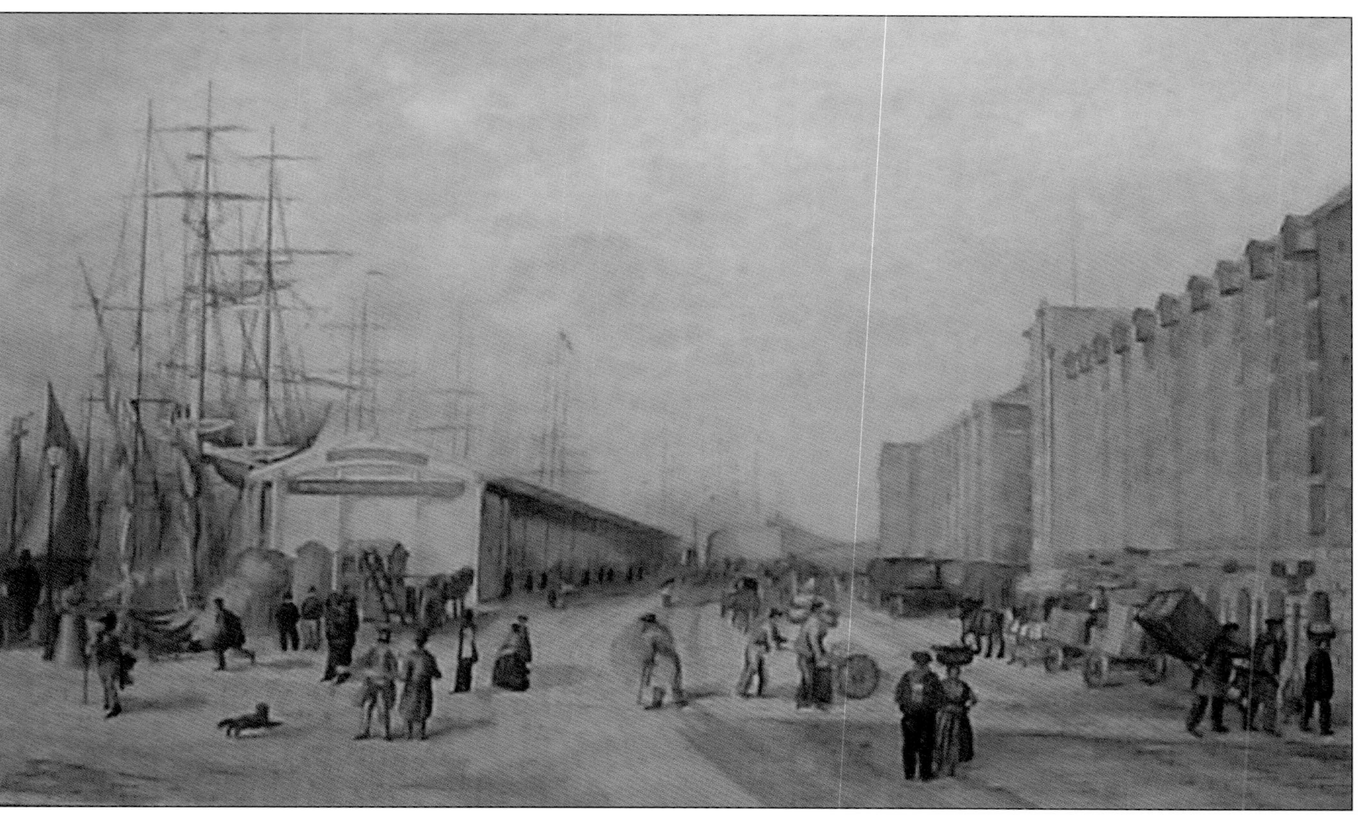

Goree Piazzas and George's Dock Quay. 1860.

Mason Street, Edge Hill. 1858.

River Mersey. 1840.

London Road. 1865

Alexandra Theatre, Lime Street. 1870.

were put up in 1802, the portico in front in 1811. The pillars of it are of stone brought from a quarry in Rathbone street. They are monolithic, and were the largest quarried in this vicinity. They were shaped in Castle street.

Castle street was widened under an Act of Parliament dated 1786, which enabled the authorities to sweep away a vast number of old tumble-down houses and ruinous tenements which were in the close vicinity of the Town-hall, in fact, abutted upon it northerly and westwardly. Courts, alleys, and passages were removed, and Fenwick street, Water street, and Chapel street were widened, as was part of Dale street. In widening Castle street it was intended at first to retire the west side of it considerably beyond its present lines and advance the eastern limit, so that the Town-hall would then have been in the centre of the street when viewed from the south. It is rather a curious circumstance that many of the public buildings facing the ends of streets are not placed in full view of the spectator. This plan was abandoned from a fear of the expense. It is to be regretted that such a want of courage existed. At the north-eastern corner of Castle street was Roscoe's Bank, carried on in the premises now occupied by Messrs. Nixon and Thew. The causes of Mr. Roscoe's failure arose from an abortive endeavour to fertilise Chat-moss, and a connexion with some extensive coal mines near Wigan. These latter eventually turned out so good a property as to enable Mr. Clarke, Mr. Roscoe's partner in them, to realise a good dividend on their joint estate. After the closing of the bank the premises remained so long unoccupied that Mr. Harvey (one of the "five liberal Harveys," as Ryley, the Itinerant, toasted them), to whom it belonged, became quite despairing about its being let again. Mr. Roscoe suggested the idea of the Exchange buildings; he roughly sketched out the plan on paper, and told those who were dubious about the expense, and were proposing some paltry expedients on the subject, that the sum required might be easily raised in shares. It is said that in a morning or two afterwards, on coming into town, Mr. Roscoe noticed a crowd of the merchants round the Town-hall, which he was told consisted of persons desirous of putting their names down for shares in the Exchange Buildings' scheme. Although no person was allowed to take more than ten shares, the list was filled up in three hours, and the £80,000 or £100,000 were raised at once. Mr. Roscoe was greatly beloved in private life, while his opponents highly respected him. In 1808 the merchants assembled in the Exchange area for the first time instead of Castle street. On the 2nd of May, 1809, the Exchange Room was first opened.

Some of the houses in Castle-street were searched for French refugees in 1798. The writer is acquainted with one family whose residence was rudely invaded for this purpose. Mr. Roscoe wrote a strong protest against this shameful infringement of the liberty of the subject. When the news of the battle of Waterloo came to Liverpool in 1815, several old soldiers who had served in the Peninsula harangued the crowd on the subject from chairs and stools in Castle-street. Heywood's Bank, one of the oldest established in Liverpool, occupied the site of the "Mercantile and Exchange Bank" until the Bank in Brunswick-street was completed. Seth Flitcroft, whose shop was in Castle-street, had a foundry in 1836 in Cook-street, on the site of the "National Bank." The Bank of England occupies the site of the "Liverpool Arms Inn," a famous hostelrie of its time. This name was changed to the "King's Arms" on that inn being given up in Water-street.

The Liverpool market was held at the High Cross at one period. The Liverpool market was only regularly constituted in 1557; but doubtless in 1112, when the first charter was granted to the town, the country people came to the High-cross to sell their produce. Within the last fifty years Castle-street used to be thronged with hucksters on market-day, who completely blocked up the thoroughfare.

Sir Edward More, in his rental, tells us about his tenants in Castle-street. He says of one Thomas Rowe "that he is pretty honest, yet trust him not, for if he sees a greater party against you, he will deceive you." In Castle-street also resided "Richard Williamson," one of a family who have been denizens of Liverpool since Elizabeth's time, and whose descendants held property on which Williamson-square and street arose, their country house being thereabout. Sir Edward calls him "a notorious knave to me and mine." He makes mention also of Mr. William Bushell, a roper, who held probably "the Old Ropery." Colonel Birch, governor of Liverpool Castle, resided in Castle-street (dying at the age of 70); as did Mr. Clayton, the founder of the Clayton family. Sir Edward More had a horse-mill in Castle-street.

Brunswick-street was opened in 1790. There was previously no thoroughfare to the river side between Moor-street and Water-street. It cleared away Fenwick-court, cut through Chorley-street (an old town family were the Chorleys) and Drury-lane, formerly called Entwhistle-street, after an old Liverpool family, one of whose members was Recorder from 1562 to 1709. Brunswick street took off a corner of the theatre in Drury-lane, which occupied a part of the present Corn Exchange. This theatre was opened in 1759. Derrick says in his letter to the Earl of Cork, "It will hold £80, and is well furnished; the scenes are prettily painted, the clothing very rich, and every thing carried on with amazing propriety. They play three times a week; behind the boxes there is a table in the manner of a coffee-house, where tea, coffee, wines, cakes, and punch are supplied. A young woman attends to accommodate the company with such refreshments as they require, on very moderate terms. It is twenty-seven yards in front and sixteen deep." Shuter, a very facetious and clever actor, was the manager. He died November, 1776. On one occasion the absence of a lady had created considerable displeasure in the audience, when the manager was called for by mingled cries of "Shuter!" "Shuter!" "Miss so and so!" "Shuter"—when the latter came forward—and declared that if they wanted to "shoot her" they must do it themselves.

In *Williamson's Advertiser* of 1756, theatrical advertisements appear without specifying the whereabouts of the place of amusement. A barn is known to have been fitted up for performances, in Moor-street, adjoining the cock pit, early in the last century. The actors of this theatre removed to a place in the Old Ropery, in 1750, fitted up for dramatic performances, and it is probable that this was the theatre the advertisement alluded to. In or about the time of Charles the First, there was an uncovered theatre of some sort, at the bottom of Redcross-street, it stood on the site of part of the Carron Iron Warehouse in James-street, (called after Roger James, a man of eminence in his time.) It is believed that entertainments took place in the Castle when "the lord" occupied it; such displays being got up to amuse his retainers and tenants.

The Corn Market in Brunswick street opened in 1818. The new Corn Exchange was opened in 1854. At one time part of Fenwick street was called "Dry Bridge," from a dry arch crossing the ropery, which was one of the earliest established in Liverpool, running up from the river side to Castle street. The street called "The Old Ropery" perpetuates the recollection of the "Walk."

Liverpool was always noteable for its extensive roperies; at one time there were several in the town, as one on the site of St. John's Market, another between St. John's Cemetery and the Infirmary. There was another on the site of Skilhorn-street, another ran parallel with Renshaw-street, another in Duke-street on the site of Parr-street, while between the end of Ranelagh-street and Berry-street, as also in, and on the site of Berry-street, there were extensive "Walks." The ropers were great men in election times, and placed a high value on their votes.

Fenwick-street was formed and so called by Sir Edward More for four reasons; firstly, because he had married Miss Fenwick, one of the co-heiresses of Sir William Fenwick, of Meldon Hall; secondly, because her dowry enabled him to pay off his father's debts, incurred during the civil wars; thirdly, because Charles II. had confiscated his estate; and fourthly, because "God haith bene pleased to blese him with 4 sonnes and 2 daughtirs."

The history of the mutations in the value of property in Liverpool would be deeply interesting and curious to read, if it could be amply and truthfully told. About fifteen years ago a house in it, near Water-street, was sold for £2,000, and was then considered to be dearly bought, or rather well sold. These premises are now worth at least £10,000. A house in Castle-street has been sold for £1,450, having only four years to run, and the rental being £210. In 1561 the rental of a house in Castle-street was £4. In 1346 an orchard and dovecot near the Castle were let for 13s. 4d. per annum. The facts connected with the Warbrick Charities are curious, and may be properly told as connected with Castle-street. In 1706 Mr. Richard Warbrick, who lived at Warbreck Moor, gave £120 wherewith to build almshouses for poor sailors' widows, and £30 to the Corporation to keep these dwellings in repair. In 1721 he gave the yearly interest in two houses in Castle-street, two houses in Moor-street, and one in Chapel-street, for the same worthy purpose. In 1744 the trustees of this charity obtained possession of the two houses and *gardens* in Castle-street, which they leased for ninety-nine years, in 1747, at a rental of £26 per annum. In 1784 Mr. John Leigh bought this lease, subject to the same rent, for £515; and in 1787 sold it, subject to the same rent, to the mayor, alderman, and burgesses for £920, under power of Act of Parliament of George III., chap. 12, that enabled them to purchase property in Castle-street for the purpose of widening it. When the lease expired in 1846 *the lease could not be found, and the house had vanished.* It appeared, on enquiry, that a portion of the property had been swept away in the improvements of that part of the town, and the remainder had been conveyed by the Corporation as freehold. About twenty years ago this case was the subject of an arbitration, when the sum of nearly £4,000 was awarded to the Trustees of Warbrick's Charity. This freehold property was sold about four years ago for about £9,000 This shows the increase of the value of property in Castle-street. In 1777 Warbrick's Charity owned the two houses in Moor-street running through the Old Ropery. These were let for £15 per annum each, on a lease for ninety-nine years, which lease was subsequently extended for sixty years longer on payment of £150, a clause being inserted in it, that a warehouse should be erected on part of the land. This property now produces a yearly rental of £150 to £200.

It adjoins and forms part of Gibbon's Bakery in Fenwick-street. It will in process of time increase the funds of the Charity double that amount. The money (£4,000) received for the property in Castle-street was invested in a freehold shop in Bold-street, which produces £200 a-year to the Charity.

The clearing away of Castle Hill, the Potato Market, Temple Bar, and the adjacent buildings was a great improvement in this locality. Some of the houses in Preeson's-row, erected by Mr. Preeson, (and others in Castle-street,) were constructed of the stones and bricks of the Old Castle. Portions of the Castle Moat have been laid open, as for instance—in digging the foundations of the North and South Wales Bank, in 1838. When the excavations for St. George's Church were in progress, the base of the south-eastern tower of the Castle was discovered. One of the houses at the corner of Castle-street, which was erected on the site of Castle Ditch, subsided so materially as to give a decided incline to the rooms in it. It was said at the time that the dining-room of this house was very convenient, "as it permitted the gravy to flow on one side of the plate."

The Castle, on which St. George's Church stands, had four towers, with battlements and battlemented walls. In the interior was a large hall, a guard room, and numerous chambers. The moat was sixteen yards in width. In 1346 the governor's salary was derived from rents of "two wind milnes and a horse milne." It amounted to £6 13s. 4d. At one time the Castle was a complete refuge for disorderly persons. The parish once occupied it. In 1700 the building was let to the Earl of Macclesfield, at a rent of £5 17s. 0d. per annum. In 1704 the Corporation obtained from Queen Anne a lease with the Duchy of Lancaster, of the site of this Castle for 150 years, at an annual rent of £6 13s. 4d., for the erection of a church, and the old materials were given in for its use. About this time the parish set up a claim to the ground, but upon what plea is not known. They abandoned it in May, 1715. An old magazine in the interior was occupied as a bridewell; it contained two large under-ground dungeons, a room above, and twenty-five cells, six feet by three, and six feet high. The Castle was ordered to be demolished in 1659, but it was not until 1721 that it was entirely removed. When the foundations for the North Crescent were in progress the base of one of the round towers was discovered.

In the open ground in front of St. George's Church (a considerable portion of which, in October 1765, fronting the south gave way, the St. George's market used to be held. Here were the stocks and pillory. There was also a fish market at one time at the corner of Moor-street. It was converted in its latter years into a general market. Redcross-street was originally called "Tarleton's New-street." It was at one time quite a fashionable locality; some of the leading merchants residing in it. Colonel Tarleton erected an obelisk on the open ground at the top of Pool-lane. This street was called at one time "Water-lane" and "Liverpool-lane." It was a very narrow thoroughfare. Previous to the opening of the Old Dock in 1700 there was a weir across the Pool with a causeway and bridge, which was "the way to the Park." In 1561 an attempt was made to form a harbour by running out two stone piers. In war time Pool-lane was a favourite resort of the privateers-men, who spent their ill-gotten gains freely amongst the dingy denizens of the locality, in the public houses, and slop sellers shops. Desperate press-gang encounters took place in it, so that it was hardly safe to pass along it at times, certainly not in the night season. The alterations took place in this street in 1836, when the name of "South Castle-street" was substituted.

In Castle-street the first newspapers were published. *Williamson's Advertiser* appeared on the 25th May, 1756, and was discontinued as the *Liverpool Times*, 1856. *Gore's Advertiser* first appeared 27th December, 1765.

In the Crescent, on the site of Dodgson's shop, was published for some years the *Liverpool Standard*. Its first office was in High street. It was started about 1832, under the highest Tory patronage in the town. It had at one time considerable influence. Its editor was Mr. Robert Alexander, a gentleman who had been connected with a Glasgow paper.

Mr. Alexander was an admirable leader writer. Any one who can obtain a few copies of the *Standard,* of say about 1832 to 1837, will find many leading articles well worth perusal, although the interest of them may have passed away. They were strong, telling, and masterly. He handled subjects in a way that could not fail to damage his opponents. About the years above-mentioned Mr. Alexander was indulging in some fierce attacks upon Brother Jonathan, neither "mollifying phrases" nor measuring his abuse. About this time a curious incident occurred, which created considerable amusement amongst the few who were acquainted with the particulars.

One day a tall Yankee walked into the *Standard* office, holding in his hand a goodly sized stick. He requested "to see the editor." He was told he was not in. He called repeatedly during three or four days reiterating his wish. At length he was asked what he wanted with the editor. "Wall, sir, in the U-nited States I guess if we want to see an editor we kin see him and *du,* but I'm darn'd if there's any catching Mr. Alexander. Look ye har—stranger, *du* you see this stick—its what we call in the U-nited States a hickory. I was dining at the As-*tor* house the day before I left New York city, and I promised some friends of mine that I would give Robert Alexander a darn'd good cow-hiding for his articles on America, and I mean to du-it, sir."—"If you can," remarked the party to whom this speech was addressed; adding that a friend of his walked ten miles to give a man a "licking," and when he got to his journey's end he found that his opponent would not let him. "Wall, sir, that may be as it may, but I mean to try,—what I say I *du.*" The following day to that, when this threat had been uttered, there happened to be a very high tide in the Mersey. Thousands of persons had assembled on the pier-heads to see the exciting sight. There were no landing-stages then. Amongst the crowd was the party who had been spoken to in the *Standard Office* by the Yankee, and also Mr. Alexander. While the two were in conversation, to the horror of the first, who should come up to them but the American, with his hickory-stick, saying, "Wall, stranger, how are you?"

At this moment Mr. Alexander, who was of a very retiring disposition, walked away, and was instantly lost in the crowd, to the great relief of the *Standard* man. As soon as Mr. Alexander was well out of sight the Yankee was asked if he had seen his victim. "Wall, sir, I haint, and I fear I must give it up. I leave your city to-morrow, sir; and I guess I shall get pretty well laughed at when I get back to New York." "Why, said his companion, that was Mr. Alexander who was talking to me when you came up." "Oh, H——!" screamed the Yankee, giving his stick a flourish, "Which is the coon; show him to me." "Not I," replied his companion; "find him for yourself." "Now, look you here, stranger," said the excited American, pulling out his pocket-book, "Here is a ten dollar note, and it's yours if you'll only show me the man." A hearty laugh was the only response. "Darned if I wont make it twenty if you'll show me Robert Alexander, Esquire." Renewed laughter was all the irate man of the west could obtain in reply to his two *tempting* offers. Fearing that he should lose his intended victim, the Yankee bolted in amongst the crowd assembled, and dodged about trying to recognize him, actually scraping Mr. A's elbow on two occasions in his progress. Again joining the *Standard* man he exclaimed, "See, stranger, if you'll show me your editor, here's a fifty dollar note; and if you don't take it and show me the coon, I'm darned if I dont cow-hide *you*." "Well, then," said the *Standard* man, somewhat alarmed, "there he is," pointing at the same time to a well-known gentleman in town, who stood at least six feet three or four in his shoes, and was strong and burly in proportion. On seeing his supposed antagonist the Yankee seemed to consider whether it would be prudent to attempt to "hickorize" *him;* and while he was reflecting on the subject his informant made *his* escape, fearing that he might receive a vicarious punishment on his chief's account. The Yankee did not succeed in carrying out his threat against the real "Simon Pure," but gave his Broadway cudgel to a well-known literary doctor of the time who used to boast of its present and his *intended* uses.

## LORD STREET.

LORD-STREET was originally part of the Castle orchard. A pathway ran through it to the ferry, across "the pool," a stream which, rising in Moss Lake Fields, after a circuitous route, fell into the Mersey, westward of the site of the present Revenue buildings.

In 1346 an orchard in the vicinity, with a dove cot, were let for 13s. 4d. per annum.

In 1668 Caryl Lord Molyneux cut a road through this orchard, proposing to construct over the little river—superseding the ferry—a substantial bridge, to enable his tenants to gain easy access to the Great Heath, lying beyond it. To this seemingly advantageous proposition, the Liverpool authorities demurred, as being likely to interfere with their rights of possession in the waste lands, to which they laid claim, under Royal authority. Notwithstanding this opposition, Lord Molyneux commenced erecting the bridge, but the Liverpool Corporation caused the work to be pulled down as fast as it was put up. Thereupon his lordship desisted in his project. He brought an action against the mayor, aldermen and burgesses, for damages. This cause was tried at Lancaster, and ended in his lordship being non-suited. The result was beneficial in the main, for it brought about amity between the litigants, for Lord Molyneux was allowed to construct his bridge at the end of his new street, paying the Liverpool Corporation two pence per annum as lords of the soil, while his lordship granted to them a lease of the fee farm of the town for 1000 years, at £30 per annum, instead of £20 as heretofore. These terms being agreed upon in 1671—they gave the mayor, aldermen, and burgesses the possession of upwards of 1000 acres of land, which enabled them to introduce the plan of letting land on building leases for three lives, and afterwards for three lives and twenty-one years, renewable on easy terms. This lease put the corporation in possession at once of a good income, and gave them free access to the pool, besides conferring on them the right to all market and town dues, and other manorial rights.

This remarkable treaty was agreed to at the house of "Mistress Margery Formby," who gave to the corporation, in commemoration of the event, a handsome silver tobacco-box, which is now used as a snuff-box at the mayor's dinners. The council-men who so successfully negotiated this most important and advantageous bargain, were Edward Tarleton, William Percival, Henry Corless, Evan March, and James Whitfield. Their names should be writ in gold in the annals of the town, as its earliest benefactors.

Lord-street was called at one time "Lord's lane," and had on each side of it cottages occupied by the retainers of the great family who resided at the Castle. The road over the great heath led to West Derby, Wavertree, Woolton, and their vicinities. There were several ferries over the Pool.

During the seige, in 1644, batteries were erected along the rising ground from the Pool at the end of Dale street to the north of Lord street, to reply to Prince Rupert's earthworks and batteries on the Great Heath.

After the seige, during which the few houses in Lord's lane were almost all demolished, a better sort of dwelling was erected than had formerly been prevalent; good substantial houses taking the place of the mud-lath-and-plaster domiciles, similar to those we see in out-of-the-way country places. The Molyneux's erected a mansion in Lord street, which they occupied when the Castle became untenantable for want of repair. Their house stood on the site of Commerce court, over the entrance to which is to be seen a shield bearing the Cross Moline. The out-houses and stables extended beyond the site of the offices of the *Daily Post* and *Journal.* Previous to the alterations made of late years, the front of the original mansion was to be seen in the same state as the Molyneuxs had left it.

Lord-street was next called "Molyneux lane." It was afterwards entitled "Lord street," and it was then paved and lighted, and had shops and dwellings in continuous lines.

The former were low buildings with bow windows. Their prototypes may be still seen in some parts of the town. They had low ceilings with beams across in the interior, and their exteriors were covered with plaster, being notable for their want of uniformity and convenience. Some of them had dormer windows in the roofs, similar to those in two houses lately taken down in Whitechapel. The approach to others was up steps, a very common entrance at the time in most parts of the town, and still to be noticed here and there.

With the profits arising out of the slave trade and privateering, Liverpool, in the middle of the last century, took a sudden start, and became of some importance in the commercial world. The narrowness of its streets was constantly intruding upon the minds of the inhabitants, but it was not till about the years 1818 or 1820 that any very material action was taken. Meetings of the authorities frequently took place on the subject, but it was not until 1825 that an act for widening Lord street was obtained. Previously to this it was only about the width of Cable street, and scarcely two vehicles could pass each other. Indeed, there were very few carriages in Liverpool in the last century. The mode of conveyance for the gentry was by sedan chairs, attended at night by link-men. The extinguishers for the links were large open-mouthed cylinders, tapering to a point. Within a very few years some of these extinguishers might have been seen attached to the lamp-irons in front of the large houses in the town.

When the scheme of improvement was first started, it was proposed to include the south side of Cable street as the limit of the new street; and, had that been done, the present thoroughfare would have been none too wide for its traffic. Then it was that John street, which terminated in Harrington street, was carried through to Lord street, and was called "North John street; while Trafford's weint and Love lane, which terminated in Cable street, were carried through to Lord street, and were entitled "South John street." Both of these streets were widened at the same time.

The cost of widening Lord street, in 1829, was £106,000; John street, £32,750; Trafford lane, Cable street, and King street, £20,382. Love lane began to be widened October 20, 1827. Trafford's weint was altered at the same time.

The Clarendon Rooms were erected in 1828, by Mr. William Statham, Town Clerk.

From being a narrow, wretchedly-paved and badly-lighted street, Lord street has been rendered as convenient and handsome as any highway in the kingdom. This line of thoroughfare, from St. George's Church to Church street, any town may be proud of.

Up and down Lord street ebbs and flows the tide of human life, without stay or stop, from early morning till long after midnight; each hour exhibiting a different class of pedestrians. It has been said that if a man will stand in Lord street for two hours a day, for a week, he will see two-thirds of his acquaintances in the town during that time.

Near the top, on the south side, is an entry skirting Messrs. Milners' Fire Proof Safe Warehouse. This passage was at one time the entrance to the meat shambles, connected with St. George's Market, held on the open ground where the cab stand is located. There was another opening to the shambles on the site of Mr. Wren's establishment, in the Crescent.

In Lord street, on the north side, near the top, stands Barned's Bank, of painful notoriety. Not far below, are the extensive offices of the *Daily Post* and *Liverpool Journal*, on the site of a court wherein at one time was published the *Liverpool Chronicle*, a paper in its day well conducted and of staunch Liberal opinions.

In front of the *Daily Post* office may be seen at all hours numbers of boys and girls, making a living by selling the *Daily Post* and other local newspapers. Laughing, chaffing, joking, sometimes quarrelling, these little people offer their newspapers to the passers-by, and it is not their fault that a man goes his way without his newspaper. Up the passage and in the office of the *Daily Post* is exhibited that portion of the newspaper devoted to "Persons wanted;" and you may at all times, especially in the mornings, see numbers of seedy careworn people, scrutinising the advertisements of those who are in want of assistance. Here you may see the young man with a rakish look, who by his appearance would not keep any place he obtained very long. There you may notice some elderly man who finds himself pushed aside by the young and energetic. Some finding a suitable situation open make a note of it, and go their way hoping against hope, that they may not be too late in making application for the "berth." Here you notice some servant girls, scanning the list of "House servants wanted." Servant girls call themselves now a-days "Young persons." They are "purtikler" about the places they are eager to obtain, but which they are not "purtikler" how they keep.

Nearly at the bottom of the street, on the north side, was once a large coaching and posting establishment, known as "Bates Hotel," and had stabling in Rainford Gardens for about 100 horses. The entrance to these stables may still be seen in the archway approaching the offices of Messrs. Anthony Jones & Co. The oldest establishment in Lord street is Messrs. Groom's, Stationers. It has been in existence since the commencement of the century.

Mr. Roscoe at one time dwelt in Lord street. It was when he was practising as a Solicitor. The offices of his firm (Messrs. Aspenwall, Roscoe and Lace,) were in Rainford Gardens, looking down Button street. Mr. Roscoe afterwards resided over the offices. Button street was called after a Mr. Button, who was previous to his death 18th, Nov., 1785, the oldest burgess in Liverpool. He lived during six monarchs' reigns, being born in that of James II. He recorded his vote in the election of 1784.

The course of the Pool river reached some distance up Lord street. The *debris* have been found in digging the foundations of the houses even as far as Messrs. Stoniers' glass warehouse on one side of the street, and Messrs. Earps on the other.

# CHURCH STREET.

Compared with Dale street, Castle street, Water street, and Lord street, Church street may be regarded as a modern thoroughfare. It was, in 1600, a mere road which wound round the foot of the rising ground, which has been since covered with the habitations of Mount Pleasant, Copperas hill, to Gloucester street. In this state it continued, as many have conjectured, at first a mere pathway, and then a country road, until 1672, when the bridge at the foot of Lord Molyneux street was built, affording facilities to those who went eastward or southward. In 1680, after the ferry was done away with, Mr. Dansie, a merchant of Liverpool, erected on the east side of the Pool river the first good house. This mansion, which until lately, stood at the corner of Manesty lane and School lane, was occupied at one period as the "Apprentices' Library" and "Milner's Safe Works," when that excellent invention was in its infancy and budding fame.

The first Milners' safes were manufactured in a cellar of a house adjoining the Blue-coat School. The *Mercury Office*, or rather part of it, now occupies the site of the old house by the Pool side, the waters of which washed the gardens belonging to it.

The handsome suite of offices called Willmer's Buildings, which has superseded the old house, was erected by the late Mr. Edward Wilmer, and is now the property of his family.

On the west side of "the Brook," as it was called, was a road which was skirted by a breast-high wall. It was called in 1721 "Common Shore," being the way to the Glass-houses in Argyle street. On the Brook being covered over, the name of "Common Shore" was changed to Paradise street. It is so designated in Eyes's map of 1768, so that the change of name must have occurred between these two dates.

In 1700 Paradise street was unbuilt upon on the west side, and there was quite marshy land thereabouts for at least sixty or seventy yards from the present street line towards

South John street. If any one looks up Cable street, Thomas street, or Atherton street from Paradise street, it will be seen that not far from the ends of those narrow thoroughfares there is quite a dip down, until a rise takes place towards the top of the streets; and it is probable that Finney lane (just above the extensive offices of Messrs. Matthews Brothers', the printers of this work,) and King street lane are the course and site of the road that was ordered in 1721 to be re-repaired and made passable to the glass-house, which stood on the site of Argyle street. In digging the foundations for the new and handsome shops at the corner of Whitechapel, the bank of the old river was laid bare, the mud of which was of some thickness. The remains of a wharf or landing place were also discovered at the corner of Paradise street, when Mr. Taylor's bookseller's shop was in progress. Several large piles were there found driven in the mud, while scattered about were a great many quarried stones. The bed of the river has on several occasions been met with. It is to be hoped that, when the excavations for the new buildings at the corner of Paradise street are in progress, a little attention will be paid to this locality, so that some authentic information may be acquired, of no little local archæological interest.

The ferry-house was originally called the "Bote House." In 1680 it was sold to a barber for £200. This man's widow afterwards refused £800 for it. In 1734 "Joe Boke," the sexton of the "New Church," resided in it, or on one built on its site. "Joe Boke's house" was known as such, long after Joe Boke had gone the way of all sextons. On its site Bullock's Museum was erected, and there carried on many years. Mrs. Bullock died in 1800, and has some verses written to her memory in the *Gentleman's Magazine* of that year. Bonaparte's carriage was exhibited in this establishment about 1816. Kind's Bazaar succeeded the museum; it was taken down to widen Whitechapel. The excavation for the new buildings thereon, laid bare the shore of the river; it appeared to consist of a strong blue silt.

The stream which ran down Whitechapel, formerly called Frog lane, must have been considerable, from a ferry being established thereabout to cross it. Boats could be built on its banks, for in 1663 it is recorded that "No more boats be built in Frog lane." Within comparatively few years Whitechapel has been so flooded as to require the inhabitants to move about in washing tubs. Even now, where the cellars of the houses are deep, they are occasionally flooded, and have to be emptied for days together. There is a deep well in the cellar under the "Old Forum," in Marble street, that is always full, and has constantly to be pumped out. This "Forum," as it used to be called, was at one period the meeting place of the supporters of Liberal opinions. Dr. Shepherd, Egerton Smith, Edward Rushton, Mulock, (father of Miss Mulock, authoress of *John Halifax, Gentleman,*) and others have frequently debated on its stage.

"Ryley, the Itinerant," a celebrated comedian of his time, used to give his entertainments in it.

In 1796 the Literary Society, which held its meetings in the Forum, gave 100 guineas to the Charities, being the profits of its meetings.

In 1725 Frog lane, (so called from the number of frogs which frequented a ditch on the south side of it,) or Whitechapel, (from the little white chapel adjacent, erected by the Dissenters,) was entirely unbuilt upon, and was then marshy land thereabouts, as it was also in 1784. The Williamson family were at one time in treaty with the authorities to give up Williamson square for a market, which would have been accepted if they had "filled up the marshy land of Frog lane." This marshy land was prevalent on both sides of the pool, and, perhaps, skirted it even as far as Trafford's weint, extending originally to the mouth of the pool. In 1725 there were scarcely any houses between Paradise street, School lane, and Hanover street, with the exception of the Workhouse and Blue Coat Hospital. St. Peter's Church was then quite in the outskirts.

Mr. Danzie's example was followed by the Claytons, Tarletons, Basnetts, and Williamsons, in laying out streets from Church street, as we find in the names of those thoroughfares. Clayton square was projected between 1745 and 1750. Miss or Madame Clayton, to whom the property belonged, was related to the Tarletons. She was daughter of Mr. Clayton, a merchant, who represented Liverpool in six or eight parliaments. He was Mayor in 1689. In 1770 Miss Clayton purchased two lots of land of Mr. Williamson (who projected Williamson street and square), lying on the north side of her property, which was previously all fields and gardens. At the back of where Compton House stands there was once a racket or tennis court, and the houses thereabout had pigstyes and cowhouses attached to them.

The fields Miss Clayton bought were probably the following, advertised to be sold in *Williamson's Advertiser*, 1769: "Two fields, or closes of land, to be let, near to Peter's church, known by the name of Williamson's fields."

Miss Clayton's mansion stood on the site of the Prince of Wales Theatre and the Temperance Hotel. She was the first who kept a close carriage in the town. Her name is the second on the list of subscribers to the Liverpool Library in John street.

The erection of St. Peter's Church in 1700, and its consecration in 1704, gave Church street a great impetus.

The Parish of Liverpool was constituted in 1699, being then separated from Walton. Two rectors were appointed to officiate, one at St. Nicholas's, the other at St. Peter's. These were the Rev. Robert Stithe, and the Rev. William Atherton.

Originally the church-yard was planted with trees on its eastern side. In the church is a small theological library, purchased in 1715 by a bequest of Captain Fells. The rectors have occasionally added to it. It will be noticed that the four doors of the church are all of different designs. Some curious stories are current as to the cause of this architectural singularity.

Church street was not paved until 1760. The parapet was not flagged until 1816. Previous to the former date, there was only a four-yard causeway in the middle of the street. In wet weather the sides were complete quagmires. Shortly previous to the present century there were very few shops in Church street. In 1800 there was a bookseller's and stationer's shop, which was kept by a Mr. Muncaster, at the corner of Basnett street; there was a grocer's shop also, kept by a man named Brocklebank, which occupied a little bit of the site of Compton House, and there was a celebrated confectioner's shop, kept by a Mrs. Furness, at the corner of Church alley. The oldest shop now in the street is Hime's Music Warehouse. The only house stood on the site of this establishment previous to the erection of the church in 1700.

In 1803, Mr. Humphrey Hime, who had a shop in Castle street, established his son, the late Mr. Edward Hime, in Church street, and under the firm of Hime and Son this concern has ever since been continued. About 1830 Mr. Woolfield converted four shops into his beautiful bazaar, which was always one of the lions of the town. He was succeeded by Mr. Promoli, Mr. Hausburg, and then Mr. Tooke. A branch of Compton House, after the fire, closed its career. On this property once stood a celebrated tavern, called the "White Dog." In the parlour of this hostlery the tradesmen used to assemble, and there concoct schemes for getting up "privateers." These vessels were generally held in shares, at a low rate, so that the risk might be spread over a wide surface. It has been asserted that, during the war time, there was not a man, woman, or child in Liverpool, of any respectability, that did not hold one or more shares in privateers. In 1777, in Liverpool, thirteen seamen received each £1328 as prize money, on account of vessels they had captured. A third of the proceeds of prizes were alloted to the crews of privateers.

At No. 10, School lane, now a warehouse, Mr. Roscoe, after dissolving partnership with Mr. Bannister, re-commenced practice as an attorney. In his advertisement in *Williamson's Advertiser*, February 23rd, 1776, he styles it as "his house in School lane."

At the commencement of the present century there was a small cattle market held once a week in Church street. A very old inhabitant recollects seeing the farmers' carts, on market days, ranged along the Church-yard wall.

The Post-office in and after 1775 was in John-street, between Dale street and Prince's street. In 1800 it was removed to Church street. In 1839 it was transferred to Revenue Buildings. The want of room in Post-office-place was the cause of constant scenes of confusion on the arrival of the mails.

Where the "Athenæum" and adjoining buildings stand there were at one time an orchard and garden, which belonged to Mr. Brooks, great uncle to Rector Brooks. Brooks' alley is named after him.

The News-room stands on the site of a large pond, whereon the lads used to skate and slide in winter. The Dispensary was erected on the site of the orchard. This charity owes its existence to Mr. Wyke, who in 1778 started it at 75, Prince's street, John street. It was removed to Church street in 1788. This property was sold in 1829, for £6,000. The Dispensary in Vauxhall road succeeded it.

Parker street was widened in 1847.

In 1821 Mrs. Cash converted the private dwellings next to the Dispensary into shops.

In Post-office-place "The Academy of Art" was held until it closed, two or three years ago, after some struggles for existence. Its decadence was attributable to bad management and contentions amongst those who ought to have been united. The first "Academy of Art" was commenced in 1769, through the instrumentality of Mr. Wyke, the Dale-street watchmaker, and it had rooms in John-street. In 1775 this society dissolved. In 1784 a new society commenced, and that year exhibited some fine pictures. There were two of Sir Joshua Reynolds' amongst the number. In 1794 this society collapsed like its predecessors, and it was not until 1810 that any attempt at an academy was again projected. In that year, on the 1st of August, an exhibition took place in the Gothic Hall, Marble-street.

Amongst the first associates were Mr. Roscoe, Mr. Gibson, the celebrated sculptor, Mr. W. D. Rathbone, Wright, the painter, Mr. Egerton Smith, and Mr. Matthew Gregson. The first exhibition was held in John-street. Next year it was held over the Union News-room, when Chantry, the sculptor, was an exhibitor. From 1811 to 1831 the exhibitions took place in the Royal Institution, Colquitt-street. In 1831 the society removed to Post-office-place, where it remained until it ceased to exhibit.

The Athenæum News-room was established in 1798, by Dr. Rutter, whose portrait hangs in the Medical Library, the books of which were bequeathed by him to the profession. Mr. Joshua Lace, Mr. Roscoe, and Mr. Currie were associated with Dr. Rutter. The idea of the Athenæum arose from the annoyances that gentlemen had to encounter at the "Merchants' Coffee House," in Old Church-yard, and at "Pontack's," in Water-street, through the boisterous conduct of the sea captains who frequented those taverns.

On the site of the Liver Drapery establishment was the Liver Theatre. It was opened about 1829 or 1830, by Messrs. Raymond and Hammond, two talented actors then attached to the stock company of the Theatre Royal. It held a prominent position for many years in the public favour. After some vicissitudes in its closing years, it was, about 1849, converted to its present purpose. It would hold about 800 people. Beneath the theatre Mr. Hodgson had extensive auction-rooms. His son is now in business in Birkenhead.

In Hanover-street, which was a sandy lane in 1725, there was only one house near the site of the present Gradwell-street, besides the farm-house and dairy opposite the end of Church-street. In Hanover-street, in 1827, the Bank of England commenced business in Liverpool. Their branch was established at the corner of Seel-street. They purchased the house of the Steers family. The Steers were descendants of Mr. Steers, the engineer, of the Old Dock. At this time Hanover-street was a fashionable locality. It will be noticed that there are the remains of some very handsome houses in it. Mr. Seel had a mansion at the corner of Seel-street. Mr. Parr had a large house with gardens at the corner of College-lane. In Hanover-street was the Excise Office. Mr. John Colquit resided in this street in 1759. In that year his house, warehouse, and garden were announced for sale at the

Merchants' Coffee House. The house is still standing. The workhouse was in College-lane, Hanover-street. At one time it could have been seen that several of the houses had their fronts placed in an oblique direction to the line of the street. This was done, it was said, to obtain a view of the river and the old dock. In Hanover-street, at the corner of Wood-street, was Sadler's Bathing Establishment, which was much resorted to. Mr. Sadler had a great taste for æronautism and made frequent ascents in this neighbourhood and in other parts of the country. He ascended from the grounds of the Pilgrim House, on the 13th August, 1812. Upwards of 70,000 persons, it is said, assembled in the vicinity to witness this ascent, which was the first that had taken place since Lunardi ascended from the fort in 1785. The balloon descended on this occasion near Derby Chapel. In the month of October following, Mr. Sadler made an attempt to cross the channel, ascending in Dublin. When off the Welsh coast the balloon dropped into the sea. The æronaut would inevitably have perished but for the timely passing of a Manx fishing-boat, by the crew of which he was rescued from his perilous position. Mr. Sadler was thrown out of his balloon after an ascent at Bolton, on September 22nd, 1824, and was killed. His body was brought to Liverpool, and interred in Christ's Church, Hunter-street.

---

## BOLD STREET

WAS called after the Bold family, who held property in it. This fashionable street, in which are so many beautiful shops with wares to minister to comfort, taste, and luxury, was nearly all private dwellings forty years ago. It was not built upon in 1785. In the last century a portion of the land on which Bold-street stands was offered for sale. The field was skirted by Mr. Staniforth's roperies on one side, and Wood-street on the other, and went as far up as Concert-street. Five hundred pounds were asked for it, but only £475 were bid—about the value of a floor of a good house in the street at present! At the top of Church-street were once some alms-houses. These were removed in 1787, with others in the town, to their present position, as being a "more healthy situation." Where Mr. Dismore's shop stands, was a dairy farm. It possessed a well of very fine water, which was retailed at a halfpanny per bucket. The proprietor was Mr. Brooks, who held the little field and orchard on which the Athenæum was erectcd. Mr. Brooks' house had a porch, and presented quite a countryfied appearance.

The Waterloo Hotel was erected by Mr. Gore, as a mansion, about 1760. Mr. Staniforth, who owned the extensive roperies, extending to Leece-street, next occupied it. Along side of his "walk" were those of Mr. Machell. After the roperies were discontinued, the land was occupied as Tobin's cooperage. This property was then sold to Mr. Jevons, the iron merchant, who converted it into arcades, which at first were complete failures, the shops being nearly all unlet and the place empty. When the lower arcade was first opened the walls were adorned by frescoes. It is greatly to be regretted that this property was not purchased in 1851, when the opportunity of widening Bold-street was available.

The Lyceum News Room was established on the site of a timber yard, in 1800. It was erected to provide accommodation for the library also, which was deposited in a Tontine Building in Lord-street, since occupied by Mr. Thornley, the tailor, who succeeded his uncle. His shop was next to Barned's Bank. This Tontine was sold freehold, in 1867, for £7680, at the rate of £65 per square yard. Mr. Robert Clay, wholesale chemist, and two others were the last of the lives.

When Newington was being laid out a deep pit was found in it, which was supposed to have been an attempt at opening a coal mine. At the corner of Newington "Bridge," as it was at one time called, in consequence of an arch crossing the Roperies, resided Dr. Parks, a celebrated physician of his day. He it was who attended the duel between Colonel Bolton and

Major Brooks, the former calling for him in his carriage on his way to the scene of conflict.

The Music Hall, erected in 1786, which stood at the corner of Concert-street, was open many years. By the celebrated John Braham it was pronounced to be the finest room for singing in, in the United Kingdom. All the first artistes of the day have appeared on the stage. It underwent many mutations, and passed through many hands before it was demolished and applied to other than musical purposes. In October, 1860, it was sold by auction for £6,900.

The present Queen's Hall was originally the learned Dr. Thom's Chapel. It has since been used for the exhibition of pictures, and other purposes. It is now a very elegantly fitted up chamber, with a pretty stage adapted for performances on a limited scale.

Some excitement once took place in Bold-street by the discovery of the bones of a gigantic animal while digging some foundations. It was suddenly recollected by an "old inhabitant" that they were those of an elephant which had died in the course of being exhibited. The field by St. Luke's Church was at one time called the "Pump Field," from the circumstance of the public pumps and corporation water-pipes, which were of wood, being made on it. The casting of iron pipes quite superseded these water ducts. Some fields in the Vauxhall-road were also used for the like purpose. The Corporation water-works were at one time situated in Berry-street. The first stone of St. Luke's Church was laid by the Mayor, Mr. James Drinkwater, in 1811, but it was not until the Mayoralty of his son, Sir George Drinkwater, in 1830, that this church was completed. The original walls stood as ghostly objects many years, and were obliged to be taken down before the edifice was proceeded with in earnest. Leece-street was called after Mr. Leece, a merchant, whose daughter married Mr. Drinkwater, the potter, in Duke-street.

# RANELAGH STREET.

THE laying out of Church-street arose from the accommodation of the bridge over the Pool inducing parties to purchase property and erect houses in the new line of way. As Church-street began to be inhabited, an outlet from its southern end was necessary, hence the formation of Ranelagh-street, or "The Way to Manchester" as it was then called, as shown by Chadwick's map of 1725. It is a curious circumstance that the line of road should have taken the turn as it did, along Lime-streeet or Limekiln-lane; but the cause of that direction was to skirt the high ground of Copperas-hill, Shelhorne-street, Gloucester-street, and Lord Nelson-street; it is, however, still more singular that Bold-street should not have at once been projected as a continuation of Church-street, and that no way, except along Renshaw-street, should have been formed at that time to the south from this part of the town. The road out of which Ranelagh-street was formed was probably at first a mere narrow lane across the "Great Comyn" as it was called, by which access was obtained up Brownlow-hill, then called "The way to Wavertree," to the south-east vicinity of the town. The tide of population took a northward direction long before it surged southwardly, for St. Anne-street, Rose-hill, Beau-street, and Cazneau-street were fashionable parts of the town long before Abercromby-square, Falkner-square, and streets in that direction became the favourite localities of the upper class of the town people.

Ranelagh-street in the middle of the last century had few houses in it. Beyond Lawton-street, southwards, were Mr. Cropper's fields (whence Cropper-street.) Mr. Shaw had two large fields where now we find the blocks of houses extending from Ranelagh-place north to St. John's-lane. Great Charlotte-street, named in honour of the Queen of George III, was occupied by roperies, and was not laid out until previous to 1785, when Queen's-square was projected. It was proposed at one time to erect a handsome Crescent on the site and southward of the present Fish Market in Great Charlotte-street, but it was not until about 1796 that this road was actually made to Ranelagh-street. The roperies which occupied the western side of St. John's Market, were in existence up to the time of the building of that market, which was opened in 1822. Lucas's Repository was originally erected to accommodate the Liverpool Light Horse, as a riding school and stables. In this street stood, previous to the widening of it about 1835, a circular wooden building, called the Sanspareil Theatre. It stood in a timber yard to the north of the carriage manufactory. The building was originally erected by a man named Marshall, and was known as "Marshall's Moving Panorama." It was converted into a theatre about 1829. It was a good property although the prices were low, and the audience of the very roughest. The proprietor, Mr. Holloway took great pains in getting up his pieces in good style; and, considering the lowness of the admission, the scenery, dresses, and appointments, were all above mediocrity. Mr. Holloway used to stand at the south or pit door, to take the money, while "missus" attended at the north or gallery entrance. Holloway was much respected, and realized an independence. Previous to the street being widened it was a narrow shabby thoroughfare. In 1776 a house was advertised for sale in Ranelagh-street, the rent of which was £2 12s. In 1802 it was discovered that a limekiln had been in operation in the streets for upwards of thirty years without its existence being known to the neighbours. Renshaw-street was at one time skirted by roperies.

Between Renshaw-street and Mount Pleasant, at the close of the last century, and commencement of the present, were numerous orchards and gardens, belonging to the tradespeople of the town. They used to resort to these gardens in the summer time, and entertain their friends in summer-houses erected on them. Some of these summer-houses were comfortably furnished. Nearly opposite Heathfield-street there will be noticed a tall thin house that seems as if it had once belonged to a row, but had run away from its neighbours till it stopped for want of breath. This curious-looking house is said to have been one of the summer-houses alluded to, only very considerably added to, since its first erection. A view of it is given in an engraved picture of Liverpool taken from the "Public Walk," which may be met with in the Binns' Collection in the Free Public Library. The proprietors of these gardens invited their friends to convivial meetings, to eat the fruit in season, and drink rum punch and "braggart," a celebrated beverage of the time, composed of ale, sugar, and spices. The writer was once treated to a glass of it by a very old lady, celebrated as a beauty in her day, and famous as a "braggart" brewer. He thought it particularly nasty. Mr. Crosbie, mayor of Liverpool in 1765, lived in the large house at the corner of Heathfield-street. In Mr. Crosbie's garden St. Andrew's Church was built. When Newington Chapel was erected about 1780 complaints were made about its distance from the centre of the town, the muddiness of the way in winter, and that there was a stile to cross over to get to it. The chapel was erected by the seceders from the ancient chapel in Toxteth Park in consequence of Mr. Hugh Anderson's appointment, he having expressed Arian doctrines.

Copperas-hill, formerly called Elliot-hill, was entirely unbuilt upon in 1802, as was Brownlow-hill. The Copperas Works belonged to Mr. R. Hughes, mayor in 1756, and others. They stood near Silver-street. The Corporation indicted the proprietors for carrying on a nuisance in 1770. The action was tried at Lancaster on the 22nd April. Thirty-five witnesses were examined, who gave evidence that the effluvium from the works was prejudicial to health and vegetation. It was agreed that the calcinery portion of the premises should be closed at once, and the proprietors have two years granted them to remove their works. Hilbre Island was suggested at the time as a fitting site for the purpose. In the *Liverpool Chronicle* of 1768 there is a letter ridiculing the writer of a communication in a former number for maintaining that the works were not injurious to health. Near White Mill-street was a mill which was blown down during a great storm that devastated this district, February 2nd, 1794. The miller was coming down the steps when the building came tumbling about him. Although he was buried in the debris, he sustained little hurt.

Where Hotham-street (formerly called Duncan-street) runs into London-road there once stood the Quaker's School, which occupied the site of a tumble-down old mill. When the foundations for the school were in course of preparation, a grave, containing a skeleton, was found in it. A romantic story was current about this skeleton at one time, purporting it to have been the remains of a miller who had been slain by his partner; but the fact was that the bones were those of one of the miller's men, who had been killed in a fight with one of his fellow-workmen, who had buried him in the foundations of the mill. The man was supposed at the time to have been carried off by a pressgang—a not uncommon occurrence for people to disappear unaccountably in those "dear, good old times." In one of the fields off Copperas Hill a well-known atrocious ruffian of his time, named "Red Dick," was hanged for murder. So countryfied was Copperas Hill, even at the commencement of the present century, that there is a story told of a hare being chased down it by Lord Sefton and his hounds; and while passing the house which stood at the corner occupied by one of the "five Harveys," Miss Harvey, then a little girl, (afterwards Mrs. Ellison) ran out at the back door so suddenly as to turn the hare and throw the dogs out, "at which," declared the lady, "his lordship and the gentlemen all swore most lustily."

At the bottom of Copperas Hill and Brownlow Hill, in the middle of the last century, and it continued open until 1780, stood the "White House Tavern" and Ranelagh Gardens. The Adelphi Hotel occupies the site of it. The date of the commencement of this establishment cannot be ascertained. It has been stated at 1759. In June, 1760, it was advertised for sale in *Williamson's Advertiser*, as it was found perhaps to be a bad speculation. The advertisement thus appeared:—"To be sold by auction, on the 14th day of July, at the Golden Fleece, Dale-street, all that messuage or dwelling house, with the outbuildings and large gardens thereunto belonging, situate at the upper end of Ranelagh-street, commonly called and known by the name of the "White House and Ranelagh Gardens." It must have been open long previous to 1775, because performances were advertised in *Gore's Advertiser*, of May, 1766, and in Eyes' map of 1768 the gardens form a remarkable feature, the shape of the flower beds and walks being laid down with the temple in the centre, and the fish-pond adjacent. In these gardens mountebanks and jugglers exhibited their dexterity, somewhat after the present fashion. Concerts were given outside, and in the large ball-room in the White House. The entertainments wound up with a grand display of fireworks. These fireworks were complained about in the latter days of their existence by the inhabitants of Ranelagh-street as a dangerous nuisance. It was the fashion of the time to frequent "Ranelagh" in the fruit season, when "strawberries buttered with crame" were to be had. Ladies and servant girls used to take children in the gardens in the day time to feed the fish, with which the pond or tank was abundantly supplied. A doggrel in praise of this establishment written at the time alludes to the practice—

> "In this delightful place
> We gain a double treat,—
> We see reflected woman's face,
> And little fishes eat."

Over the garden door was this distich—

> "You are welcome here all day :
> But if fruit or flower you pluck
> One shilling you must pay."

The admittance appears, by the old bills extant, to have been 1s. Round the walks were alcoves, in which tea and other refreshments were served. In the Chinese temple the company used to sit and watch the promenaders below.

After the closing of the White House Tavern, towards the end of the last century, and previous to the property being converted into the Adelphi Hotel, there were four large houses erected on the site of it. The entrance to one was in Brownlow Hill, and other in Copperas Hill. The two centre houses were entered from Ranelagh-place. The house in Brownlow Hill was occupied by a Miss Pearson, a Quaker lady; it was famous as being the habitation of some of the young and leading bachelors of Liverpool. The house next to it in Ranelagh-place was at one time the residence of Mr. Charles Lawrence, father to Mr. George Hall Lawrence. It was next occupied by Mr. Anthony Molyneux, of the firm of Greaves, Molyneux and Co., eminent brokers. About this time, 1817, Dr. Carson took possession of the next house, where he remained till 1830. The Golightly's resided at one time in the house on the Brownlow Hill side. They were a very old and highly respectable family. The family were horrified by discovering one Sunday morning, on returning from church, their footman hanging in a well staircase. He had destroyed himself through a love affair with one of his fellow-servants. The house in Copperas-hill was occupied by Mr. Hughes, of the firm of Rathbone, Hughes, and Duncan—the former gentleman being father of the late venerated Mr. William Rathbone, and grandfather to our present member. A Captain Phibbs succeeded Mr. Hughes. He was a large landed proprietor in Ireland, and married Miss Renshaw, daughter to the then rector. Mr. Bulmer, the parish curate, next lived in it with his son-in-law, the Rev. Mr. Horner. It was about the year 1827 that Messrs. William and Joseph Ewart purchased the house on Copperas-hill, and the one adjoining, converting them into the Adelphi Hotel, and placing the late Mr. Radley therein as their tenant. About 1830 they acquired the two adjoining houses. After the death of Mr. Radley the Adelphi became a joint-stock property. The shops opposite the hotel in Ranelagh-place were at one time extensive stables, kept by Mr. Peter Burns. They extended along the whole side of that vicinity. The stables were succeeded by houses, which gave way to the present handsome establishments. Mr. Burns occupied the house at the corner, where his wife kept lodgers.

Ranelagh-street was considered at one time to be a very genteel street, their being only private houses in it, occupied by the most respectable tradesmen and professional gentlemen.

# LIME STREET.

Lime-street in 1790 was called Limekiln-lane, from the lime-works which stood on the site of the Railway Station, near Lord Nelson-street. These limekilns were suppressed in 1804, the proprietors being indicted for a nuisance by the authorities, the physicians attending the Infirmary giving evidence of the injurious effects of the azotic gas on their patients suffering from pulmonary complaints. Lime-street does not seem to have been a favourite locality for the erection of private residences, for up to even 1812 the land was unbuilt upon on the east side beyond Skelhorne-street, which was at that time, and had been for years previously, an extensive ropery. In the fields thereabout disgraceful exhibitions of brutality took place in cock-fighting, dog-fighting, and pugilistic encounters, when the "roughs" of the town, who were fond of assembling there, had their little differences to settle. On Shrove Tuesday, in "the good old times," it was a favourite pastime to turn cocks loose, in the presence of boys, who had their hands tied behind to prevent them seizing the poor birds in any way except with their teeth. The boys used to run the cocks down and then cast themselves on them to prevent their escape. Tying a cock to a stake and throwing at it, Aunt Sally fashion, was also a favourite pastime in this locality. Many are now living who can recollect such scenes taking place in Waterworth's fields, on the site of Gloucester-street. On the site of the Concert-hall, Lord Nelson-street, two or three of the rebels of '45 were hung, their graves being made at the foot of the gallows. The nuisance of the brawlings that took place in the Lime-street fields, especially on Sundays, called forth at length interference by the authorities, and strong measures were taken to suppress such unseemly scenes. Gloucester-street, although projected in 1802, was not built upon until 1814. The cattle market was held in a large yard on the site of the Railway Station. In 1567 we find it "held out of town, over against the Castle." That would be in the open ground now occupied by the top part of South Castle-street. In 1572 it was removed to the bottom of Chapel-street. In 1780 a cattle market was established in the present St. James's-place, opposite the church. Next we find it mentioned that a small market was held in Church-lane; next we find it in Lime-street; then it was taken to Netherfield road, at the west end of Everton Valley; and in 1830 to its present location at the Old Swan.

The destruction by fire of the Caxton Printing Office on January 31st, 1821, created a great sensation in the town. These extensive works occupied nearly the whole of one side of Bolton-street. The fire was in existence for months; and it was only finally subdued by the bricks being carted away in a hot state to Mosslake fields, where they were left to cool. So intense was the heat, that men were employed to rake out the bricks one by one, with portions of the burning matter, as they could lay hold of it. Thousands of bibles and prayer-books were destroyed. The damage was estimated at about £36,000.

At one time a large room on the ground floor of the printing office was occupied by a schoolmaster, who was wont every morning to range his boys in rows before their forms in a kneeling position, to receive punishment for their previous day's shortcomings. He made them adjust their nether garments, so that the twig from the tree of knowledge could have its due effect. This cruel domine then went slashing up and down the ranks, till every boy had received his full share of correction; nor was any one allowed to rise until the whole process had been completed. One of the lads having mentioned this atrocious proceeding to a benevolent gentlemen, he determined to be present to witness one of these wholesale flagillations. Walking one morning into the school he was so horrified at the yells uttered, and the scene before him, that he forthwith made the whole affair public, and such was the excitement on the subject that the school was suddenly closed, the domine being obliged to decamp and take to shop-keeping, in Paradise-street, for a living.

The London and North-Western Railway Station occupies the site of Waterworth's-fields. The Liverpool and Manchester

Railway was in the first instance suggested, it is said, by a Mr. James, a London engineer, who called a meeting of gentlemen together, who entered into a subscription to defray the expenses of a survey. In 1823 Mr. Hartley made the survey of the country, but nothing was done until 1824, when Mr. Joseph Saunders, who it is said really originated the idea of the line, published a clever pamphlet on the subject, urging the attention of the Liverpool and Manchester merchants to it. The sum of £300,000 was then raised, and a prospectus in October issued. The scheme met with great opposition at every step. Lords Derby and Sefton opposed it. Mr. Huskisson opposed it; and numerous parties, whose interests were supposed to be affected by it, combined against it; but nevertheless the railway was opened on the 15th September, 1830, on which occasion Mr. Huskisson was killed. Mr. Huskisson, the day before his death, received a deputation from Hyde, who wanted him to support a railway from Manchester to that place, when he told them in the Mayor's (Sir George Drinkwater) room that, though he voted for the Liverpool and Manchester Railway as *an experiment*, he would never consent to see England *grid-ironed by railways!* A curious circumstance may be here related connected with the Liverpool and Manchester Railway not generally, indeed perhaps not known, to but few now living. In or about 1829, previous to the opening of the line between Liverpool and Manchester, the late Mr. Bartholemew Bretherton, the eminent coach proprietor, made an offer (which was then thought a good one) to farm the railway passenger traffic for ten years for £20,000 a year, so little was at that time known as to how the profits of the line were to be derived. It was then anticipated that the goods traffic would yield the most income, and that the transport of passengers would be only a secondary consideration. At that time, or about that time, a Mr. Miles, a Yorkshire gentleman, who had been instrumental in getting up the Stockton and Darlington Railway (called the "Quaker's Road," from the Pease's and other "*friends*" being largely concerned in it), being in Liverpool, he waited on an influential director and offered to render assistance in promoting the

Liverpool and Manchester Line, or giving any information he could, that might be useful to the directors. Mr. Miles' services were accepted, and he was requested to draw up a report upon any subject he thought might prove useful. He selected the passenger traffic, and showed that the probable receipts for the first half-year would be upwards of £60,000. This statement so astounded the directors that they laughed at it, and refused to receive the report. Mr. Miles was urged to reconsider it, the directors assuring him that he was "completely wrong." Mr. Miles, however, stuck to his report, and had an interview with the board, letting them into the secret of the bases of his calculations, which were so feasible that the report was at length accepted, and Mr. Miles received a complimentary fifty guineas for his trouble. The result of this was, that the board, relying on Mr. Miles' statements, broke off their negociation with Mr. Bretherton, and resolved to stand or fall by the result of keeping the line in their own hands. To show how near Mr. Miles was to the mark, the first half-year's receipts for carrying passengers amounted to over £70,000. Mr. Miles's calculation was thus worked out:—Take the number of inhabitants between A and Z, and of each intermediate station, and divide by three, and you will obtain the number of yearly railway passengers. Query: How does this work now!

When the Manchester and Liverpool Railway first opened the passengers were landed in Crown-street, and conveyed down to the town in cabs, coaches, and other vehicles, along Myrtle-street, then all open ground.

At the entrance to Lime-street, on the western side, there were originally some small shabby-looking dwelling-houses, which were entered by steep steps. These domiciles were all swept away when the street was widened in 1845, and the late Mr. Tuton commenced erecting the first block of his noble buildings from Back Lime-street to Messrs. Forrest's glass warehouses. The land was obtained from the Corporation on a seventy-five years' lease, at "a peppercorn rent, if demanded, on the Feast of St. Michael the Archangel." These buildings were completed in 1846. The shops and houses hereabout occupy about 1,200 square yards of ground. They were then valued at £20,000. Mr. Tuton next erected the Liverpool County Court. This court, which stands on about 280 square yards, was opened September 1st, 1848. It is leased to Government for seventy-three years. Mr. Lowndes was the first judge; Mr. Park, treasurer; and Mr. Statham, registrar.

The next building undertaken by Mr. Tuton was the "Teutonic Hall," now the handsome "St. James' Hall," and the shops and houses round to Mitchell-place. These buildings stand on 1,213 square yards, including the County Court. The value of this property was then about £30,000. The shops and houses in the Quadrant were next erected by Mr. Tuton, in 1847. It was that gentleman's intention, but for some reason the design was objected to, to make both sides of the Quadrant alike. Mr. Tuton gave his workmen a dinner in the Hall on the completion of his buildings, at the time of the meeting of the British Association, which had engaged his new Hall. At the corner of Rose-street stood Mr. Lister's Baptist Chapel, erected in 1802-3. This chapel stood on the site of Hellewell's premises, and on the side-path in front. The Rev. Mr. Lister was highly esteemed as a pious Christian and a learned man. His chapel was taken down in 1844. The materials were removed to Bootle, wherewith to erect the Baptist Chapel there, which somewhat resembles the original. Mr. Lister opened the handsome chapel in Myrtle-street and Hope-street on the 10th January, 1844. He remained there till 1857, when he was succeeded by the present greatly esteemed and highly-talented minister, Rev. Hugh Stowell Brown. Mr. Lister died in 1857, aged seventy-three.

When Elliot-street was widened there was at the corner of Back Lime-street a disreputable house, in which a skeleton was found buried in the basement. Considerable excitement was caused at the time in consequence, but no discovery was made as to the identity of the individual who was supposed to have been "put out of the way." Previous to this time Elliot-street was very narrow and inconvenient for the increasing traffic of the town. At one time there was a row of isolated houses on the east side of Clayton-square, which it was necessary to pass round to get into Elliot-street. Until commenced by Mr. Tuton, the land all the way to St. John's-lane was unbuilt upon.

The hotels, the Washington and the Queen's, were next erected, and also the handsome ironwork warehouse of Mr. Alderman Bennett. This ground when vacant was a favourite resort for mountebank shows, menageries, and such like displays. Opposite the top of St. John's-lane there was at one time a large book stall, and a capacious stall for the sale of herbs and quack medicines, the proprietors of which were Messrs. Startup and Brown, one of whom sold the drugs, while the other, dressed in a "mortar board" cap and a stuff gown, delivered short lectures to the gaping crowds which assembled in front of the stall, on the *medicamina artis*.

Not far from this was the "Fall Well." It was a square enclosure covered by rude stone arches. When this well was filled up the water was diverted to the garden at the back of Mr. Rowe's house, now the Stork Hotel, where for some years it appeared in the form of a fountain.

St. John's Church-yard was originally intended as a cemetery only. It was consecrated in 1767. There was a chapel at the southern corner. St. John's Church was not completed till 1784, although the first stone of it was laid as early as 1775. The burials in St. John's Cemetery were very numerous. Up to 1820, for the preceding twenty years, they amounted to 27,080. This ground was closed December 31, 1854. All sorts of people were interred in St. John's Cemetery. Those who had "gone to their death" by mischance, or committed suicide, or died in prison. In 1806 there was a huge pit dug in it which was covered by folding doors, or flags. The dead were deposited in the pit, and the earth was thrown upon each layer of coffins as it was completed. In 1816 a writer in the *Mercury* complains of the frightful stench arising from the public grave in the Parish Cemetery, suggesting that a similar contrivance to that used in St. John's Yard should be constructed to cover it. The Lunatic Asylum stood at the top of the cemetery.

In the open ground opposite the Railway Station at one time were some almshouses; these were removed, with the other buildings of a like character, to the back of Hope-street. The Hay Market was held in the open ground here about 1814, when the number of carts coming into the town had so much increased as to block up the Old Hay Market. The Hay Market was continued here until 1841, when it was removed to Great Homer-street and Olive-street, the site of the Botanic Gardens. The latter market proving a failure, was soon closed. The Infirmary and the Seamen's Hospitals stood at the top of Shaw's-brow, on the site of St. George's Hall. The first was erected in 1748, the expenses being defrayed by public subscription. The Corporation granted for it, a lease of the land for 999 years. The first president was Edward Earl of Derby. The gardens for the use of the convalescents extended to where are now the steps leading to the esplanade in front of the hall. The building was of brick. The wings of the Infirmary were occupied as the Seamen's Hospitals. They were receptacles for decayed seamen and their wives. The seamen sailing from Liverpool contributed sixpence per month, by Act of Parliament, for their support. They were erected in 1752. The Lunatic Asylum and Infirmary on being closed were used as barracks.

In digging the foundations for these buildings, remains of Prince Rupert's batteries and trenches were met with to some extent; and in them many little articles, such as portions of flasks, balls, bones, pots, &c., were discovered.

---

## LONDON ROAD.

The London-road, although in reality an ancient way out of Liverpool, is quite modern in respect to its dwellings. Up to a comparatively recent date it could only have been a mere bridle-road over the heath. The erection of the bridge across the Pool, at the foot of Lord-street, gave an impetus to the spread of population on the south-eastern side of the stream, and consequently caused the opening of a road to the interior of the country in that direction. London-road was formerly called the "Way to Warrington." It was traversed only by pack horses, which went in strings. The old road of 1720 could at one time have been clearly made out, and was so narrow that only three animals could have made use of it. It is said that even now some portions of this old way may be traced by turning off to the right-hand from near the furthest end of Edge-lane, and, after crossing Mill-lane, by going to the right of the footway running across the fields towards Wavertree Nook. In these days of change all traces of it may, however, now be lost. In 1775 there were only two turnpike roads out of Liverpool, viz., the London-road and the Prescot-road through Ormskirk. In 1725 the stage-coach came no nearer to Liverpool than Warrington. We hear of the pomp and state in which the nobility and gentry used sometimes to travel with their six and eight horses; but it was not pride but necessity that compelled them to have that number of steeds to drag the cumbrous vehicles of yore through the mud and mire of the country roads. On the widening of the London-road waggons came into use, superseding pack horses for the transport of goods. In 1774 the introduction of mail-coaches to London took place from Warrington. The first mail-coaches were small vehicles carrying only four passengers. They were drawn by two horses, which were changed every six miles. The coachman and guard were well armed to provide against highwaymen. The communication with London was reduced from forty-eight to thirty hours. In 1790 a horse road formed to Liverpool from Warrington was spoken of as being a great convenience and "luxury." London-road, after the general use and improved condition of the stage-coaches, became a thronged thoroughfare. Those who can recollect the old coaching days cannot fail to have pleasant reminiscences of the pretty sight these vehicles and the royal mails presented to view; the former dashing along with their four horses full of life, blood, and bone, and the latter, equally well horsed, with their coachmen and guards in scarlet liveries and gold-laced hats. The race of coachmen, like that of the Dodo, is extinct. The stage-coachman with his many caped coat was a remarkable object. He generally sported a flower in the button-hole of his outer garment, the gift of Mary or Fanny at the Saracen's Head or the Talbot. To see him mount his box, "ribbons" in hand, amidst a group of admiring spectators, was equivalent to beholding a monarch in all his glory ascending his throne. Then the downy-looking guard taking charge of bank and other parcels, sometimes of great value, spruce, active, full of jest, and no end of chaff, was a man of note. He knew everybody "down the road," and everybody knew him. These good fellows made a deal of money by fees and gratuities, and generally finished their career in a "public." The writer once stood in the London-road talking to a very old coachman, one whom he had known many years. This man had been in his day noted in "working" the Oxford line. Looking at the 'bus drivers, he said, "There ain't no drivers now-a-days, mister, them's only horse whackers." There certainly was a scientific style and neatness in the driving of the old coachmen that we do not now see. The old man continued:—"When I was on the Oxford line I used to get many a 'half sov.' for letting the gents tool along for a few stages. They was joking gents, mister, them was. The team I drove into Oxford they called the 'Classics,' sir. One horse they said was 'Homer,' cos he knew his way home to the stable so well the moment he got out of the traces; another they called 'Odye'see,' cos he'd only von heye, sir; a leader they said was 'Jerkses,' cos he had a sort of jerking step with him; and a wheeler was 'Arterjerkses,' cos he come'd arter him. Them chaps is only horse whackers." About one hundred stage-coaches a day used to go in and out of Liverpool along London-road just before the opening of the railway.

Beyond Commutation-row there were no houses at the close of the last century and the beginning of the present, as far as the Gallows Mill public-house, lately taken down, which stood at the corner of Stafford-street. Beyond it were fields to Low-hill, scarcely a house intervening, except the "Green Man Still," and a few cottages near it. Between Commutation-row and the present Norton-street there were at the side of the road some deep dingles or hollows. In these dells or hollows the Folly Fair people used to have "wrastling" and "tustling" matches, the sides of the road being crowded with the ginger-bread booths and shows, the fair extending up to Prescot-street. The once celebrated "Blue Bell Inn" stood at the corner of Norton-street and London-road, on the site of Mr. Cooper's ironmongery warehouse and Mr. Hobb's hatter's shop. All the coaches used to stop at the "Blue Bell," either coming into or going out of Liverpool. Adjoining the Blue Bell was an old stone building which was partly used as a provender and corn warehouse. In April, 1813, in consequence of overloading the upper floors, the whole building fell into the road, crushing Mr. Barton the proprietor, who was in it at the time, to death. Mrs. and Miss Barton, who were in the lower part, escaped. It was rebuilt as a shop, and was about the first that made its appearance in the road.

Commutation-row was so called, it is said, in consequence of some "commutation" that took place in the terms of the purchase of land on which it stood. The houses in it were all private dwellings, and were constructed with very large windows, to evade, as it was hoped, the window-tax; but in 1785 the Legislature prescribed the limit for windows, in consequence of this plan of making large windows spreading throughout the country. It was intended that the large windows should only count as one in the jotting up of the houses' number. The Blind Institution was first commenced in 1791 in Commutation-row, occupying two of its houses. It lingered for a time in a forlorn way until taken in hand by Mr. Pudsey Dawson, of Rodney-street (Pudsey-street is named after him) in 1798, when, by the great exertions of this benevolent gentleman and others, it was put into a healthy state. In 1800 it was removed to the London-road, and was situated between Pudsey-street and Hotham-street (then called Duncan-street). The workshops, school-rooms, and dormitories are now occupied principally by the Road and Railway Omnibus Company as one of their sets of stables and yards. The chapel connected with it stood on part of Messrs. Cope's premises and St. Simon's Schools, the access for the pupils to it being from the school, under-ground. Some years ago, before Liverpool became so full of "lions," the Blind Asylum was considered to be the most interesting of those mythical animals,—all strangers coming to see through the town attending its concerts and crowding its chapels on Sundays. In 1850 this institution was removed to Hope-street and Hardman-street. The chapel was taken away stone by stone, and rebuilt entirely of the old materials and in its original form. The portico is a copy of that attached to the Temple of Jupiter Panhellenus, in the Island of Ægina. A mill once stood at the eastern corner of Hotham-street, on the site of Ray and Miles' bedding warehouse.

There are several claimants to the honour of suggesting the School for the Blind; one was a Mr. Christie, a blind gentleman; another was a Mr. Arnold, a blind Ormskirk youth, who was in the school from 1791 to 1798; another was the Rev. Henry Dannett, the minister of St. John's Church; while the Rev. Dr. Shepherd, in his edition of the Poems of Edward Rushton (father of the late stipendiary magistrate), claims for that gentleman all the merit of the admirable idea. Mr. Rushton, senior, was a blind man. It has been, however, asserted that the first notion of it was started by an anonymous writer in *Williamson's Advertiser*. While on the subject of the Blind School two little anecdotes connected with two blind persons, once well known in Liverpool, may be, without impropriety, told as showing the extraordinary intelligence exhibited by those afflicted with the loss of their sight, or, as Samson pathetically terms it, "total eclipse." The writer was, some years ago, walking up London-road with an acquaintance, a local artist of some celebrity, when Mr. Platt, the then organist to the Blind Chapel, was seen approaching. "Here's Platt," said the artist; "I wonder if he will remember me,—it is three years since I last spoke to him. How are you, Mr. Platt?" said he. "Bless my heart!" instantly replied Platt. "Why, Mr. H., I have not *seen* you for the last three years!" The second anecdote is still more singular. This Mr. Platt had a brother, also blind. These two men were crossing the London-road by the Monument, one from the right and the other from the left-hand side; they met by the railings, and heartily greeted each other without the slightest hesitation, when they were even some feet apart.

Between Pudsey-street and the Legs of Man there was once a coal-yard and weighing machine, and it is said that in consequence of an accident, by which a child was killed through the kick of a horse, the owner of the machine shut it up and built on it the shops now standing. The shop of the late Mr. Sorge, the tobacconist, was the machine office.

It will be noticed that the streets in this locality are mostly called after some illustrious men, whose names are quite "household words" amongst us. Such as Lord Nelson, St. Vincent, Bridport, Camden, Hotham (late Duncan), Trowbridge, Stafford, Seymour, Anson, and Great Newton-streets. Pellew-street, out of Copperas Hill, was proposed to be called *Trollope*-street, after the admiral of that name, but the *ladies* beginning to be residents in its vicinity objected to the title, as being too demonstrative of their calling.

The picturesque old Mill public-house was a fair specimen of our ancient roadside baiting places. There was a good joke told of a trick played there at one Folly Fair time, by some loafing fellows hard up for "tin." There were above the Gallows Mill public-house, on the site of Mr. Hughes's pawnbroker's shop, some stables and a shippon. The fellows got a large bill made, bearing an inscription to this effect:—"To be seen within ALIVE a horse's head where his tail should be." This was placed over the door of the stables, and when the public were admitted they found a horse with his tail tied to the manger! As the crowds that were passed through (at two-pence each) were obliged to go some distance round to get back into the London-road, the deception could not be exposed to the people in front until a good sum had been realised. Those who had been "sold," enjoying the joke, tried to "sell" their friends.

There were three mills hereabout at one period. One stood in a field near Audley-street, with a wheel outside to turn the sails to windward, another adjacent to it, and a third on the opening to Stafford-street. This latter was called the "Gallows Mill." This arose from the circumstance that four Jacobites were hung in front of it in 1715, after the defeat at Preston. These men were named Barnet, Drummond, Hunter, and Collingwood. The latter was a Northumbrian gentleman of large estate, which was confiscated in 1716. These, with about 160 other rebels, were tried by special commission of Oyer and Terminer, for high treason, at Liverpool, before Mr. Justice Eyre, Mr. Baron Montague, and Mr. Baron Bury. Of these, twelve were found guilty, and hung at Bolton; seven at Wigan; seven at Manchester; four at Garstang; four at Lancaster; and the above four at Liverpool. Seven were acquitted; others were reprieved on pleading guilty, and were sent by their own desire to the West Indian "Plantations;" others were imprisoned, and died in captivity—in some cases of hunger and privation. When the news of the rebellion first came to Liverpool, the utmost enthusiasm was excited amongst the inhabitants, who enrolled themselves into regiments, constructed batteries at the north side of the town and the river approaches, arming them with upwards of sixty cannon. The seamen of the port volunteered to man them, and every exertion was made to place the town in a defensive state. Liverpool, in fact, became the head-quarters of the Hanoverian party in this district. At the back of the Gallows Mill was at one time a large quarry, afterwards converted into a mill dam. It was in shape like a "Rupert's Drop," the thin end extending up London-road. The Gallows Mill, and land on which it stood, was purchased by the Corporation in 1788 for £700, for the purpose of effecting improvements thereabouts. The materials were sold by auction at the house of Mrs. Murphy, in Whitechapel, and realized £71.

The statue of George the Third was erected by subscription, but the amount fell so far short of the sum required, although a great deal of squeezing and pressing took place, that the completion of the testimonial was delayed until after the monarch's decease. The first stone for the pedestal was laid in Great George-square garden on the 25th October, 1809, being the fiftieth anniversary of the king's accession to the throne. It was deposited with great pomp and ceremony by his Worship the Mayor, the Cheshire yeomanry keeping the ground. The survivors of the original committee in 1822 decided on altering the original site for the monument to London-road, in which year the figure was set up; but it was not finished until the year following. It is said that it was only by nursing the original amount subscribed, and allowing it to accumulate, that the cost was eventually defrayed. The statue is a copy of that of Marcus Aurelius at Rome, with the exception of the head, which is by no means indicative of great intellectual powers. The modeller was Mr. Westmacott. Near the site of the Monument once stood a small thatched public-house, known as "Polly Tittle's." It had a garden behind it. The entrance to it was approached by stone steps cut out of the rock, and was much resorted to by the townsfolk, who went out on holidays for a "little country air." They used to have wrestling matches and boxing bouts there at fair time. "Polly" was a woman of masculine stature and habits, and was wont to boast that she could "tittle up any of the chaps who wanted to cut up rough." And she could do it too.

Stafford-street was unbuilt upon in 1807.

The shops above Norman-street, in the London-road, to within two doors of Daulby-street, have only been erected within the last fifteen or sixteen years. The land was then enclosed within a wall. Just where is now Mr. Watson's cabinet-maker's shop, against the wall, stood the first milestone from the Exchange. The value of property in the London-road may be said to have been improved through calamity. The accident at the weighing machine has been mentioned. The predecessor of the eminent builders, Messrs. Haigh and Co., had his workshops and timber-yard, fronting the London-road, destroyed by fire about 1819, which resulted in a total loss from the fact of the fire insurance policy expiring a few days previously, and not having been renewed.

This fire caused the frontage to London-road to be covered with shops and houses, now occupied by Messrs. Evans and Co., drapers, and Mr. Goold, outfitter. By the falling of a wall of Mr. Johnson's timber-yard at the corner of Stafford-street, resulting in the death of a youth, the owner's attention was turned to erecting thereon the handsome shops of Messrs. Leigh, Wilkinson, and Kerrison. At the top of Gloucester-street remains of batteries and trenches were found, as also in the London-road by Norton-street, in which a cartouch-box, musket, and other war materials were discovered. In 1864 trenches were discovered at the bottom of the London-road, opposite Mr. Routledge's shop. These were about five feet deep, and three in width. These trenches commenced there, as the only indication of them was found on the south side of the excavation then making to receive the large pipes for the transmission of the Rivington water. These batteries must have commanded Dale-street, the batteries of which were erected to defend the pool at the bottom of the brow. Several cannon balls, of small size, have been dug up in the yards of the houses that stood on Shaw's-brow.

---

## WILLIAM BROWN STREET AND ISLINGTON.

---

WILLIAM BROWN-STREET was within the last few years known as "Shaw's-brow," and is still so named by many who have objected to the change, or who cannot forget its old appellation. It was the main outlet from Liverpool in the olden time by way of Dale-street, and the "Towns-end," as that part of Liverpool was called. It was a narrow steep street. It derived its name and title of "Shaw's-brow" from being the road to Mr. Alderman Shaw's extensive potteries on the rising ground. When Mr. Shaw was Mayor in 1794 he gave away the whole of his allowance of £800 to the charities. After

Mr. Shaw had settled on the Brow, other "banks" or potteries were opened, and increased in number, until the vicinity became quite a potters' colony. According to the census of 1790 there were seventy-four potters' houses, inhabited by 374 persons, on the Brow, all connected with the manufacture of earthenware of various descriptions. Mr. Chaffers had extensive works on the north side of the Brow. His moulding-houses were on the site of Islington-terrace. He resided in Dale-street. His manufacture was celebrated for the elegance of the ware and the beautiful colours it exhibited. He introduced a higher class of ware in Liverpool than formerly, it being made of a clay discovered by him, or through his agency, in Cornwall, which was shipped to Liverpool on his account. Mr. Chaffers died of typhus fever caught while visiting an old and respected workman in his employ named Podmore, who was his foreman. Mr. Pennington had large works also on the Brow. His eldest son, James, had a manufactory on Copperas-hill. John, his second son, had a "bank" near St. Anne-street; while Seth, his youngest son, had large works on the Brow, extending to Clayton-street. The Penningtons were famous for making ornamental ware and large and handsome punch bowls, some specimens of which may be seen, with numberless other descriptions of Liverpool pottery, in "Mayer's Museum"—that wonderful collection of rare and beautiful objects. It is a rather curious circumstance that after so many years' service, and since these wares were manufactured, that they should have returned to the precise spot where they were originally made. Higher up the Brow Mr. Phillip Christian had extensive works which stood on the site of Islington-flags or terrace. After the death of Mr. Chaffers, he took the lead as a manufacturer amongst the Liverpool potters, producing many very elegant and elaborately designed sets of dinner, dessert, tea, and breakfast services. Another famous potter was Mr. Zachariah Barnes, whose works were in the Old Hay Market. Part of his premises may still be seen in Mr. Price's provision shop, which was his show-room. The pottery was at the back, on the site of part of Mr. Pooley's foundry. Barnes was born in 1743, and died in 1820.

It is to a Liverpool man we are indebted for the discovery of printing on earthenware. The art was accidently discovered by, or rather suggested to, a Mr. Sadler, an engraver, who resided in Harrington-street, by seeing his children stick prints of pieces on broken pottery. The secret of it was kept for some years between himself and a Mr. Guy Green.

The bottom of Shaw's-brow, facing the Haymarket, was called St. John's Village. Up the south side of Shaw's-brow were the potters' dwellings. It is said that some of these men, in the time of resurrectionism, were in the habit of getting over the church-yard wall and exhuming any newly interred bodies, taking them into their houses, and selling them to the medical students and others who purchased such *subjects*.

On Shaw's-brow there was once a well of famous water, which was advertised for sale in the *Weekly Advertiser* of the 17th November, 1758, at nine-pence per butt. It is recommended by Mr. Parker, the proprietor, as being "so soft as to be excellent for washing and boiling peas!" It may be recollected by many as a never-failing well, supplying the engine of an emery-mill. In the same yard was one of the cones of one of the old pottery works. A view of it is given in "Herdman's Ancient Liverpool," whose beautiful sketches by the way often aptly illustrate the text of this work.

Water was for many years hawked about the town in barreled carts, driven by women, who sold the fluid at so much per bucket, or "Hessian," as these receptacles were called. The slop and mess made by the water-carts in the streets, and the saucy behaviour of the women attending them, were constant sources of grumbling amongst the town's-folk; but when the water was about to be supplied by pipes, in 1799, an outcry was actually made against the plan, as having "the effect of throwing so many poor people out of employment!"

On Shaw's-brow at one time were the alms-houses, erected by the Richmond family, and to which Mr. Scarsbrick contributed.

The widening of Shaw's-brow took place in 1852. The houses were in some cases of rather a picturesque appearance, some being constructed of wood, lath, and plaster, and others of timber and brick.

The triangular piece of ground on which stands the by no means beautiful Wellington testimonial was purchased by the Corporation in 1780. The Townsend Mill stood at the western end. It was taken down about that date. Mr. Peter Rigby received £300 for his lease, and Lord Derby £300 for his reversion. There was a large mill on the opposite side of the way in Mill-lane, which derives its name from the circumstance. It was burnt down in 1852. Previous to the establishment of Old Islington Market, Folly Fair used to be held on the vacant ground, extending up to Islington or Folly-lane, and in the London-road beyond the Gallows Mill. It took place at Easter and Whitsuntide.

It was an unauthorised gathering, suggested probably by the owners of public houses that then began to be opened in the neighbourhood. Folly Fair was discontinued in 1819, being put down by the magistrates, urged on by one of that body who declared that in his young days he frequented it, to his shame, and knew the wretchedness it originated, and the sorrow it engendered. The disorders and disturbances that were practised during Folly Fair time were said to be unparalleled in any similar gathering.

The market established on the triangle in 1827, was discontinued in 1843, on the opening of Gill-street Market.

Islington Market was encompassed by a wall, having gates at the ends and sides. Those to the west were approached by flights of steps. There was a fine well of water in the centre, the brick-work of which was discovered in excavating the foundation for the Wellington column. Along each wall shops were arranged, the farmers' tables and stalls being in the middle. There was a colonade on one side. The area of the market was about 3,000 square yards. In 1818 the market was partially covered over. The shops, on the closing of the market, were taken to Gill-street Market, and were put up in the yard for pedlars. They are now used as styes in the pig market.

In Islington, on the site of Christian-street, Hunter-street, and thereabout, there was once the celebrated public garden called the "Folly." In it was the tavern known as "Gibson's Coffee House." This consisted of a long low house of one storey above the ground floor, and a tall tower, six yards square, of eight stories high, with a gazebo on the top, whence the place obtained the name of the "*Folly.*" The view from this tower was exceedingly fine, especially seaward.

The cock-pit discovered in 1861, when the ground was being levelled for the use of the Wholesale Vegetable Market held near the Free Library, doubtless formed part of the garden amusements. Some doubt has been thrown over the generally received opinions as to the arrangements of the Folly Gardens, as there is no plan of them in any of the Liverpool maps from 1768 to 1786, whereon the Ranelagh Gardens are distinctly shown, with their walks and flower beds. Gibson, the landlord of the Folly, was a brother to the lessee of the White House and Ranelagh Garden. One of these gentlemen obtained the grant or license to open the Theatre Royal, in Williamson-square, for twenty-one years after its erection, in 1771. The grant enabled him "to form, entertain, and govern privilege, and keep a company of comedians for his Majesty's service in the borough of Liverpool."

The entrance to the Folly Gardens was from Islington or Folly-lane, up an alley skirted by hedges. The Folly Tavern stood on, or not far from, the site of Christ Church. The closing of the Folly Gardens, about 1785, caused great regret in the town, as they were liberally patronized by the middle and even higher classes. "Braggart" was a favourite beverage at the Folly, made of ale and spices, and for the compounding of which Gibson was famous.

Mr. Phillip Christian purchased the materials of the Folly Tavern, and with them erected his house at the corner of Christian-street (named after him), now a druggist's shop. Islington-terrace presented a handsome appearance when first erected. The style of the entire row may now be judged by looking at three or four of the houses at the west end which appear to be unaltered, having steps to the doorways, as was usual in dwellings erected in Liverpool at that period. Folly-lane or Islington was a mere country lane, leading to West Derby, having hedges on each side. Here and there was an old cottage, the inmates of which cultivated garden produce for their support. One of these old cottages was laid open to the public view, on the erection of the "Friends' Institute," a few years ago. It was evidently of great antiquity. Folly-lane, in 1802, commenced only at St. Anne-street. In 1814 we find the name of Islington carried up to Moss-street. Brunswick-road was the last remnant of "Folly-lane."

About half way up Islington was "Birchfield," at one time quite a suburban retreat. In it were three large mansions, embosomed amidst fine old birch trees, some of which it was said were part of the old forest of West Derby. In the southern mansion at one time resided Mr. Roscoe, and in it he wrote a large portion of his well-known works. These mansions were afterwards converted into barracks for artillery. The whole of the site of Birchfield is now covered with small property.

A curious circumstance took place in Islington some thirty-five years ago, which may now be told, as all parties immediately connected with it, it is believed, have passed away. It created great wonderment amongst the immediate circle of those who were cognisant of the matter. About the year 1830, a widow lady residing in Islington, near the square, with her only daughter and young son, was in want of a female servant. Upon the recommendation of a respectable widow woman who kept a smallware shop in the London-road, a young woman applied for the vacant place and obtained it. She went to it in very shabby attire; and although she had evidently endeavoured to deteriorate her good looks by a strange mode of *coiffure*, she evidenced the possession of rare lovliness. She remained with the lady nearly two years. She exhibited an exceedingly grave, humble, reserved manner; seemed timid and uneasy previous to the advent of strangers, which emotions however disappeared on becoming acquainted with their features. She fulfilled the duties of house servant in the most scrupulous, exact, and exemplary manner; and on one occasion exhibited, although left alone in the house, a dauntless spirit when it was attacked by burglars. During the time she was residing in the house she displayed a considerable knowledge of medicine and the treatment of the sick, watching with intense care a case of disfiguring and contagious disease. On unpremeditated and unlooked for occasions she proved herself to be well versed in several Continental languages, was discovered to be highly accomplished in drawing and music, and was evidently a person in intellect far above the ordinary run of females. She went away as mysteriously as she came, and all traces of her were lost until two months after her departure, when a package was received by her late employer containing presents of the most costly description for all who had been kind to her. She gave the name of "Hannah Brade;" and it was a common question to ask in the circle acquainted with this curious affair, "Who was Hannah Brade?"

The majority of streets leading out of Islington are named after the owners of property in that neighbourhood, as "Christian-street," "Gerard-street," "Gildart-street," "Salisbury-street," "Frazer-street," a mode of nomenclature that it is a pity is not followed up in the present day, instead of introducing the unmeaning titles affixed to many new thoroughfares. Calling new streets after those who projected them, or of men well known at the time, forms a pleasing feature in town history.

---

## BRUNSWICK-ROAD.

BRUNSWICK-ROAD, the approach from Liverpool to Rake-lane or West Derby-road, as it is now termed, has borne several appellations. In 1802 it was known as "Folly-lane," being a continuation of that ancient thoroughfare. In 1807 it was called "Mill-lane," which name it retained until 1820, when it became "Brunswick-place." It was then also called

Brunswick-road, and into this last title it has of late years resolved itself. The change from Mill-lane arose in this wise. If the story is not true it is well told. About the latter year a young lady, having strong proclivities towards the reigning dynasty, observed that the painter who was re-inscribing the names of the streets had left his ladder against the house in which she resided while he went to his dinner. She availed herself of the opportunity of his absence to rub out "Old Mill-lane," and chalk up "Brunswick-place." On his return, seeing the latter name boldly written, he considered that that was the title he had to inscribe, and accordingly "followed his copy." Brunswick-road was much steeper originally than it is at present, a very material cutting down of it having been carried out about 1838. On the north side of the way the houses originally were prettily situated, with gardens before them. The air being then pure and salubrious, it enabled the inhabitants to cultivate horticulture in a small way, which produced pleasing effects in the appearance of the road. When the court-houses were erected, which will be noticed about half way up the north side of the street, when a shop or two, about 1837 or 1838, made their appearance, and houses began to be built on the fields on the south side, deep regrets were indulged in at these innovations. One after another the pretty gardens disappeared, the chance of widening the street cheaply was lost, and now that Brunswick-road has become an immense thoroughfare the mistake has become palpable, if not formerly perceptible. There are no less than five lines of omnibuses, making from ten to twenty journeys a day, besides the numbers of carriages of the West Derby gentry, the traps, carts, and all other sorts of vehicles and conveyances, to be found passing up and down continually. A pecularity in Brunswick-road has been noticed by a wag, which is worth telling. He says it is "the most depressing thoroughfare to reside in, to a sensative mind, that he knows;" for, says he, "there is the Necropolis at the top, where they bury you, there are two coffin shops about half way down, then below these there is a tombstone manufactory; nor is that all, for there are two or three establishments in the street where the people are *dye*ing all day long."

Erskine-street was planned about fifty years ago, and was called after the great law lord of that name. It was widened at the top about 1840. The houses at the bottom were erected in or about forty years ago, as was also the cottage at the corner of Low-hill. The houses on the southern side are all of a much later date. Childwall-street and Chapel-place were laid out about 1800. At one time there were fields and gardens skirting Prescot-street, or lane, as it was then called. Just on the spot where the bridewell stands there used to be a large stone quarry, open to Prescott-street. Near the northern brink of this delf was a small building, in the shape of a summer-house, called by the people about "Rats' Castle." The occupier of the garden in which it stood was an eccentric person, a Mr. Harrison, who feasted his friends, if he could persuade them to eat at his board, on strange dishes, composed of cockroaches, spiders, rats and mice, snails, slugs, and even earth-worms, which he used to have cooked in a variety of tempting ways. This delf was much complained of thirty years ago, as being exceedingly dangerous. Several severe accidents at one time took place from people falling into it. On one occasion an over-driven bullock cleared the low wall that protected it, and was found frightfully hurt at the bottom of the excavation.

Harper-street was called after Mr. Harper, who lived in a large house, with a garden, opposite the end of Phythian-street. He erected the houses adjoining the public offices, which were formerly used as a bridewell. On these premises there is a deep well, which was at one time open to the public. The paupers in Low-hill Workhouse, which stood on the site of St. Jude's Schools, used to go through a passage cut in the rock, on the site of which the houses opposite the school were erected, to draw water.

Previous to 1807 there were no houses on the south-side of Brunswick-road to Low-hill. Mr. Plumpton's mansion stood alone for many years, near the corner of Low-hill. There were houses in Low-hill in 1820, built at the corner of Gloucester-place, facing Erskine-street. On the west side was an old cottage, lately replaced by a row of shops.

Within the last few years near the southern corner of Phythian-street, in Low-hill, there was a pretty place called "Halcyon Cottage," erected by a sea captain, who so called it after the name of the ship in which he had "ploughed the salt ocean." The tablet bearing the name of the cottage has been inserted in the wall of one of the houses which occupy its site. To the south of Gloucester-place was Stringfellow's nursery, which extended from Low-hill to the fields. The houses at the rear of St. Jude's Schools are erected on part of its site.

Previous to the passing of the Municipal Reform Bill, which came into operation in 1835, it was customary for the mayor, attended by the aldermen, some of the councillors, and personal friends, on horseback, to perambulate the boundaries of the borough. The party was accompanied by a band of music and a number of the Blue-coat boys, who bore wands wherewith "to beat the bounds." The procession always halted at Low-hill for refreshments, which were laid out in a tent on the vacant ground. Beating the bounds took place usually on the Monday previous to St. Luke's Day (18th October), when the mayor was elected. Some of the old boundary stones of the borough remain, bearing upon them the names of the mayors in whose year they were put down. Of late years neat iron slabs have been erected instead of the old stones.

Here is a bill of the expence of the cold collation in 1775, October 18th:—To cost paid expenses at Low-hill on Liberty Day, £2 13s. 8d.; to H. Forshaw, expenses on Liberty Day, £3 10s. 0d.; to do. Thomas Morrias, £7 9s. 10d. Forshaw kept the Black Horse and Rainbow in High-street. Morrias, Pontacks, Water-street.

In 1800 Mrs. Jane Barrow supplied the refreshments. Here are some of the items of the bill:—Roast and boiled beef, £1 13s. 6d.; hams, tongues, and fowls, £2 15s. 0d.; veal pies, 8s.; pigeon ditto, 15s. 6d.; potted and fresh shrimps, 11s.; milk punch, £2 18s. 6d.; rum and brandy punch, £1 15s. 0d.; wine, 17s. 6d.; brandy, 17s. 6d.; rum, 19s.; ale and porter, £1 8s. 0d.; labourers work, canvas, &c., £1 12s. 0d.; total, £16 10s. 6d.

Mr. James Aspinall was the last of the mayors who performed the ceremony of "beating the bounds," as it was called. Amongst the other places the party went to was Beacon's Gutter, where the mace-bearer at low water used to stretch his arm out as far as he could, so that the utmost extent of the shore should be included in the borough limits. Respecting boundary stones, those that indicated the confines of Everton were called "Mere Stones," some of which are still in existence. There used to be one at, or near the end of Boundary-road, in West Derby-road, within the last few years. It may be there still, unless some sacrilegious hand, or one not acquainted with its history, has removed it. Near St. Domingo Pit at one time were several "mere stones," which noted its "high-water" mark.

Phythian-street was named after a publican who erected some houses in it. Beyond Vivian-street, this street ought to have been called Donison-street, as it was originally projected by Mr. Donison, a builder. In fact, some of the deeds of property in this part of the street term it "Donison-street." There was, some thirty-five years ago, at the eastern end a gate, which enclosed an occupation road to the back of the Gilead House grounds. At that time only the north side of the street was built upon, with the houses having gardens in front. Those numbered 149 and 151 were constructed out of the old materials of the old infirmary sold to Mr. Kilshaw, of Gloucester-street, and resold to Mr. Tolson, by whom these houses were erected. The cottage, No. 147, was at one time a shippon and stable. Within the last three years all the vacant land about Phythian-street has been covered with cottage property; hundreds of dwellings thereabout having sprung up like mushrooms. The classical name of "Phythian" is by no means an uncommon one in this part of Lancashire, several families bearing it. There was a "John Phithian," who was one of the original Everton copyholders of the waste lands enclosed in 1717. Whether the Phythians of Lancashire are descendants of the ancient Python, or of Apollo, who took his name after killing him, or of the lady who told fortunes in a cellar, sitting on a three-legged stool, or of Pythias, the chum and cater cousin of Damon the Pythagorean, or whether they trace back to those who at the Phythian games sold "oranges, apples, ginger-beer, and por*ter*," and vended "bills *of* the play," is left for the distinguished geneologists of "these diggings" to determine.

The sites of "Emly-street" and "Vane-street," which are intersected by Walker-street and Lower Baker-street, are on the course of a brook, which forty odd years ago was green with water-cresses, flags, and forget-me-nots, and on the brink of which little boys on fine summer days cried out, "My eye," to tittlebats.

West Derby-road was originally called "Rake-lane," and not so long ago either. After passing the present Belmont-road it was called "Rocky-lane." At the corner of West Derby-road and Everton-road is the Necropolis, or "Low-hill Cemetery," as it was termed at first. In consequence of the filling up of the Fabius little cemetery which they had given "to the Baptists" for ever, and no other convenient place being specially provided for the dissenting body, wherein to inter their dead, a meeting took place in 1824 of the leading ministers and gentlemen of the various denominations, when it was determined to purchase a piece of land which should be converted into a burial place, whereat any form of burial service could be used, or no service at all if desired. A large market garden at the corner of Everton-road, the property of Mr. Plumpton, having been fixed upon as an eligible site, an offer was made for it, which that gentleman accepted. The total cost of the cemetery was about £8,000. Having obtained possession of the ground, comprising about five acres, the proprietors of the undertaking (which was divided in shares) set to work and laid out the premises neatly, but without any pretensions to picturesque effect or taste. The first interment took place on the 1st February, 1825, when Miss Martha Hope, sister to Mr. Wm. Hope, of Hope-street, became the first denizen of the Dark City. The Rev. Dr. Raffles addressed those present on the occasion, pointing out the advantages of such a cemetery over a churchyard, at the same time condemning all intermural burials, and especially those within churches. The Rev. Dr. Raffles himself sleeps in this cemetery. His grave and mural tablet will be found in the enclosure on the east of the chapel. This excellent and much loved pastor, who for forty-nine years ministered to the congregation of the Great George-street Independent Chapel, was born 17th May, 1788; died August 18th, 1863. In the same enclosure is the grave of Thomas Coglan, who took a leading part in municipal and local affairs. He died 30th March, 1831, aged sixty-one. He was an honest reformer, and set his face against all abuses. He was highly respected, He served twice in the Liverpool Town Council. His epitaph, probably the production of his old friend Egerton Smith, does him ample justice. Mr. Egerton Smith, the founder and editor of the *Liverpool Mercury*, is interred about the middle of the cemetery, between the east side and middle walks. He died November, 1841. Mr. Egerton Smith occupied a prominent position for many years in public estimation. He was a thorough reformer, and a man of undoubted ability.

In the open ground near the arcade or covered way is a granite obelisk erected to the memory of Dr. David Thom, a man of great merits, as a courteous gentleman, a distinguished scholar, and an eloquent, earnest, truth seeking and preaching divine. Beside the usual inscription, the significant line appears "*Exuo et induam.*" A few years ago public indignation was very much aroused by the discovery of certain nefarious and most discreditable practices pursued by the sexton and other officials of this cemetery relative to the interments—bodies, after having been interred in one part, considered the better portion of the ground, being removed the following morning very early, and unknown to the relatives, to another and inferior portion. This was supposed to have been done for the purpose of leaving continuously plenty of space for the better class of interments, from which higher fees were derived. The discovery led to the discharge of the sexton and the resignation of the then chaplain.

There are many very pretty monuments to be found in the cemetery. One is remarkable for its originality. It consists of a block of stone, on which is lying an anchor in bronze or iron, with one of the flukes deeply embedded in a mass of iron, representing a rock sand or beach. It is in memory of Mary Wilson, who died at Marseilles. There is a very chaste and pretty monument dedicated to Mrs. Whyte, and two very handsome granite obelisks in memory of the Greenshields. Of obelisks there are several—there is one of large size to the memory of Mr. Watson Peck. There is a neat tomb, erected by friends and fellow-servants, to the memory of Mr. Capes Ashlin, who was for many years treasurer to the Health Committee. He was highly esteemed by all who knew him. He died 4th November, 1856. On the tomb of a Mr. M'Dowall we are told that he was a most "exemplary" man, who was "twenty-nine years a total abstainer from all sorts of intoxicating drinks," dying at sixty-one years of age. This tomb rests on two railway bars. On the monument of Mr. Swain, a Wesleyan missionary, who died at the age of thirty-eight, are these quaint lines—

> Go to the grave at noon, and labour cease,
> Rest on thy sheaves—thy harvest work is done;
> Come from the heat of battle, and in peace,
> Soldier, go home! With thee the fight is won.

Another tomb will be noticed constructed of iron, and is shaped exactly like a child's crib, without a bottom. One grave has over it a large iron cover, like an immense domed top rat-trap. It is intended to preserve flowers from sacrilegous hands. Alas, where are the flowers! The cage is a bitter satire on posthumous affection. There is a very handsome tomb in the shape of a broken column, with a wreath; and another, near Mr. Capes Ashlin's, has in front of it a stand on which is a collection of ferns. The inscription on the cross inside the case is peculiar.

# WEST DERBY ROAD.

West Derby-road was widened about 1823 or 1824. The line of the original road, which was narrow and winding, may be traced by following up the railings of Brougham-terrace, Wellington-terrace, and those of the Licensed Victuallers' Asylum, until it reaches the site of the present Bourne-street, whence it proceeds for some short distance straight forward. From Belmont-road it was and is still called Rocky-lane. The north side was lineable with Brunswick-road, until the Necropolis was laid out, when a good piece of open ground was secured. The road hereabout was skirted by fields extending to Mill-lane, now laid out in Aber-street, Ogwen-street, Lavan-street, Caird-street, and other streets teeming with neat cottage property. The line then followed the course of the churchyard railings, on the south side, and at the east end took a decided curve. Hereabout were some neat cottages with gardens in front of them. All along the road side from the Necropolis were hawthorn hedges, which in spring time were white with fragrant blossoms. Previous to the building of the Licensed Victuallers' Asylum the fields were all open as far as the back of the Phythian-street ropery. Brougham-terrace (erected in 1832) is in Everton township, the gardens at the back being in West Derby. The boundary line crosses the road at the west end, and returns on the east end. There was at one time a stream at the back of Brougham-terrace. Within the last eight or nine years there were two excellent houses and gardens on the site of the shops adjoining Walker-street.

The fields, where Upper Baker-street, Schomberg-street, and other streets in that neighbourhood are now to be found, were very dangerous to cross at nightfall, from the vagabonds, both male and female, who prowled about seeking whom they could plunder, especially those from the Zoological Gardens who had been imbibing strong drinks too copiously. In 1856, in one of the ponds at the back of the gardens the plate of

St. Chrysostom's Church was recovered, having been thrown in by some thieves. West Derby-road was at night a scene of sad confusion and uproar previous to the straightening of it. The parapet under the hedge was so narrow as scarcely to admit two persons to walk abreast; consequently the road had to be resorted to, and was crowded with people on their way home after the gardens had closed. Accidents sometimes occurred to pedestrians from the reckless conduct of the car-drivers, then the most unmitigated set of ruffians under the sun—they have vastly improved of late years. It was only wonderful that accidents were not more frequent, considering the narrowness of the road and the awkward turn it took thereabout, as the parapet on the south side of the road began only at Wellington-terrace end. What with badness of lighting, the noise of men shouting, the screams of terrified women, and the hurrying of vehicles through the mud or dust, as the case might be, a return from the Zoological Gardens on foot in olden times was always an undertaking attended with disagreeable contingencies.

Emmanuel Church was consecrated and opened in 1856. It was erected at the sole cost of Thomas Darnley Anderson, Esq., by whom it was also liberally endowed. It is handsomely fitted up. The chancel is decorated with costly foreign marbles, and the windows of it are of stained glass in beautiful and rich devices.

The Licensed Victuallers' Asylum was erected in 1852. It was projected in consequence of the original asylum, in St. Anne-street, now the Oddfellows' Hall, proving inconvenient for the purposes intended. When this building was determined upon, only £460 could be totted up on account of the building fund; but finding Mr. Plumpton willing to sell some land advantageously, and on a good site, the worthy victuallers, who had the direction of the affairs of their Association, went manfully to work, subscribing £200 amongst themselves, and commenced forthwith this building, having procured a set of very beautiful plans from the late Mr. William H. Daish. The first stone of the present building was laid by his Worship the Mayor, Mr. Thomas Littledale, on the 28th October, 1852.

The total cost of it was £7,000. £2,000 were raised the first year of its erection, and the rest was made up by the exertions of the friends of the institution, and from the proceeds of a fancy fair and bazaar that were held for four days in 1854. The late Mr. Daish presented the whole of the plans of the building to the institution. This talented architect was called away too soon to establish that fame which would doubtless have been meted to him had he lived. The present asylum is a specimen of his great taste and ability. There are at present twenty recipients of the asylum funds. Several of the houses are occupied by licensed victuallers' widows, the other houses are let advantageously to tenants, thereby providing funds for the institution. Of the children under its fostering wing, some are received in the house, in the care of the inmates, and others are placed out in respectable schools. The land on which the present asylum stands is now for sale, and doubtless will fetch, in consequence of the increased value of property in the neighbourhood, a good price, which will materially assist the committee in erecting their proposed new premises. The school of the asylum is occupied rent free by the incumbent of Emmanuel Church, Rev. H. Carpenter, for his Sunday schools. The Licensed Victuallers' Association affords the following benefits to its members in adversity:—The privilege of admission into the almshouses, free of rent and taxes. A weekly allowance in money (at present ten shillings per week for married couples, and seven shillings for single adults), with the addition of coals, gas, water, and clothing. The maintenance and education of the children or orphans of deceased members up to an age when they can be placed in suitable situations to earn their livelihood. The committee can also, if they think fit, in special cases, grant out-door relief, or temporary assistance, to unfortunate members, as well as to the widows, children, or orphans of deceased members, being in needy circumstances.

In connection with the West Derby-road ought not to be omitted mention of a worthy woman who, for nearly thirty years, has made her appearance in it, and who must be known to all passers by in that thoroughfare. At the corner of Lynedoch-street may be seen a tidy-looking fruit-seller, who, when the Gardens were in their prime, used to stand with a little stall selling ginger-beer and fruit, near the garden gate of a cottage, which had a ditch standing before it. This good woman maintained a sick husband, now dead, for years, brought up respectably three or four children, and has been good to some sick relatives. She used to stand through the afternoon and evenings in this locality when the Gardens were in their glory, but on their decadence, in the week days, she located at the corner of Washington-street, Great George-street. Every Sunday, however, she comes up to her old neighbourhood, whether it be sunshine or storm, winter or summer; and during all these years, she has scarcely ever missed a Sunday vending her fruit. Neat and tidy, with her green shade over her head, she prettily decorates her stall, and sells the best of articles in her small way.

Another "old stager" in the West Derby-road is a blind man, who sits under the Necropolis wall selling matches. For the last twenty-four years has this old worthy taken his stand in one position; and if the inhabitants of the neighbourhood have not given him due encouragement, it is not his fault that he has not made his fortune.

A little to the east of the Derby Hotel once stood a small ale-house, in which was a collection of objects of natural curiosity, entitled "Seaman's Museum." To the east of this were the Zoological Gardens, now passed away for ever, without one vestige remaining of them. This once famous and popular establishment was originated in May, 1832, by Mr. Atkins, who possessed the largest and most valuable travelling menagerie in the kingdom, whether for number, rarity, or the value of the animals contained in it. Stimulated by the success of the London Zoological Society, in the Regent's Park, and the Surrey Gardens, Mr. Atkins looked about for a locality wherein his extensive collection of animals could rest. Mr. James Plumpton provided him with the very place required. This was the piece of ground now rapidly being covered with cottage property. It was called "Plumpton's Hollow." It consisted of a disused brick-field and pit, from which the clay had been excavated. At that time this part of West Derby-road was all open fields, which were the resort of all the rowdeys and loafers in Liverpool, who came out on fine summer evenings, and on Sundays, to indulge in pugilistic encounters, dog-fights, rabbit running, and such like pastimes incidental to civilisation. Mr. Atkins engaged about five acres of these fields on a twenty-one years' lease, with the option of purchasing, at five shillings per yard, within seven years. The cost of laying out the gardens was about £2,000. The novelty of the undertaking created quite a *furore* in Liverpool, crowds of persons going out in the evenings to inspect the fine collection of animals, listen to the band, and view the displays of fireworks. Those who saw the place in its melancholy decadence, when it had become nothing more nor less than a drinking and dancing garden—a vulgar and dull imitation of *La Chaumiere* or *Mabille* in Paris, can form no idea of the respectability of the company that first patronised it. The leading families in Liverpool might have been seen at that time promenading the walks, while, in an afternoon, ladies with children and servants were present in numbers, strolling about or seated on the grass, or amusing themselves with a sight of the numerous and rare animals. The fireworks then were really objects of admiration, not mere lettings off of squibs and crackers and a few rockets. In Mr. Atkins's time the most beautiful set pieces were exhibited, with wonderful displays of coloured lights and complicated devices, exciting the admiration of all who beheld them. At that time no loose characters were admissable; and if a gay lady should chance to have gained admission, she was speedily ejected. For several years after the opening of the Gardens great interest was taken in augmenting the collection; and paragraphs were constantly to be read in the newspapers announcing the arrival of animals, birds, or reptiles by such and such a ship, which were presented to Mr. Atkins by some worthy captain who had thought kindly of the pleasant gardens over the sea in which he had happily spent some of his on-shore hours. Mr. Atkins, senior, thoroughly understood the management of wild animals. He was much noticed by the Earl of Derby, who frequently consulted him about his own collection, exchanged animals with him, purchased from him, or made him presents from his own duplicates.

In 1848 the destruction of a fine Elephant, Rajah, that had cost Mr. Atkins, senior, £300, was subject of public regret, this animal, certainly provoked by the cruelty of the men who had charge of him, having on two occasions killed his keepers. It was thought advisable to have him shot.

As a description of this place of amusement may be read with interest some few years hence, the following statement will show what were its attractions. At the entrance to the Gardens were two rustic lodges for pay-places. To the left of the entrance was a broad walk which led to some pretty flower-beds and a wide lawn; here was the elephant's house and pens for large animals and birds. Further on was another cage of birds. Near it, skirting a private kitchen-garden, was a cleverly contrived labyrinth, whence sounds of laughter constantly arose from those who, like Sterne's starling, "could not get out." In another part of the grounds was a large area in which there were archery butts, gymnastic machinery, swings, climbing-poles, and leaping-bars. Near here were cages for vultures and eagles presenting a melancholy picture of captivity. It was a pitiable sight to see these freedom-loving birds cooped up in a dull dark corner fretting their hearts out for the mountain top and the pure air of heaven. All animals in captivity have a tinge of the miserable about them, but these birds were deeply dyed in it. There was an aviary dedicated to the use of cockatoos, parrots, small rare animals requiring heat, and singing birds. Descending some rustic steps from an open ground, the picture of the season and lake were visible, and there it was the fireworks were let off.

The fire-work gallery was erected on the edge of a capacious and deep clay pit, the bottom of which formed "The Lake." At the back of the lake, stretched on immense frames, was a large expanse of canvass, on which was depicted some well-known mountain view, capable of pyrotechnic displays—such as Vesuvius or Etna, or a representation of a locality in which public interest had been recently centered. The effect produced on the picture, by the distance of it from the shore of the lake, was extraordinary and sometimes very beautiful, especially when strong lights were thrown upon it, giving the mimic scene all the appearance of reality. These pictures cost about one hundred pounds each. The expense of the fireworks on ordinary nights averaged about ten pounds; on extra nights as much as twenty pounds and even thirty pounds have been expended in these displays. Near here was the theatre, to the performances of which the admission was free, except to the gallery, whereat a small extra charge was made. Vaudevilles and light farces were represented by a small company, of sufficient talent to play the pieces respectably. Near the theatre was the Rotunda, in which were confined the larger descriptions of animals, such as lions, tigers, leopards, &c. These, in the elder Atkins's time, were very fine specimens. A lion would be worth £150, a tiger, £100, and so on for smaller animals. The expense of feeding these beasts would be about ten to fifteen pounds per week. Some people fancy that menagerie animals are fed upon anything—carrion, and such like. This is a misconception. To keep caged animals in good condition the best food should be given to them. The leading menageries use only first-class meats, not choice pieces, but the most profitable of the other portions. Animals in menageries are not usually fed on Sundays, as it is considered that one days rest from food in the week is beneficial to their health.

In the front of the Rotunda was the promenade ground, with the dancing-platform, and orchestra. It was from this part of the gardens that balloon ascents took place. The quantity of gas required for inflating a small sized balloon would be about 20,000 feet. The Liverpool Gas Company's gas is not fit for æronautical purposes, it being far too rich and dense. Balloon ascents generally are not very profitable exhibitions, from the uncertainty of success and the many chances of failures. Several very pretty ascents have, however, taken place from the Zoological Gardens by Mr. Coxwell, Mr. Green, and others. Blondin made his appearance here in 1860, and again in 1863, attracting immense crowds to witness his very hazardous, foolhardy, and by no means entertaining performances. To the right of the promenade was the centrifugal railway, which consisted of a tower about twenty feet high, from which a substantial car, to hold one person, was despatched down a steep decline, whence the vehicle was hurried round a ring, from which it was projected up an incline, from the crest of which the car speedily ran round the gardens on a rail back to the tower base. This apparently dangerous journey was in fact a safe one with common care. The railway was made of the best material, and accidents rarely if ever took place. Behind the railway tower was the monkey cage. On the west side of the garden was a model of Shakespeare's house, and near it was the Bear pit, from which once a bear escaped into the West Derby-road. It was followed by crowds of people. As the bear every now and then stood at bay, his pursuers fought shy of seizing him; but a man named Mayman, who afterwards kept a public-house opposite the gardens, closed with Bruin, who was at length secured, after lacerating his captor's arm so fearfully as to need amputation. The public-house was known for many years as "The Bear;" and there was a picture as a sign of the bear's capture. From the top of the bear pit wound round a shady walk, overlooking a little pond in which were some aquatic birds and two melancholy pelicans, which pouched food of all sorts offered them. Many of the trees were very beautiful; there was one magnificent hawthorn on the left of the orchestra, which, when in bloom, was a perfect miracle of beauty. The fair hand that set it, is still flesh and blood, but "where's the tree she planted." In the song the hand went first and the tree remained, but here the reverse is the case. In 1857 a spirit license for the gardens was obtained, and from that hour the place degenerated. Two drinking saloons were then erected, one near the Rotunda, and the other on the left of the lake. Mrs. Atkins, after some years, sold her interest in the concern to Mr. Durandu, who, after working the Garden for a year or two unsuccessfully, sold it again to Mr. John Atkins, who again sold it to a company of proprietors. These gentlemen disposed of the animals and converted it into a dancing garden, which became the resort of all the loose fish that had come to colonise the neighbourhood, after being turned out of their localities in the town in consequence of the improvements that had been carried on. Boaler-street runs through the centre of the gardens, Goldsmith-street, Bourne-street, and Empire-street intersecting them. Not one of the new streets have been designated in some way to perpetuate the recollection of this once famous locality. It is to be regretted that no effort was made to secure the gardens for public use. The beauty of the trees, the richness of the lawns, and the picturesque appearance of the place would have at all times made it a favourite public resort.

Kilshaw-street was projected by Mr. Councillor Kilshaw, about 1845. Hygeia-street in 1830. It was called after a ship of that name. Within the last fifteen years the whole of the neighbourhood eastward of the Zoological Gardens was open ground, fields, and gardens. In Boundary-lane, which twenty-five years ago was a dirty narrow thoroughfare, with a dangerous and stinking ditch on one side, was a large strawberry garden, famous in its hey-day for the fineness of its fruit. In the western corner of Sheil Park stands a large white house. In March, 1826, it was a ladies' school, kept by the Misses Daulby. Amongst other scholars was a Miss Turner, aged fifteen, the daughter and heiress of Mr. Turner, of Shrigley Park, Cheshire. A Miss Davies (who afterwards was married to Mr. E. G. Wakefield's father) meeting Mr. E. Gibbon Wakefield in Paris, told him of Miss Turner's large expectations, and proposed to him a scheme for carrying her off, and marrying her, which, if successful, should be rewarded by the payment to her (Miss Davies) of a large sum of money as *honorarium*. Mr. Wakefield consented to Miss Davies's plans. A forged letter was indited, addressed to the Misses Daulby, requesting them to deliver Miss Turner into the hands of "the bearer, Mr. Edward Gibbon Wakefield," as an escort home to Shrigley Park, where Mrs. Turner (Miss Turner's mother) "was lying dangerously ill, and who was anxiously desiring her daughter's presence." Upon this, after packing up a few necessaries, Miss Turner was delivered to Mr. Wakefield's charge. She was handed into a chaise in waiting. After a short time, finding that they were not proceeding in the direction of Cheshire, Miss Turner inquired whither she was being taken, when Mr. Wakefield informed Miss Turner of his intentions, stating that by her compliance she would save her father from utter and irretrievable ruin. Miss Turner was taken first to Manchester, next to Kendal and Carlisle, and thence to the borders, where she was married to Mr. Wakefield, border fashion. They next made their way to London, and then proceeded to Calais, where Miss Turner was found by her friends and taken home. Mr. Wakefield shortly after being seen in Brighton, was arrested, tried for the abduction of the lady, and sentenced to transportation. The whole of the affair had some remarkable features about it. Miss Turner seemed passively to acquiesce in Mr. Wakefield's scheme, for at not one place where they rested or slept—in separate apartments—between West Derby-road and the Border, did the young lady make any complaint to any one, nor apply to any body for protection; while, on the part of Wakefield, he conducted himself towards his fair captive more like a tender father than a lover, treating herself and person with the utmost politeness and respect, and in no one instance taking the slightest liberty that could be wrongly construed. This case and trial created in this neighbourhood, and in fact all over England, the utmost attention. It was for long the sole sensational topic of conversation and remark, and may be justly classed as one of the *causes celebrés* in English criminality. Mr. Edward Gibbon Wakefield was a perfect stranger to Miss Turner previously to their meeting. Miss Davies was tried with two of Wakefield's brothers, for complicity in this affair. On Wakefield's arrival at Sidney he exhibited so much talent and energy and usefulness that he eventually became the Government commissioner there. He was said to be a natural son of Lord Sandwich. He was unquestionably a clever man.

# PEMBROKE PLACE.

IN 1800 Pembroke-place was called "Wavertree-road" on the south side, and "Edge-lane-road" on the north side. In 1807 it was nearly all unbuilt upon between the present Monument-place and Boundary-street. Mr. Dansey and Mr. Daulby held the fields therein, which were of triangular shape. Mr. Dansey's widest side of the triangle extended along London-road to the corner of Boundary-street; Mr. Daulby's being in Pembroke-place. Gill-street was named after Mr. Gill, who held land in the vicinity. At the corner of this street, on the site of the handsome shops between Gill-street and Moor-place, were three excellent houses on a terrace. In that next to Gill-street Mrs. Prior kept for many years a ladies' school, Mr. Prior having a boys' school also on the same premises. The little chapel in Gill-street was for many years occupied by the Sandemanians, or "beef-eaters" as they were termed, from the custom of the congregation, who were few in number, and some of whom lived at a distance, having beef-steaks cooked on the premises, which were consumed between the morning and afternoon services. Gill-street market was opened in 1843. It was closed in 1861.

At the junction of Great Newton-street with Dansie-street, where the latter runs into Brownlow-hill, in 1816, resided Dr. Soloman, the inventor and proprietor of the "Balm of Gilead." His house was at the corner of the street, his gardens extending into Brownlow-street. This part of the street was then called "Solomon's-place." From this place the doctor removed to Gilead-house, Kensington, where he hospitably entertained his friends. On one occasion a guest, when the bottle had circulated freely and "all went merry as a marriage-bell," asked the doctor why he did not treat them to the celebrated "Balm of Gilead." The doctor replied that he should be most happy to do so, if those present wished it. The price of the "Balm" was a guinea a bottle. The party expressing a desire to taste the famous compound, half-a-dozen bottles were ordered in, which were duly consumed and highly relished. On the party breaking up, each guest was favoured with a little bill of his share of the expense of the "Balm." On the doctor being taunted with wishing to make his company pay for their entertainment, he reminded those present that it was by *the sale of his Balm of Gilead* that he was able to treat them so hospitably, and to make them welcome to his well-spread board. He therefore insisted upon being paid for his balm as specified in the "bills delivered." When the fact oozed out, the doctor's conduct was highly applauded, while the guests at the feast were heartily laughed at. Dr. Solomon drove four horses in a dashing carriage. On one occasion he followed the coach of Lord Sefton (who was one of the most expert whips of his day), to Heywood's Bank, where the two vehicles pulled up together. The doctor in flourishing his long whip contrived to get the thong so inextricably entangled round his body that he was obliged to call his groom to extricate him from the predicament into which he had involved himself. Dr. Solomon once played off a good trick on a Custom-house Officer. The doctor having shipped a case of Balm of Gilead to go abroad, the Custom-house Officer, finding the value declared so much below the usual selling price of the article, seized the package. On the doctor finding his "balm" had been detained, he became very wroth, and determined on revenge. He thereupon sent another package to the docks for shipment, which was made up precisely like the former, with the same description of bottles, labels, and wrappers. These bottles, however, only contained common spirit, sugar and water. Supposing that they contained the real stuff, the man seized the package. The doctor refusing to release it, it was thrown on the officer's hands, who found afterward, to his cost, of what the contents of the bottles consisted. The doctor chuckled gaily at the success of his scheme, declaring that he "vood teach dem to seize his goots." Dr. Solomon started Lord Sefton in the election of 1818. The flags were all painted at Gilead House, and cost at least £1,000. Such a quantity of ribbons was given away by the Doctor of his Lordship's colours that there is one family now residing in the town who have still quite a large stock remaining of what was then given them. It is said that Dr. Solomon gave the land for the Wesleyan Chapel in Moss-street.

A good story is told of some medical students stealing a favourite broad brimmed white hat of the Doctor's, who, on the discovery of his loss, had the town placarded with savage bills offering a reward for the apprehension of the offenders.

Dr. Solomon erected a mausoleum on the Mossley-hill estate, for the reception of his wife and children's remains, and for his own resting-place. It stood on a picturesque delf, and was for many years an object of remark. It is now entirely swept away.

Brownlow-street is said to have been called after Mr. Lawrence Brownloe, a gentleman of some standing and of very old family in Liverpool. This gentleman was one of those who was concerned in the leasing of the manorial rights to the Corporation of Liverpool, and is said to have purchased a considerable quantity of the land on the east hill after the settlement of the sale. Mr. Joseph Boult, however, considers that the term "Brownlow" has been derived from the term of "Brown Law," mentioned in the Survey of Toxteth Park.

Part of Brownlow-street was originally a footpath over the fields, from the back of the quarry. This path ran out to the corner of Pembroke-place.

Daulby-street was called after Mr. Daulby, to whom the land belonged. He resided in the house at the corner. The third house from it was erected by Mr. Thomas Oakes, who was a chemist, having a shop at the corner of Atherton-street and Pool-lane. He married Miss Harrison of Cranage Hall, Cheshire. Mr. Oakes built also the cottages nearly opposite to Ashton-street (called after the Ashton's, at one time large shipowners). This property is still in the Oakes' possession. Oakes-street was a lane at the back of their premises. In 1800, to the east of these houses, there was a large market garden and florist's nursery, kept by a man named Fielding. It was a celebrated place in its day. At the corner of Oakes-street was a Jews' cemetery. Crown-street was laid out about

1800. All about there was called Mosslake Fields. In winter these fields were famous skating places. In the summer the Volunteers were drilled and reviewed upon them. The Mosslake-brook ran through these fields about the course of Crown-street on its way to London-road. There were several large pits in these fields, in one of which, near the present Little Woolton-street, a couple of thieves came to grief. Not far from where the opening to Crown-street now is, there was a large pond, to the south of which was a stile. In 1780, one dark night, a jolly son of Neptune was rolling along the path from Smithdown-lane, when, as he was about to cross the stile, two footpads attempted to seize him, demanding his money, but the tar, drawing his hanger, which at that time it was customary for sailors to wear, cut lustily at the robbers, who, seeing a sword flashing before their eyes, took to their heels. In the obscurity of the night they ran straight into the pond, where they floundered about calling for help. The sailor dashed in after them, administering to them both a sound ducking, and a drubbing with the flat of his sword, leaving them to get out as they could when his vengeance had been appeased. Mosslake fields were not wholly built upon until as late as 1844, and even as late as 1835 some portions of them were open ground. On digging the foundations for the houses, in some parts excellent turf was found, which, on being properly dried, burnt well. Mosslake fields were part of the ancient turbaries of the town, and belonged to Sir Edward Moore. They extended from the top of Copperas-hill, along the upland, to Parliament fields, being skirted on the east by Smithdown-lane.

At the corner of a field bounded by Love-lane and the site of the present Hardwick-street, was fought the duel between Colonel Bolton and Major Brooks, in 1805, which caused at the time immense excitement in Liverpool, from the high standing of both parties in society. Colonel Bolton was a merchant of great eminence and wealth. At his own expense he entirely raised, clothed, and accoutered a regiment of Volunteers, consisting of ten companies. In consequence of this exhibition of loyalty at a time when the

Throne needed the strongest support, from the prevalence of sparks of sedition in the country that were only wanting to be fanned to become flames fierce and hot, Colonel Bolton had considerable influence with the Government. He exerted this at the close of the last century to obtain for Major Brooks, who had been adjutant of the Lancashire Militia, the post of Customs Jerker in Liverpool, on the death of Mr. Bryan Blundell. After holding this office for some time, Major Brooks applied for an increase of salary, a step that Colonel Bolton, on being consulted by Major Brooks, did not approve, stating that he considered £700 a year quite a sufficient remuneration for a single man, and for the duty he had to perform. The application, however, of Major Brooks was referred to the West India Association of Liverpool, then a very influential body, consisting of all the first West India merchants in the port, and of which Colonel Bolton was the president. The decision of the association was adverse to the raising of Major Brooks' salary; at this he took umbrage, blaming Colonel Bolton as being the cause of it, and at the same time using very insulting and abusive language towards his benefactor. Major Brooks, not content with abusing Colonel Bolton behind his back, carried his animosity so far as to insult him personally on 'Change, and so publicly, that a hostile meeting could not be avoided. The Major, who all through his life appears to have been a quarrelsome, turbulent man, and constantly in broils of some sort or another—fighting not long previously a duel on Bootle Sands with Captain Carmichael, of Earle's regiment, as already mentioned—seized the opportunity of taking revenge upon Colonel Bolton, with the utmost avidity. A meeting was therefore arranged to come off at Mather's Dam, in the Park, then a lonely, unfrequented place. The meeting having got wind, Bolton and Brooks were taken into custody, the latter storming and abusing his antagonist, and charging him with being the cause of the interruption to their encounter—a charge utterly untrue, as it was satisfactorily proved that the authorities received the information on which they acted from a friend of Major Brooks. Both parties were then bound over to keep the peace for twelve months. During this time Major Brooks never spared an opportunity of behaving contumaciously towards Colonel Bolton; but on the 25th of December, 1805, the day that the bail bond expired, meeting Colonel Bolton walking along Castle-street with Colonel Earle, his violence completely got the mastery of him, and he again grossly insulted the Colonel, leaving no other alternative than an immediate meeting, which was fixed to take place that very evening. The disgraceful conduct of the Major becoming known, he was taken into custody and detained some hours, but was eventually released without giving any assurance of keeping the peace towards Colonel Bolton. No sooner had he been set at liberty than he sent that gentleman a message to the effect that he should that evening, at five o'clock, await his appearance in the field skirted by Love-lane, above Fielding's nursery. Punctual to the moment, Colonel Bolton, attended by Mr. Harris as second, and Mr. Park, an eminent physician, who resided at the corner of Newington-bridge and Bold-street, whom he had picked up in his carriage on his way, came upon the ground; but it was so dark before preliminary matters were arranged that candles had to be procured to enable the parties to see what they were about. Colonel Bolton, remarking that it was the custom of the *duello* for the challenger to fire first, requested him to do so. Brooks instantly discharged his pistol. The ball, however, passed Colonel Bolton without touching him, but the Colonel's shot entered his antagonist's right eye. Brooks fell and died immediately. The Colonel was hurried away by his friends and went into retirement until the affair blew over. Although a verdict of "Wilful murder" was recorded by the jury at the inquest on Major Brooks, that gentleman's friends so strongly represented his ferocity and disgraceful conduct towards Colonel Bolton, that no steps were taken to proceed further with the affair. Colonel Bolton was a most amiable gentleman, and stood high in the estimation of his townsmen. It was said that this unhappy duel greatly affected his spirits in after life. He died in 1837. In 1836 he gave 2,000 guineas to the charities of the town, in the following proportions:—Infirmary, £500; Blue-coat Hospital, £400; Dispensary, £300; Marine Society, £300; School for Blind, £300; Ladies' Charity, £200; School for Deaf and Dumb, £100. Major Brooks lodged in the house at the corner of Daulby-street, where the pistol shots were distinctly heard by the inmates of it, who little conjectured the cause until his dead body was brought home.

West Derby-street was called at one time "Pembroke-road." It was skirted by hedges and beautiful elm trees, some of which stood at a late date a little way up on the north side, near Mount Vernon-street. A street hereabout is called Elm-street. In 1840 each side of Paddington was unbuilt upon. At the bottom, on the north side, there was a pretty white house in a garden, with palings skirting the road. Some of the streets hereabout are called after the Gascoyne family, as Bamber-street, &c. In 1760 a long reservoir extended under the hill westward of Smithdown-lane. It commenced near Pembroke-place, and ran nearly half-way to the present Grinfield-street. Mount Vernon had at one time only Mount Vernon Hall standing on it. Mount Vernon-green was at one time called Cheetham-green. On the west side of Hall-lane, within the last four years, was a large field on which the Volunteers were accustomed to parade and drill. It was called Cheetham-brow. It belonged to Colonel Tempest. It is now covered with cottage property, shops, and spirit vaults. The extensive conventual establishment in Mount Vernon-street was commenced about 1835. At the corner of Hall-lane and Prescot-street, adjoining Mr. Tipping's garden, was once a famous bowling-green. Some curious anecdotes are told of Mr. Tipping, who was a member of the Society of Friends. Some time before his death he sent for Hargreaves, the builder, who worked for him. Taking him up to the lobby, near his bed-chamber door, Mr. Tipping said to Hargreaves: "Look here, dost thou think that a coffin could go through that doorway and into this passage?" "I don't," replied Hargreaves. "Well, then, send thy men and make it, so that one can be got out if I should be in it." Great changes have taken place about Edge-hill of late years. Where Mr. James Mullineux's mansion stood there are now numbers of houses. To the east of Edge-hill Church in 1816 was a spacious stone quarry, which was in 1780 an open green called "Greenfield." St. Mary's was erected, at the sole cost of Mr. Mason, in 1813. This gentleman resided in Mason-street, not far from Paddington. This thoroughfare at one time was only an occupation road to a lonely farm-house which overlooked the valley below.

## MASON STREET, EDGE HILL.

THIS was a very pretty street twenty-five years ago. On the east side were long gardens, which were most prolific in anything grown in them, whether flowers or vegetables. The erection of a set of court houses over an old delf, skirted by Upper Mason-street, about 1845, commenced the deterioration of the street. An old inhabitant could scarcely now recognise this once pleasant thoroughfare, where he had heard the birds singing in the morning, and could see from the top room windows of his house at night the Rock light with its alternating red and white flames. A few houses have still gardens in front of them, but their green glories have sadly faded. The houses on the west side are not changed outwardly in aspect in front, nor at the back, although between them and Smithdown-lane there have been great alterations of late years. The once peaceful and pretty terrace gardens are now full of signs of grim-visaged war in heavy guns, the deep excavations being filled up, the marvellous arches and mysterious tunnels closed or removed, and the subterranean wonders of the place no longer accessible. Mr. Mason's mansion stood near the Paddington end of the street; his garden extended to Smithdown-lane, and is now occupied by the small short streets on the south side of Paddington. The site of his stables is occupied by the row of houses near the corner. Miss Mason, who was a most bountiful lady, resided in the house after her father's death.

She had a school for poor girls, who were taught house work, and received a useful education. It stood at the bottom of her garden, on the south side of Paddington-lane.

Several gentlemen of considerable local celebrity have resided in Mason-street. The Rev. Edward Hull, who for forty years and more was chaplain to the Blind Asylum, dwelt in the first of the series of houses erected by Mr. Joseph Williamson. It is now the storehouse of one of the artillery corps. In the house but one adjoining dwelt Mr. Cornelius Henderson, who died about 1846. He was an artist of considerable merit. His portraits were extremely faithful; and in other branches of his profession he attained some fame. Near Grinfield-street, in the house now occupied as St. Anne's Industrial Schools, resided the Rev. Dr. Raffles, who for nearly half a century was pastor of Great George-street Chapel. In some of the intermediate houses the Artillery Volunteer Corps, and also the Engineers, at present have their store-houses and head-quarters. Nearly opposite Bolton-street, now called Shimmin-street, resided Mr. Joseph Williamson, by whom nearly all the houses on the west side of the street were erected, and which, whatever they may be now, were at one time some of the most singularly constructed and contrived habitations ever man dwelt in. Mr. Williamson was called "King of Edge-hill," for at the time, when his works were in full operation, he employed at least one half of the labouring portion of the Edge-hill community. He held a great deal of property in Mason-street, and also about the neighbourhood, chiefly under the Waste Lands Commission. It went out of lease in 1858. In all his property he exhibited his peculiar taste for excavating and vaulting. He was a curious tempered man. He never seemed so happy as when he was in his excavations and grubbing under the surface of the earth. In the house in which he resided he literally lived in the cellar. It was his sitting-room, while his bed-room was actually a cave. Mr. Williamson came from Warrington. He said of his parents, "My mother was as decent a woman as ever lived. She started me in life with a good box full of clothes, and sent me to Liverpool to make my fortune. My father was a regular rip." Mr. Williamson was largely engaged in the tobacco trade. He served his apprenticeship to Mr. Thomas Moss Tate, tobacco merchant, in Wolstenholme-square, whom he succeeded in business, after marrying his daughter, Miss Elizabeth Tate. The wedding took place at St. Thomas Church. Williamson, who was a member of the Liverpool Hunt, had his hunter and groom in waiting for him at the church door while the ceremony was proceeding. At its conclusion, Williamson told his wife, "to be off home," and that "he would be with her in the course of the afternoon," whereupon mounting his horse he joined "the hunt." Some one noticing his *debonnaire* appearance, remarked, "Why, Williamson, how smart you are." "Smart, lad," replied he, "I should think a man ought to look smart on his wedding-day." At this his companions pricked up their ears, and some of them exclaimed—"Wedding-day! why, where is your wife?" "My wife," replied the newly made Benedict, "my wife, why, where a good wife ought to be, looking after her husband's dinner."

It has been said that from some information he obtained from General Gascoigne, connected with the tobacco trade, he cleared an immense amount of money. Mr. Williamson in person was tall and portly, having a handsome face. Although he usually assumed a rough and bearish manner, no man could be more courteous, appear better dressed, or make himself more agreeable in a drawing-room. In fact, it has been stated as a fact, that when the Prince of Wales was in Liverpool, in 1806, Williamson, on being introduced to him, was by his highness pronounced to be "one of the few gentlemen he had met with in the town." To ladies, and especially to children, he was extremely engaging; with the latter he was very fond of playing and petting them in all sorts of ways. "Ah," said he once to a friend who saw him with a little one holding each of his hands, "ah," said he, "if I had any of these of my own I should not have been the old rip I am." No one who saw him in good and select company could have credited that he was the same man that might be seen lounging about Mason-street, attired in an old brown coat, wearing corderoy breeches, hob-nailed boots, and a shabby old hat. He did many very odd things. He once invited several gentlemen to dine with him. They were shown into a poorly furnished apartment, in which was a bare table with common forms around it. On it was a large tureen containing porridge, and for each guest was provided a soup plate. Of this they were invited to partake. One guest, however, who did not know his host's queer ways, resented the proferred food as an indignity, expressing great disgust at Mr. Williamson's conduct in inviting him to partake of such ordinary fare, intimating his intention of instantly quitting the house. Mr. Williamson, in the most courteous manner, showed him to the door without a word of explanation. The guests remaining, who suspected what was to follow, quietly pretended to partake of the first course. On Williamson's return he requested them to follow him. He led them into a large apartment, where they found a table blazing with glass and plate, and a banquet spread that would have been fit for Amphitryon or Heliogabulus, or any other master in the gracious art of good living. To this feast the party was invited to partake without any comments as to the meaning of the curious "first course."

In respect to his tenants Mr. Williamson did out-of-the-way things. A gentleman, the father of a respected "boy of the broad sheet," of long standing in Liverpool, once went to see Mr. Williamson about a house of his in Parr-street. "Well, sir," asked Williamson gruffly, "Who, and what are you?" The reply was, "I am an officer in his Majesty's Excise." "Oh, you are! Are you? Well, you are just the man for me. You can look after your neighbours. They want it, I can tell you." "What will be the rent of the house, Mr. Williamson?" "Oh, never mind the rent; you get into the house, and we can talk about that afterwards. I know we shan't disagree." "I would rather have the amount fixed before I take possession." "Well, I thought of getting fifteen or eighteen pounds for it; but from you I shall not ask more than ten pounds. That's quite enough for you to pay." The gentleman, of course, being well satisfied—rents have considerably risen since those days—took the house. When the first quarter's rent became due, he went to his landlord and tendered it. "Be off," said Williamson, "With your paltry quarter's rent. I don't want it till it is worth receiving. You bring it at the end of the year, if you like; and if you don't, never mind until I ask you for it." This gentleman occupied Williamson's house for some years, until circumstances obliged him to change his locality. Some time after he had done so, he met Williamson, who asked him "Where he lived, and what rent he paid?" He was told. Williamson remarked that he was paying more rent than he ought to do. "Now," said he, "As you were a good tenant of mine, and as I think you are a worthy man, I'll buy the house you live in, and let you have it for less than you are now paying." This promise he actually performed; for he purchased the house forthwith, and reduced the rent, as he said he would, fully twenty-five per cent. Williamson was, at times, very suspicious, and once exhibited this phase in his character in a curious way. On one occasion he put bailiffs into the house of a man for whom he entertained but little respect. A friend of this person called on Williamson with the greater part of the rent in arrear, begging him to accept it, and relieve his tenant of the unwelcome occupants. Williamson seemed to agree to the terms proposed, and was just handing the receipt to his visitor, when, looking him fixedly in the face, he drew back the document, saying, "You are up to some trick, sir. Why should you meddle in another man's affairs? Take your money, sir, and come to-morrow; but here is a discharge for the bailiffs. You bring the money to-morrow. You want to trick me." The man tried to persuade him to accept the rent, but he would not take it until the following day, when he had satisfied himself that no artifice was intended to be put in practice. With the people he employed he did strange things, and put them to strange occupations, as laborious as purposeless. One man who asked him for work he sent to a pump, and told him to go on pumping till he bade him stop. This man he kept pumping for days, all the water drawn running away. At first the man put a bucket to catch the fluid, and inquired what he was to do with it? "Why, drink it if you like," replied his em-

At the corner of Bolton-street it will be remembered by many that there was once a strange-looking tall house of three stories, or rather two stories and a ground floor, having immensely long large windows. Without stating his intention respecting this house, Williamson went on building it, superintending its progress with great care, and employing many men in its erection to expedite the work. On its being completed, he sent for Mr. Henderson, the artist, whom he much patronised, often giving him commissions for pictures. On that gentleman's arrival he took him to the new building, and after showing him the rooms, told him that he had erected it purposely for him to paint in. Mr. Henderson, astonished at this generous act, respectfully pointed out to his patron that the windows, as they were then constructed, were utterly useless to an artist, who required only "a top light." At this Williamson flew into a violent passion, swore at Henderson, and charged him with ingratitude, that "he had built a house for him that had cost upwards of a thousand pounds, and after all for nothing." Just at this moment the Rev. Mr. Hull was seen passing along the street, when Williamson shouted, with a voice like Boanerges, "Hi, hi, hollo! Parson Hull; hi! come here." On Mr. Hull joining them, Williamson said, "Now, look here, Parson, I've built Henderson a house on purpose to paint in, and he says its of no use to him. He's been talking a lot of d——d rubbish about 'top lights.' Did you ever hear such nonsense? Here's light, plenty for everything and anything, and yet he says its of no use to him. Did you ever hear such regular nonsense?" "Parson Hull" and Mr. Henderson endeavoured to appease the roaring lion, and strove to explain to him how unnecessary was such an exuberance of light to a painter, but all to no purpose. He would not, or could not understand, and the consequence was that the house was never occupied or used for any purpose. In fact, as a habitation it was untenantable, there being no kitchen, scullery, or any domestic convenience whatever. It was a mere building consisting of three immense rooms, one over the other, with a deep basement or cellar.

On sewering Mason-street about 1846 or 1847 a tunnel was discovered, five feet high and three feet wide, running from the cellar to Williamson's house opposite.

The yard in which the house stood was built the same as when it stood in the south-east corner. Williamson, speaking of his wife, said that although they led a cat and dog life, he missed the old girl at last. Once, after a little matrimonial tiff, Williamson vowed he wished he was a bachelor again, to be at liberty. Opening the doors of his wife's aviary, he let all the birds out, saying "There! see how the poor little devils like to get free." "Many a married man would like to have wings and the door of wedlock thrown open, so that they might fly away and be at rest." One severe winter a meeting of the inhabitants of Edge-hill took place, to consider what could be done for the poor. Williamson was invited to attend. After some discussion, and a variety of modes were proposed to alleviate the distress then prevalent, Williamson was asked to head a subscription. "Now," said Williamson to the incumbent of St. Mary's (Mr. Barker) who was in the chair, "how many men do you employ?" The incumbent replied "None." He put the same question to another of the leaders of the meeting, and also to others, some of whom had a man at work, and some two. "Now," said Williamsom, "you all come and see what I do for the poor, and don't bother me with your charity." Thereupon, leading the way, he took the whole party to his works, called up all his men, told the meeting to count them, and "go and do likewise;" showing them at the same time an old man who was slowly turning a grindstone, without any tools to be sharpened, merely as some occupation for him.

As Joseph Williamson's extensive excavations and astonishing underground works are every year disappearing, and their memory becoming dimmer in men's minds, a brief notice of them may prove acceptable. Very few persons but those actually employed in their construction have seen much of them, for Mr. Williamson was singularly reluctant to allow anybody to go through them. Persons of some standing and distinction occasionally applied to see the excavations, but were almost always refused, either politely or surlily, as the whim of the moment arose in the mind of their eccentric proprietor. He seemed jealous that other people should be gratified by a sight of them, and appeared to carry his works on solely for his own gratification. It has been conjectured that Mr. Williamson must have expended at least £100,000 on these extraordinary works—works utterly purposeless, without design, and useless. What their projector's idea was in constructing his stupendous undertakings can never now be known, for he said little about them to those with whom he was intimate. He certainly did not get out the stone from his quarries for profit, for he often declared that he never sold a ton of it. He contributed, it is said the material, for the construction of St. Jude's Church, and he would, if he was in the humour, give any one as much stone as might be wanted on application; and, in not a few instances, he has been known to cause the blocks to be dressed, without charge, in the way suitable for the purposes for which they were intended. It has been thought he had some notion of creating a posthumous fame—that after his death when the excavations were examined, people would cry aloud with wonder at their originality and vastness. He certainly did not covet fame through them living, as has been shown. It is a curious circumstance that after his death no interest was taken by the public in them, no curiosity raised to see through these works,—his representatives, caring nothing for them, shutting them up until year after year they had become considerably circumscribed, by filling up and decay.

Amongst the few who were taken through the works by Williamson was the celebrated Robert Stevenson, who declared that what he had seen were marvels in underground construction, and he gratified their projector by highly extolling them. When the tunnel was in formation from Edge-hill to Lime-street, about 1834, and was passing through and under his property, Mr. Williamson actually drove a tunnel under the railway tunnel, appearing himself in the aperture made, to the amazement of the navvies, who were told that if "they wanted to know how to tunnel he could give them a lesson in that polite art." Mr. Williamson, through the intercession of one of his tenants, for whom he had a great regard, gave an order to inspect his works to Dr. George C. Watson, a physician who practised in Liverpool some five and twenty years ago, and who was the writer of some admirable letters on sanitary reform in the *Liverpool Standard,* signed "Medicus," which were in fact the Pioneers of that great movement in this town. The order for admission ran thus:—

"Dr. Watson is not to be interrupted in his walks on my premises, either on the surface or under the surface.
"January, 1839. J. W., E. H."

Dr. Watson's account of the works when they were in their prime was, that they were perfect marvels, not only for their great extent, but for the excellence of their construction, and their inapplicability to any possible purpose. Mr. Williamson always said his prime motive in all he did "was the employment of the poor; for if you give them something to do, no matter what, it keeps them out of mischief." He certainly always seemed to have a great many people about him; and at times the place was like a hive, as might be seen when he would order all the people up to give them a drink, tapping for them a half barrel of ale or porter, of which little would remain after all had been supplied. He said "they worked all the better for their throats being wetted." Williamson's property in Mason-street, besides some portions on the east side of the street, commenced at Miss Mason's land, continuing along the street to about two houses from Grinfield-street. It was bounded on the west by Smithdown-lane.

In Williamson's lifetime the western side of the lane was open ground, and nearly all unbuilt upon. Williamson's land was enclosed by a strong stone wall, portions of which still remain, exhibiting its solidity. Nearly at the northern end of this wall there was a strong archway, with solid folding doors. A rickety gate stands in their place at present. This was the entrance to a tunnel, or vaulted passage, through which the carts brought up the stone from the great quarry. It would admit of two waggons abreast. It was higher at the eastern than at the western end. On the outer surface was soil with bushes growing. This vast arch or passage is now destroyed. On the left of the eastern end of this passage or vault there was another lofty vault running to the northern limit of the property. It must have been originally at least forty or fifty feet high. In one corner of it, in its eastern wall, was an aperture about six feet from the ground, about five feet in height, and four feet in width. This was the entrance to a passage or gallery which led under the terrace and branched off in different ways. Any one in it made good haste to get out of it, for the stench that existed thereabouts was frightful. Several attempts were made in 1844 by a party to explore it to its termination, but without success. This large vault is destroyed or filled up, no vestige of it remaining. Here was also an enormous chasm, now filled up, which would be about thirty to forty feet wide, and at least sixty in depth from the surface. This was uncovered. At the eastern extremity was a stupendous brick arch thrown over from side to side of the chasm or quarry. This arch supported the terrace above, brick work being run up to the surface. From a yard occupied by a carter may still be seen the remains of this immense cavern. About forty feet from the entrance there was a solid pier run up in the middle of the arch. About three-fourths of the distance from the bottom there was on the left hand side an arch thrown over from the pier to the side of the vault, and above that was another arch thrown from the top of the pier. On the other side of the pier, between the first and second arches, was an arch thrown to the right hand side of the vault, and over that was a smaller arch on a level with the top arch of the left hand side. Between the top arches was brick work, which was continued to fill up to the top of the vault. In this pier itself were three arches. On the left hand side wall of the vault, near the bottom, was a vault or tunnel that ran to the northern limits of the property. It would be about twenty feet high. Over it, near the top of the arch, was another passage running in the same direction. The passage in the vault, near the entrance tunnel, communicated with these vaults, steps leading to the upper one. In the eastern, or end wall of the vault, were two openings, from which extensive passages ran under the Mason-street houses. In the south or right hand side wall, about twenty feet from the ground, was an opening from which commenced a series of other passages or galleries under the terrace and the houses to Mason-street. The Artillery Volunteers' battery overlooks the site of the entrance tunnel and the quarry opening to the great arch. To the right of the entrance to the quarry there were two large arches. At the northern extremity of the property there was a small tunnel or gallery about six feet wide and ten feet high, which commenced in the orchard (part of the area between the terrace and Smithdown-lane being so appropriated) and ran up to the back premises of Mr. Hull's house, in Mason-street. About halfway up this gallery were two flights of steps, having a landing-place between them. At the second flight of steps there was a recess. Above it was a funnel or spout through which rubbish from the garden above appeared to have been shot down. At the top of the passage or tunnel there was a door, which opened to a back yard. This tunnel crossed over the other tunnels. At the first flight of steps in the right hand wall the crown and part of the arch of one of the vaults leading from the great vault previously described was visible. Why it was thus open appeared inexplicable, unless it was for the purpose of shooting through it the garden refuse. In the garden or orchard to the right of the tunnel just described, there were four lofty recesses cut out of the solid rock. In one of them was a stove and flue, which communicated with the terrace above. It was supposed to be intended to heat a greenhouse. Near these recesses there was a passage or vault running eastwardly. It was about 120 feet in length, and ten or twelve feet high. The approach to it was by a path cut between two high banks. This gallery crossed over the tunnels running northward and southward. The entrance to it was neatly finished. When the writer saw it there were some huge blocks of stone at the furthest portion of it, which had lain undisturbed either upon Mr. Williamson having abandoned the idea of continuing the tunnel to Mason-street, or the work was stopped by his death. Some eccentric and unaccountable-looking arches were to be seen under the terrace at the southern limit of the property. Some of them were fitted with bins similar to those in a wine cellar. In this part of the ground there were several sets of arches, one over the other, which it seemed impossible to account for. They are now buried under the surface of the Corporation stable yards. The effluvium hereabout at one time was very obnoxious. There was a run of water from the lowest of one of the arches. In one place a deep well was excavated, into which a woman one night fell and was drowned. In one of the vaults that occupied the ground near where the present blower or fan for ventilating the railway tunnel is placed, there were some fine stalactites observable. In the vicinity of the Corporation stables and yards there was once a deep delf, in the side of which were excavated several rooms—one on the top of another, communication between them being obtained by a spiral stair, or flight of steps, cut out of the solid rock. This delf has been filled up at least thirty years. In this neighbourhood were some long arches, one on the top of the other. They seem to be of no earthly use. When seen by the writer they were in a ruinous state. In one of these vaults were several deep niches, as if it was intended to have run out passages from them. The terraces of the Mason-street houses, on which the gardens were laid out, are now used as Volunteer drill grounds. They are built entirely on arches, some of which are of notable construction, and of bold and just proportions. In the house where Mr. Henderson, the artist, resided were some remarkable instances of Mr. Williamson's constructive peculiarities. To accommodate the artist, who was at that time making a large copy of Rubens' "Descent from the Cross," Williamson cut away the two floors of the house to form a large painting-room, roofing it over by an immense sky-light. Attached to the western wall of this spacious apartment was a banistered open staircase, by which access could be obtained to a bedroom. At the top of the stairs there was a passage which ran over the top of the next house, leading to the two attics appropriated to the use of Henderson's family. The kitchen was vaulted. Passing the kitchen door was a flight of steps which led to a lofty arched vault. Passing through a doorway was found a long gallery wide enough for two carts to pass; and about half-way down it a vault, secured by an iron-open work gate, which ran to the limit of the property northward. At the end of the main vault was a long narrow passage, which shot off at right angles. It was lighted by a grid, which was let into the walk of the garden above of an adjoining house. The end of this passage came out on a terrace which overlooked the great quarry, the bottom of which seemed to be a terrific depth. A fine view was then obtainable from this terrace. Considerable changes appear to have taken place hereabout, as during a late visit many of the former features of the place seem to have disappeared. It seems as if part of the houses at the back had been removed, and had been substituted by an open space of ground, used by the artillery to drill upon. A fire which took place here a few years ago perhaps originated this change. The backs of the houses in Mason-street are of the most varied character. Some have projecting rooms, some are recessed. Here are long large windows, there will be noticed small square ones. When in their prime, and occupied by respectable families, the Mason-street houses were unrivalled for their want of uniformity. They are now uglier than ever they were. Mr. Williamson seldom had any plans to build by, of either his houses or his works. He told his people to go on building this wall or that till he bade them to stop. Cases have occurred where, in his houses, it has been found he had omitted the two essentials to a room, of light and entrance. There is, or was, a room in one of the houses in Mason-street, in which it was discovered, while in course of construction, that there was no door provided, no fire-place, and no window. The light had to be obtained by making a shaft through an upper room, at the top of which was a sky-light. As for the door, the utmost ingenuity was obliged to be exercised to introduce it at all. The fire-place proved to be an insurmountable obstacle, and therefore was abandoned altogether. The Mason-street houses have in them lofty, large rooms, with long passages leading to them. These rooms would be exceedingly suitable to any one with a large circle of acquaintance, with ample means to entertain them.

As store-houses for Volunteers they are admirably adapted, as may be supposed by several of the leading corps of artillery and engineers mustering in them, and making them their head-quarters.

In some of the houses in High-street, which were erected by Williamson, there are cellars that would contain fifty tons of coals, and Cloacinian receptacles, that it would take half a century to fill.

The houses which have their backs to Back Mason-street were erected by Mr. Williamson. They are all vaulted to an immense depth. Some of them have five and six tiers of cellars, one over the other. The baker's shop at the corner of High-street, and that adjoining, have very deep foundations. They are as low in depth as they are in height. It may be noticed that one of them has four stories. This is a regular barrack, from the number of rooms it contains. The rats swarmed in the excavations, vaults, and passages. Some of them, once encountered by the writer were of immense size. They actually ran in droves. He once saw one that was pure white—a most beautiful animal. He tried to catch it, but the rat objected to be impounded, and fled into the dark recesses of a long passage under one of the houses, in which it would not have been prudent to follow. These excavations, vaults, and passages, left unprotected, were, undoubtedly, highly dangerous places. They might have been applied to various unlawful purposes. Strange and unaccountable noises have occasionally been heard proceeding from these excavations by the inhabitants of the houses in Mason-street. Many years ago the writer was told by a gentleman residing in one of them, that one night he and his family were terrified in the extreme, by the horrible yells and sounds of agony that appeared to proceed from the vaults under his house. He endeavoured to unravel the mystery that hung about the circumstance, but without avail. The passages that were then somewhat accessible were searched, but nothing was found in them that could clear up the matter. The orchard has disappeared with the arches that were erected in it. Great accumulations of soil have been heaped up between the terraces and Smithdown-lane, and scarcely a vestige is now perceptible of the great works of Joseph Williamson, who, although he employed numbers of persons, has left but little to show how his money was expended. That which he perhaps anticipated would be a local wonder, seems to be now almost forgotten. His costly excavations and galleries are filled up, his vaults are destroyed or covered over, and his great delf is a tradition. Had he spent his money usefully on the surface, instead of uselessly under it, those who came after him would have doubtless had more satisfaction. Williamson was very hospitable. In his sitting-room, or vault, or cellar, were casks of wine laid up, out of which he drew draughts in mugs and jugs wherewith to regale his visitors. Wine glasses appeared to be taboo'd in his establishment. He died in May, 1841.

Amongst the things that were in this neighbourhood may be mentioned the old Botanic Garden, which occupied about ten acres of land towards Myrtle-street. The Deaf and Dumb Asylum stands nearly on the site of the entrance. It was suggested and supported in its establishment by Mr. Roscoe, who seems to have been first and foremost in numberless public institutions tending to the general welfare. Under his directions, it was first laid out in 1800, and opened in 1803, when he read to those assembled a very graceful and elegant address, replete with point and happy suggestions. The old gardens were laid out somewhat similar to the present Botanic Garden in Edge-lane, having hot-houses for tropical productions, and a small ornamental water for the growth of aquatic plants and gold fish. Dr. Foster's extensive collection of dried plants, collected by him in his southern voyages, were amongst its attractions. These gardens were discontinued in 1836.

# RODNEY STREET.

Towards the close of the last century the district of Rodney-street, Upper Duke-street, and Hope-street was all unbuilt upon, being in some parts cultivated land, and in others growing nothing but furze and heather. The fields, for instance, that skirted and overlooked the great quarry on the east side, belonging to Mr. Crosbie, were of this wild description. Along the site of these fields, Hope-street was cut to Parliament-street. The site of St. Mark's Church, in 1799, was a field, which extended to Rodney-street. During the residence of Prince William, of Gloucester, in Liverpool, he once attended St. Mark's, when the Bishop of Chester preached. During the service a report arose that the gallery was giving way, when the utmost confusion took place, but happily without loss of life. The originator and principal proprietor of St. Mark's was a Rev. Thomas Jones, of Bolton, who was a very popular preacher. He died suddenly, while on a journey to London, just previous to the opening of the church, in 1803. St. Mark's was not consecrated till 1815.

Upper Duke-street terminated at the entrance of St. James's-road, on the south, and a few yards above Rodney-street, on the north. Just above this spot were a tavern, a windmill, and a bowling-green, which stood to the south of Sir Foster Cunliffe's field, at the back of which was an occupation road, leading to Mr. Kent's fields. This bowling-green stood on the site of Mornington-terrace. Beyond this were fields, and as late as 1823 there were extensive roperies on the site of Canning-street. Just above Rodney-street was a little lane, which skirted the public-house and the bowling-green. This lane ran up eastwardly to a lane called Crabtree-lane, now Falkner-street, named after Mr. Falkner, who held a considerable quantity of property hereabout. Crabtree-lane was only an occupation road at one time, which terminated somewhere about the site of the present Grove-street. From it ran a foot-path into Smithdown-lane. Falkner-square was formed upon Mr. Falkner's property, about 1830. Blackburne-place was named after Mr. Blackburne, who erected a mansion there (now Blackburne House), and had much land in the vicinity. Between the Unitarian Chapel and where the Philharmonic now stands, in 1768, there was an Observatory erected, which, it was expected, would prove of great importance and advantage to the port. Although the Mayor laid the first stone with much ceremony, and the building was completed, nothing came of it, and it went to decay. By the end of Mr. Maddocks's field the lane took a turn, skirting a bowling-green and tavern, which stood nearly on the site of the open ground between Oxford-street and opposite the Workhouse wall. In this tavern, as elsewhere stated, Roscoe was born. The road again turned until it entered Brownlow-hill-lane, as it does at present. The cause of this serpentine road is supposed to have originated from its skirting, at an early period, the marshy ground of the Moss Lake Fields.

The "Moss Lake" is supposed to have occupied the locality of Abercromby-square. The fields in the neighbourhood of Crown-street and the present Grove-street at times were under water, and when frozen over in winter time was the favourite resort of skaters.

To show how little traffic there was at one time (within the last sixty years) in Hope-street, a worthy gentleman now dwelling amongst us recollects, when a boy, that on leaving his parents' home one snowy morning, between nine and ten o'clock, to go to Lewin's school, his own footprints were the only indentations to be seen in the street on the whitened surface. Hope-street was called after Mr. Hope, who resided in it.

In 1826 a horrible disclosure took place connected with Hope-street, that filled the minds of the inhabitants of Liverpool with horror. One morning, in the month of October in that year, three barrels were taken down in a cart to the Pier, and were put on board the Glasgow packet. After they had been on deck a short time, the captain of the packet and some of the passengers noticed a disagreeable odour prevailing in the vicinity of these casks, which had been shipped as "salted hides." The passengers insisting upon the barrels being put on shore, in the act of doing so, one of them burst open, when a human body was found closely packed in it, in salt. In the other two were also human bodies. The carter who conveyed them to the vessel having been discovered, the police authorities were communicated with, by whom it was found that the barrels had been brought from a house in Hope-street, which on being searched was found to contain no less than thirty-three other corpses, regularly salted and cured. The bodies had been taken from the parish cemetery in Cambridge-street. These subjects had been obtained for the use of medical schools with which, it appeared, a regular trade was carried on.

Hope-hall has seen some mutations. It was at one period a dissenting chapel, in the basement of which "Love Feasts" took place, of so extraordinary a character, as to excite the attention of Mr. Samuel Warren, Q.C., the author of the "Diary of a Physician," "Ten Thousand a Year, &c.," who, while on circuit, visited the place, and afterwards described the proceedings that he had witnessed in a very clever and amusing article in *Blackwood's Magazine*, which had the effect of calling public attention to the case, and causing a discontinuance of the strange doings. The chapel was afterwards converted into a church, under the designation of "St. John the Evangelist." The alms-houses in St. Mary's-lane were erected in 1787, for old and indigent persons, as a substitute for the alms-houses that had been erected in divers parts of the town, and which had been taken down, for the improvements in their immediate neighbourhoods.

Rodney-street was projected about 1780. When this line of streets was first marked out it extended to Mount-pleasant only. It is a current tradition that it was at first proposed to call the new street "Schlink-street," to perpetuate the name of a Dutchman who had purchased a considerable portion of the land. The name, however, being very objectionable, as one that was in connection with prematurely and newly born calves, converted into veal, it was changed in 1782 to "Rodney-street," the gallant Admiral Rodney having, in that year defeated a fleet of French line-of-battle ships off Guadaloupe.

In 1807 there were many portions of Rodney-street unbuilt upon, on which grew heather and furze about the sandpits abounding in the vicinity. The first house erected in it was by Mr. Pudsey Dawson, who had so benevolently and successfully taken the Blind School in hand. His house stood at the corner of or near Hardman-street, which was called after Mrs. Hardman, who had much land thereabout. In Rodney-street have resided many of those who may be truly placed on the list of Liverpool "Worthies." Without regarding dates, a few names may be given of those who have dwelt in this at all times fashionable thoroughfare. Between Knight-street and Upper Duke-street resided Mr. Robert Gladstone, who afterwards lived at Parkfield, near the Dingle, where he erected a beautiful lodge, which is said to have cost £800. Parkfield is now "Alexandra Drive." Mr. John, afterwards Sir John Gladstone, resided in Rodney-street, between Leece-street and Knight-street. In this mansion, which had a centre and two wings, the gifted sons of this eminent Liverpool merchant-prince were born—men who have proved themselves to be the first of foremost men, in national and local histories. From the balcony of this mansion George Canning in 1812, after each day's polling, addressed tremendous crowds of people, charming them by his graceful eloquence, his polished oratory, his happy allusions to passing events, and his withering sarcasms directed against his adversaries. Here it was that he uttered the remarkable declaration, that "He would not support the question of Parliamentary reform, because he felt persuaded that those who were most loud, and, apparently, most solicitous in recommending it, did mean, and have for years past meant, far other things than these simple words seemed to intend; because he was persuaded that that question could not be stirred without stirring others, which would shake the Constitution to its very foundation." In Rodney-street Mr. D'Altera—"little Joe," as he was called amongst his familiar friends, resided with his mother. He was a leading member of the "Committee of Taste," a celebrated society of its time. The Rev. Mr. Cardwell, who officiated at St. Paul's Church, dwelt in this street. He was uncle to the Right Honourable

Edward Cardwell, member for Liverpool, 1847. The reverend gentleman bore the soubriquet of the "Pier Head Parson," from being seen there day by day walking up and down, in all weathers. He usually was attired in black coat and knee breeches, with gold buckles, silk stockings, and low quartered shoes, and he always carried a neat little silk umbrella.

Rodney-street has always been a favourite locality of the medical profession. There are at present upwards of twenty practitioners residing in it, either physicians or surgeons. Dr. Gouldie, a celebrated physician of his time, lived in it, as did Dr. Scott, the celebrated lecturer, and Dr. Brandreth. Dr. Manifold, a highly esteemed physician, had a house in it. The late Mr. Bickersteth, who dwelt near Mount-pleasant, was considered as skilful and dexterous in the conducting of an operation as Sir Astley Cooper. At the corner of Mount-pleasant dwelt Mr. Churchwarden Dennison, at whose expense was erected the beautiful gate of St. Nicholas's Churchyard, at the bottom of Chapel-street. Stirred up by Mr. Egerton Smith and Mr. Edward Rushton, the parishioners grumbled so much that the vestry refused to meet the cost, and left their churchwarden in the lurch, although attempts were made to reimburse him, but without effect. Mr. Counsellor Fletcher Raincock resided in Rodney-street. He had an immense chamber practice. He was the agent for the Lowther family at their Appleby elections. He was a man with very plain face and ungainly gait. On one occasion, in cross-examining a female witness, who had used once or twice the then newly-coined word "humbugging," Mr. Raincock inquired what she meant by "humbugging?" "Whoi if oi war to ca' yer a handsome mon, that ud be humbugging." In 1832, died in Rodney-street, by Maryland-street, Mr. Hammerton, who bequeathed £5,000 to four of the Liverpool charities. Sir George Drinkwater, who was Mayor in 1829, and who was present at Mr. Huskisson's accident, resided near Mount-street; Sir Thomas Brancker, who was Mayor in 1830, and afterwards dock treasurer, dwelt between Hardman-street and Maryland-street. Mr. Counsellor Henry Lawrence, the last of the old Commissioners in Bankruptcy, occupied a house on the west side, near Mount-pleasant. The celebrated Lieutenant Maury was born in Rodney-street; his father resided in the house next to Mr. Bickersteth's. Mr. Maury was the first American consul appointed in Liverpool. He held the appointment fully twenty-six years. On his retirement the Liverpool merchants presented him with a service of plate as a testimony of the high respect and appreciation of his conduct, Near him resided Mr. James Aspinall, a most remarkable man. He was Mayor in 1834 and 1835. He did not go out of office until the new Municipal Reform Bill came into operation. In January he was succeeded by Mr. William Wallace Currie, the first who filled the office of chief magistrate under that Act. Mr. James Aspinall was a borough magistrate also. He was of immense bulk both in height and breadth, weighing, it is said, twenty-four stones. His face was singularly handsome, while his manners were exceedingly pleasant, kindly, and courteous to all who had intercourse with him. He was always remarkably well and fashionably dressed. In fact in Liverpool he was the "observed of all observers." On the 12th July, 1834, some silly orangemen parading the town with their flags, swords, ribbons, and such like trumpery, excited the anger of the Catholic community to such an extent, that in several parts of the town serious disturbances were anticipated. Word having been received at the Town-hall that a large and turbulent mob had assembled in St. James's-street, Mr. Aspinall, attended only by a small force of police and a few friends, confronted the crowd, and deliberately walked into the midst of it. Singling out the most noisy of the lot, he ordered one man to go to his work, and another to "be off about his business;" and told a violent woman to "go home to her children." Mr. Aspinall's dauntless and authoritative bearing had the desired effect of dispersing the mob. A good joke, of which Mr. Aspinall was the originator, was current once in the town. A well-known tailor in Lord-street had been extensively advertising complete suits for "gentlemen at three pounds" something, when one day Mr. Aspinall, accompanied by a worthy alderman of nearly equal bodily proportions to himself, and a town councillor, next in degree of size to his companions, walked into the tailor's shop, and to the dismay of the Clothier ordered suits for each of them at the advertised price. The cloth alone for the three would have been more than sufficient to cover the backs of six ordinary sized individuals, to say nothing at all of the expense of making such capacious garments.

In Rodney-street resided at one time one of the largest women in England, the widow of a wine merchant. This lady used to say that if Daniel Lambert had been a woman they would have been a matchless "pair." In Rodney-street have resided the families of the Tobins, Grants, and Heywoods. Many of the houses on the east side were erected by a company, the shareholders of which were in the building trade. They built houses also in Great George-street and St. Anne-street on the same plan. In the middle house of the row to the north of the Scotch Church, in 1837, Grace Avery, a cookmaid, was found brutally murdered by a man named Duffin. The case excited great interest at the time.

The Scotch Church was commenced in 1823. The learned Dr. David Thom was the first minister. He and Rear Admiral Murray laid the first stone on the 17th June. The Church is held, with the adjoining grave-yard, under the Corporation of Liverpool, for a lease of seventy-five years, renewable for ever on payment of a nominal fine. Disagreements having arisen between Dr. Thom and a portion of his congregation, in June, 1825, the reverend gentleman was brought to the bar of the Presbytery, in Glasgow, by thirty-five members of his congregation, on a charge of holding and propagating sentiments inconsistent with the Westminster Confession of Faith. Nine articles were specified. This commission sat three weeks in July. At a cost of a thousand pounds, at least, the enquiry was conducted; the report of it being adverse to Dr. Thom, he thereupon ceased to be minister of the Scots Kirk. Those of his congregation who held with him followed him to the Music Hall in Bold-street, until 2nd October, 1825, when his chapel in Bold-street, now the Queen's Hall, was opened, and where the great scholar ministered until a few years before his death, the property having been purchased for his benefit by a few of his much attached and devoted friends.

## EASTWARD.—CLARENCE STREET, RUSSELL STREET, AND SEYMOUR STREET.

THE line of thoroughfare from Rodney-street to St. Anne-street was cut between 1786 and 1790. A field belonging to Mr. Bromfield, in Mount Pleasant, was first broken up for the formation of Clarence-street, which was not named until 1809, when the Duke of Clarence visited the town, in company with the Prince of Wales.

Mount-pleasant was formerly called Martindale's-hill. At the suggestion of Mr. Roscoe the name was changed. In its young days it must have been a very pleasant suburb. On the site of Harford-street was a bowling-green, and a well-frequented tavern, near which was a windmill. On each side of the hill were pretty gardens belonging to the tradespeople, who went visiting them in the evenings, when in their summer-houses they entertained their friends. Mr. Roscoe's father kept a public-house, to which a bowling-green was attached, on the site nearly of the present Hope Hall. It stood at the corner of May-lane. Roscoe's career is so well known that it need not be detailed here. The following paragraph from the *Liverpool Mercury*, of October, 1816, will be read perhaps with some interest:—"Mr. Roscoe's sale.—Mr. Coke, of Holkham (afterwards by the way Earl of Leicester) was the purchaser at Mr Roscoe's sale of the fine portrait of Leo the Tenth, for 500 guineas. The library sold for £5,159, the prints for £1,880, and the drawings for £736, a circumstance highly flattering to the taste and discernment of their classic collector." Small comfort this compliment for the ruined poet. The writer of this book may mention one fact respecting Roscoe's popularity in Liverpool, that cannot but be considered curious, and carries out the notion of the prophet having little honour in his own country. When he (the writer) first came to Liverpool, all London was ringing with Roscoe's name, and he was there looked upon as an author of the highest rank. Many persons the writer first met in Liverpool were asked particulars about Roscoe as to where he was born?—where he lived?—where his bank was? It is a fact that the replies were for the most part unsatisfactory. One man only knew him as having been a "person who once had a bank that broke," and knew nothing of any books he had written; another had never heard of him; while a third actually described him as keeping a watchmaker's shop in Church-street! thus confounding "Roscoe" with "Roskell."

The houses that were erected on Mount-pleasant were commodious and handsome, especially towards the middle of the rise and the top. A celebrated Roman Catholic physician, Dr. M'Cartney, who had a large practice, resided in it. Dr. M'Cartney's house was afterwards occupied by Mr. James Dawson, who, on giving up practice, went to reside at Wray Castle, by Windermere Lake. Next to him dwelt Rector Renshaw. At the corner of Rodney-street dwelt Sir George Dunbar, at one time the leading colonial broker in Liverpool, and who had an immense business. In his office Messrs. Rutson and Ewart were brought up. On Sir George declining to take these gentlemen into partnership, they started on their own account, and, it is said, drew away nearly all their late employer's business. The firm of Ewart, Myers, & Co., sprang out of this firm, all the principals of which acquired large fortunes. Their offices occupied a large portion of Exchange-court, on the site of the Phœnix Fire Office. There would be between fifty and sixty clerks employed in their business.

Mr. Hunter, an eminent tobacco merchant, lived on Mount-pleasant, in the large house with the portico. He had large gardens at the back of it, extending to Maryland-street, which was his property, and so called by him in compliment to his trade. South Hunter-street, as distinguished from Hunter-street Byrom-street, was called after him. A large conventual establishment occupies his grounds. The ornamental pebble pavement laid down in front of his house was executed by a blind man, and was at one time exceedingly pretty and elegant, both in execution and design. In this part of Mount-pleasant in 1827 it was that the first application of Macadam's system of road-making was tried in Liverpool. A portion of Church-street was also "macadamised" at the same period. It will be noticed that many of the houses in Mount-pleasant have porches at the doors. There is one of very elegant design, near Rodney-street. In the house now occupied as the Eye and Ear Infirmary (originated by the late Mr. Hugh Neil, an eminent practitioner in this branch of medical science), dwelt Dr. Carson after his removal from Ranelagh-place. He had a board put up near his late residence intimating the alteration in his "whereabouts." Just at that time Dr. Carson was recommending the copious use of water to his dyspeptic patients at meal times, and was insisting upon it that it was "a perfect cure" for that dreadful complaint. One night the doctor's signboard was removed, and replaced on the following morning, with the addition to the address of —"Take notice, opposite the pump," referring to the pump in the street facing the doctor's house. The trick caused a good deal of joking at the time at the doctor's expense. Where the institution stands there was at one time a stile from which a footpath led to a foot-bridge that crossed the Moss-lakes brook. The path on the other side of the stream divided, one way going to Edge-hill (then called Cheetham's-hill), and the other to Smithdown-lane. There was a stone bridge also which connected Mr. Howard's fields to the southward of the foot-bridge. It was laid bare a few years ago, at the corner of Grove-street and Oxford-street, when the course of the brook was plainly to be made out.

The line of street from Rodney-street was next cut through the Powder-house Fields, adjoining the fields belonging to Mr. Gildart. The Powder-house stood exactly on the site of the opening of Russell-street, or rather a few yards from where is now the Brewery. It was a square brick building, having a court-yard round it, enclosed by a high wall, with large folding gates. Not much account of the Powder-house is obtainable, but it was erected previous to 1737, as we find, by a lease granted by the Corporation, dated 14th January in that year, by which it was let to Thomas Pearse, Samuel Underhill, and Robert Norman, for three lives and twenty-one years, at two shillings per annum. The owners of vessels complained much of the expense and risk of conveying gunpowder through the town and up so steep an aclivity as Brownlow-hill Lane, while the inhabitants entertained considerable apprehensions lest an explosion should take place at some time, and cause destruction in the town. They evidently considered the Powder-house as a very disagreeable neighbour. The removal of the powder magazines to Liscard, previous to 1768, was a great relief to the public mind. They were constructed on a piece of land called Warrington Close, which was purchased by the Corporation from a man named Richardson for thirty pounds. During the American Revolutionary War the Powder-house was used as a prison.

Brownlow-hill was formerly called "The Way to Wavertree." Where the Workhouse stands there was once an extensive quarry. The road ran through it. The largest and deepest portion was on the right hand side, and the smallest on the left, where now stands the Lunatic Asylum, erected in 1771.

Mr. Neild, the Philanthropist, in 1803, visited the Workhouse at Brownlow-hill. He says there were 700 persons in it. Although the female children were taught to read and write, the boys were neglected. There was a pin manufactory in the building, which provided employment for forty-two children. Mr. Neild complains that they were kept too many hours at work, the result of which was that they were suffering from sore eyes to a great extent.

The workhouse twenty-five years ago presented a different appearance to what it does at present. There was then a spacious lawn in front of it, on which was a small battery of guns, which was fired on great occasions. The house was four stories high, constructed of red brick ornamented with stone. It had projecting wings. Over the principal entrance was a pediment with a good clock. Above was an octagon tower or turret. This was surmounted by a cupola and vase.

Mr. Neild, in 1802, after visiting the House of Correction, which stood at the back of the Fever Hospital on Brownlow-hill, states that it was erected in 1776. He complains of the bad management throughout the building. He mentions the existence of a whipping-post in the yard, at which every week females were chastised. He describes also a ducking-stool. On Neild's second visit there had been some diminution in these two punishments, owing to the care of Mrs. Widdows, the matron, whose salary was only thirty-five pounds per annum. She had procured the abolition of the ducking-stool, and obtained some relaxation in the use of the whipping-post. The pump in the mens' yard was the place of punishment. Mr. Neild found in the House fifty-seven women and nineteen men, all of whom were without any religious or secular instruction. No chaplain attended the Gaol. The prisoners were allowed a twopenny loaf, two pounds of potatoes and salt, daily.

Russell-street was next cut through the fields of Mr. Parr and Mr. Hughes. The chapel in Russell-street has had many occupants of various denominations of Christians. It was erected in 1808 by the friends of a Mr. Ralph, who had been pastor in Bethesda Chapel, Hotham-street, which he had left under peculiar circumstances. It was first called Salem Chapel. It next became "St. Catherine's Church," a Mr. Pearson occupying its pulpit. He had been formerly an auctioneer. He held it from 1812 to 1817. The Rev. Thomas Stretton next took it on lease from the proprietors. He greatly improved it, erecting a vestry, and putting porticoes over the entrance-doors. He covered the seats and pews with cloth or baize, and had painted windows introduced. He also established a cathedral service, hiring twelve choristers, who were attired in surplices. In his progress on Sundays from the communion table to the pulpit the train of his robes was held up by two youths acting as pages. He and his lady cut a great dash in the town for some time, the one in full clerical costume, and the other in the most expensive silks and satins procurable, with jewellery corresponding. After a time Mr. Stretton's creditors began to be anxious to see a little of his money as well as his divinity. Although the church was always well filled by the attraction of the rev. gentleman's capital choir, and certainly clever reading and preaching, little profit seemed to have accrued therefrom. One day, as the pressure became great for a settlement of sundry "small accounts," Mr. Stretton was taking the air in Church-street, when, to his horror and consternation, he encountered a lady who was said to be his lawful "partner." A regular commotion took place near Basnett-street, the upshot of which was that the parson took to his heels, ran home, packed up bag and *baggage* to boot, leaving his congregation uncared for, and debts to the amount of £2,600 unpaid. A Mr. Crookenden next took Salem Chapel in 1818. A small body of Lady Huntingdon's connexion next became tenants. Some Independents followed. In 1829 a body of Baptists took the building. It was next "consecrated" by the American or pseudo American Bishop, named Montgomery West, who raised some theological dust in the town. He dedicated it to "St. Clements," and ordained several gentlemen as priests to officiate in the service. In 1832 Salem went into the hands of a body of Scotch Dissenters. In 1838 the Swedenborgians took possession of it, and called it the "New Jerusalem Church." After fourteen years' occupancy, a body of Warrenite Methodists became tenants. It is now a United Methodist Free Church.

In 1803, in expectation of the French invasion, Russell-street was fixed upon as the rendezvous for carts, horses, and vehicles, to carry movables into the country. However much we may now ridicule the fears of the people at that time, it was no joke to expect the landing of the invaders.

In 1807 Seymour-street was unbuilt upon. In the field skirted by London-road and Copperas-hill the Volunteers used to muster for drill and parade. On the 12th June, 1804, a serious fracas took place thereabout that led to the court-martial of Captain Carmichael, the adjutant of Colonel Earle's regiment of Fusileers. This gentleman had been formerly adjutant in Colonel Bolton's regiment. The unpleasantness arose in consequence of Carmichael gesticulating offensively, and making use of insulting language to his colonel, in the face of the whole regiment. The court-martial sat for five days, the result of which was, that Carmichael was found guilty, and sentenced to be reprimanded at the head of the regiment. This Captain Carmichael not long before had been "out," as it was then called, on the Bootle sands to fight a duel with the Major Brooks, who was killed by Colonel Bolton on the 20th December, 1805. In this duel Carmichael fired in the air, when Brooks called out, "Why don't you fire at me; we don't want child's play."

---

## ST. ANNE STREET.

In 1818 Norton-street had no houses built in it between Finch-street and Islington. It was projected about the commencement of this century, or at the close of the last. It was cut through Mrs. Gildart's field. At the corner of the London-road stood the once famous Blue Bell Inn. Parallel with Norton-street ran the brook, crossing Islington to supply a mill dam which stood at the corner of St. Anne-street, at the back of the present grocer's shop. This mill was burnt down, when a brewery was erected on its site. In Norton-street was Dr. Pulford's day academy and boarding-school. It was a celebrated establishment in its time, and to it most of the leading people of the day sent their sons to be educated. The schoolhouse may be remembered by many as standing in Frazer-street, the open space of ground visible in Norton-street being the playground, now occupied as slate works. Dr. Pulford resided in the house in Norton-street, at its southern corner.

At the west corner of St. Anne-street, where there is now a spirit vault, was at one time the mess-room of the officers of the regiments quartered in the town. It was kept by a Mr. and Mrs. Burgess. The officers then, as they always have done, played havoc amongst the ladies' hearts in Liverpool. One of them, a very young son of Mars, captivated a middle-aged lady, resident and having considerable property in St. Anne-street. This lady bestowed on the young gentleman her hand and fortune. He contrived in a short time to dissipate the latter, leaving the lady to wail her sad fate in connection with "one who loved and rode away."

St. Anne-street was projected previous to 1786. At the commencement of the present century it was the most distinguished thoroughfare in Liverpool, and was looked upon as a rival to Rodney-street. It so continued until 1835, when the tide of fashion began to sweep southward, and afterwards extend towards Aigburth. It then commenced declining, the mansions being cut up into smaller tenements, and subsequently shops making their appearance. The first house in it was that erected and occupied by Mr. Samuel Sandbach. After, this eminent merchant, who was mayor in 1831, went to reside at his mansion at Aigburth, the house was occupied by Mr. Thomas Colley Porter. He was a painter and plumber in a very extensive way of business, principally amongst the shipping. He it was who, in 1827, contested with Mr. Nicholas Robinson, an eminent corn merchant, the honour of the chief magistracy. The election lasted six days, and was carried on with intense energy and at an enormous cost, every exertion being made to obtain votes for love or money by both sides. The expenses were said to have amounted to over £10,000. Mr. Porter obtained 1,880 votes, Mr. Robinson 1,765. The contest was considered as a fair struggle for supremacy between the tradesmen and the mercantile body. It was asserted, at the time, that the principals in it would have willingly settled the matter between them at an early stage of the election, but for the interference and persistence of their supporters and friends. In consequence of their notorious culpability in receiving bribes, three freemen in 1828 were disfranchised. A service of plate value £650 was, in 1829, presented to Mr. T. C. Porter. Mr. Nicholas Robinson, his opponent, in 1828-9 succeeded Mr. Porter in the office of mayor. Mr. Porter, during his mayoralty, laid the first stone of the new Custom House, with great public exhilaration and ceremony, August 12, 1828. It would have been wiser, it was said, "to have mourned over the death of the old dock than rejoiced at the erection of its monument."

Until recently the mansion was occupied as the Judges' Lodgings. In it, July, 1846, the late Prince Consort resided, during his brief sojourn in the town, upon the occasion of the opening of the Albert Dock and the laying of the first stone of the Sailors' Home. Mr. Tinne, Mr. Sandbach's partner, resided in St. Anne-street, as did Dr. Traill, Mr. Sandbach's brother-in-law. His house was near or on the site of Mr. Fairhurst's establishment. Dr. Traill was an eminent physician and a ripe scholar. On leaving Liverpool he went to Edinburgh, where he became Professor of Medical Jurisprudence, and was the editor of the last edition of the *Encyclopœdia Britannica*. There is a fine portrait of this gentleman in the Royal Institution in Colquitt-street. There is also a bust of him extant. In St. Anne-street resided Dr. Rutter, a celebrated physician of his day. He was of the Society of Friends. He has been already mentioned as the founder of the Medical Institution and Library. The Rev. Dr. Vause, the incumbent of Christ Church, dwelt in this street. He was of a particularly irritable temper. Many droll stories are told of him in which he manifested it. On one occasion he was sent for in a hurry, just as he was sitting down to breakfast, to marry a couple. On arriving at the church he found the bride and bridegroom far advanced in years, whereupon, rating them soundly for disturbing him at his meal, he ordered his sexton to turn them out of the church, telling them to get married somewhere else as they had waited so long before entering wedded life, he thought they could wait a little longer without detriment. Dr. Vause published a book of excellent sermons, a copy of which may be seen in the Lyceum Library. Christ Church was erected in 1797 by Mr. John Houghton, who endeavoured to introduce a reform in the church service, which failed. In 1800 the church was consecrated by the then Bishop of the Diocese. Mr. Rutson lived in St. Anne-street; he, in conjunction with his partner, Mr. Ewart, paid into the subscription to support the

Government, in 1790, £250. Mr. Ackers, Mr. Overton, and other eminent merchants resided in St. Anne-street. Mr. Wright, who was mayor in 1816, dwelt in a house a few doors from Springfield, as did the Rev. Mr. Blundell, the incumbent of St. Anne's Church. A well-known schoolmaster of his day, the Rev. Mr. Prince, resided in St. Anne-street, as also did Parson Tetlow, Dr. Lewin, Mr. Gibbon, and Mr. Lassells the dancing-master, as famous for fly-fishing exploits, as for his skill in teaching the Terpsichorean art. In holiday time he generally went to fish in Norway.

In the middle house in Trinity-place, in 1808, resided Mr. Charles Angus, a surgeon, or, at least, one who was in some way connected with the medical profession. With him lived a Miss Burns, his sister-in-law, who acted as his housekeeper and governess to his children. Mr. Angus was a widower, and had been to sea. Miss Burns, in the month of March of the above year, was taken unwell, and it was suspected that she was *enciente*. On the 23rd March she remained in the breakfast-room all day, suffering from excessive thirst and vomiting. Mr. Angus sat up with Miss Burns the night of that day, watched over her the following day, and again tended her on the next night, allowing no one to share his task. On the 25th Miss Burns told the inmates of the house that she was much better, and expressed a wish to have some Madeira wine. A servant having been sent for some, on her return found Mr. Angus asleep in a chair, and Miss Burns dead in the corner of the room. Mr. Angus was taken into custody, charged with the murder of the young lady. He was tried for this alleged offence at Lancaster on the 2nd September, before Sir Allan Chambre. Sergeant Cockle, with Messrs. Holroyd, Raine, and Clark, were for the prosecution; Messrs. Topping, Scarlett (afterwards Lord Abinger), and Cross for the prisoner. The evidence was most conflicting, but there was evidently no case against Mr. Angus, for it was proved that during the whole period of Miss Burns's sickness the door of her chamber was open, anybody could have access to it, that no sounds of pain were heard, no cries of any description, no dead child was found on the premises, no signs of childbirth visible, and that Mr. Angus had never quitted the house for a minute while his sister-in-law was lying ill. It was conclusively proved that Miss Burns's death was attributable to internal disease, under which she had suddenly sunk. A verdict of "not guilty" was recorded. After the trial a hot controversy arose on the medical features of the case, in which the late Dr. Carson, whose name has occasionally been mentioned in this work, took a prominent part. His evidence at the trial completely upset the testimony of the adverse witnesses, especially that of his medical brethren. Dr. Carson wrote an admirable and masterly vindication of his own evidence, which had been attacked. He hit his opponents heavily. It was endeavoured to show that Miss Burns's death arose from an attempt to procure abortion. Mr. Angus frequently declared that he loved and respected Miss Burns too well to do her any harm. The case created immense excitement at the time, not only in Liverpool, but throughout the kingdom, especially amongst the medical profession.

Mr. Matthew Gregson, the most laborious of our local historians, author of "Gregson's Fragments," a work in constant use for reference, dwelt in St. Anne-street. In 1813 he was treasurer to the Blue-coat School. He presented in that year a handsome flag to the school, which is described as being "after the Roman custom." The "Blue Boys" on the occasion marched to Mr. Gregson's house, where, on presenting the colour to the head master, Mr. Gregson made a speech, advising the lads "to venerate the Church, be loyal to their King, and love their country, assuring them that they would never find a better land to live in." The boys then sung "God save the King," departing with three cheers. They then went to the Mayor's house, in Richmond-row, where they saluted his Worship (Mr. Nicholson) with three cheers. They then, as "a *treat*," were marched through the streets to witness the preparations that were making to illuminate the town, on the occasion of the success of the British forces over the French. They then proceeded to the Exchange, where the head monitor made a speech, exhorting the boys "to be faithful to their God, their country, and their

King." Three times three cheers were given by the boys, 130 in number, who were marched back to school to be regaled on plum-pudding. The merchants made a subscription on 'Change, which produced a shilling for each of the boys and a shilling for each of the girls at School.

Between Springfield and Queen Anne-street dwelt Mr. Huddleston, a gentleman whose heart and purse were ever open in a good cause. During his lifetime he was a constant contributor to the local charities.

On the 24th March, 1847, Mr. Huddlestone walked into the office of the Blue Coat School, wherein Mr. Forster the master was writing at his desk. He carried under his arm a parcel, which he placed before Mr. Forster, requesting him to peruse the contents, stating that they related to a donation he was desirous of bestowing to the School. Saying this, he went away. On opening the parcel, to Mr. Forster's amazement, he found a deed of gift to the School, of property in houses in School-lane, Manesty-lane, Peters'-lane, and Hanover-street, with a warehouse in College-lane. The value of these houses amounted to £10,000! The Trustees of the School, considering that a mere vote of thanks to Mr. Huddlestone, and a simple record of his bounty insufficient, intimated to him that a deputation from the Board of Trustees would wait on him, when convenient, to thank him. As a characteristic of the man who thus did "good by stealth, and blushed to find it fame," he declined the visit, stating that the vote of thanks passed by the Board was a quite sufficient acknowledgment for him.

At the corner of Richmond-row and St. Anne-street resided Mr. Joseph Hadwen, a Quaker. His garden extended in a southward direction up the street. He had a bank in Church-street, doing business with the tradesmen of the town, especially with the leather and hide dealers. His bank stood about the site of the shop of Messrs. Johnson, the chemists. It was approached by a flight of steps, being on the first floor. The Misses Hadwen, his sisters, kept a tea shop below. Mr. Hadwen, in consequence of some imprudent advances, was obliged to stop payment, bringing down with him some of his customers. His estate eventually paid twenty shillings in the pound. He had plenty of assets, and would not, it was said, have stopped but for undue pressure. He was much respected by all who knew him. Dr. Bainbridge, author of the well-known "Fly Fisher's Guide," lived in this street. Springfield and Queen Anne-street contained many very handsome and well-built residences, which were occupied by leading people in the town. The evidences of this being the case may still be seen by any one passing along these once fashionable streets. St. Anne's Church was erected in 1772. It will be perceived that it stands in the unusual position of north and south instead of east and west. At its first opening, and for some years afterwards, it was the most aristocratic church in the town. The pews at one time sold for sixty and seventy guineas each. When it was proposed to extend this line of streets to Kirkdale-road, now Scotland-road, it was desired to take down St. Anne's Church, but the idea was so decidedly opposed by the then Bishop of the Diocese that the plan was abandoned, although its merits were unquestionably great, as any one may perceive. It is from this cause that Great Homer-street was opened, being a continuation of Trinket-street, now Fox-street. Great Homer-street was originally a sandy lane. The removal of St. Anne's Church will open up a great improvement in this vicinity. At the house with a bow window at the corner of Richmond-row, now occupied as a funeral establishment, resided Mr. Dobb, who, in connection with some other gentlemen, erected Richmond Fair, or Linen Hall. This took place in 1787. This Linen Hall is constructed after the plan of the Cheese and Linen Halls in Chester. It retains much of its original appearance. The shops are now let as cottages, there being tenements on the basement, or ground floor, and rooms above approached by a gallery running round the interior. The entrances to this queer place are from Fox-street and Richmond-row, by passages. On its first being opened a large trade was done in it by the Lancashire, Yorkshire, and Irish dealers; but, in consequence of the interference of the authorities, stirred up by the linen and woollen drapers in the town, the use of the Linen Hall was discontinued.

Nearly opposite the entrance to the Fair in Richmond-row is a public-house called "The Loggerheads Revived." The original "Loggerheads" was a tavern of great note in its day. It had a nice garden attached to it, and was much frequented. The sign exhibited *two* stupid looking fellows with this inscription beneath: "We *three* Loggerheads be." The reader of the legend of course made up the third. The trade in it from some cause falling off, it became a private house, and was occupied by Mr. Nicholson, who was Mayor in 1813. In this house resided constantly, with Mr. Nicholson's familv, Felicia Browne, afterwards Mrs. Hemans. Under this roof many of her early poems were written. After Mr. Nicholson left the house it became again a tavern under the present title. This fact was once mentioned to a person who was "fond of his beer." He afterwards told the writer that he never passed the "Loggerheads Revived" without going in to drink "a glass of bitter to the blessed memory of the gifted poetess."

Everton-crescent was for many years, and is still so called by some very old people, "Loggerhead-lane." At one time it was known as Causey-lane. It was originally a steep sandy road, having ditches and hawthorn hedges on each side. The fields adjacent were called "Richmond Meadows." When the Crescent was erected, in 1807, by Messrs. Highfield, Bibby, and Webster, it was proposed to run up a corresponding set of mansions opposite to it. Where Soho-street now commences there used to be at one time a dyer's yard and pond, surrounded by willow trees.

Richmond-row was called after an old Liverpool family, of considerable eminence in the last century.

The Adelphi Theatre, in Christian-street, has seen many mutations. It was originally erected by "Old Astley," in 1795, and was called by him "the Circus, whence Circus-street. It was entirely re-built in 1825, in consequence of the foundation proving insecure, when it was called the "Queen's Theatre." It was next entitled the "Adelphi." When first erected there were very few houses about, and some of the adjacent streets were only then projected. It has been also called the "Victoria." At one time Mr. Banks, one of the lessees of the Theatre Royal, had possession of it, and opened it when that theatre was closed. When the late W. J. Hammond was lessee, in 1843, he endeavoured to raise the standard of the performances, by engaging Miss Cushman and other leading performers. On the occasion of Prince Albert's visit to Liverpool, a very funny farce was got up, specially for the occasion, in which Hammond, Browne, and other local favourites had capital parts. Two mornings previous to the evening when the performance was to take place, and while a dress rehearsal was convulsing the few persons present with laughter at the drollery of the dialogue, the absurdity of the "situations," and the admirable get-up of two of the leading performers, Mr. Hammond received from the Lord Chamberlain a prohibition to produce the farce, in consequence of some allusions in the plot to Royalty. In this predicament, although appropriate local scenes had been painted, there was nothing to be done but submit. However, as the expense of the getting-up of the farce should not be quite thrown away, the baffled manager and unlucky author put their rueful heads together, and after rumaging the stage library over, fell in with the old farce of "John-street Adelphi," which the pair cut and contrived so as to localize it, and introduce the new scenery, songs, and choruses with the closing exhibition of the "Seamen's Home" in all its glory. This notable interdicted work was entitled "H.R.H.P.A., or the Royal Guest."

## SOUTHWARD.—THE PARK.

Toxteth Park, until the last seventy or eighty years, was entirely arable and pasture land. In 1775, and towards the close of the last century, there were very few houses in it, and these were not congregated together or in clusters, but were lonely farm dwellings, or cottages occupied by labourers and small gardeners, who raised produce for the Liverpool market. Toxteth Park at that time belonged wholly to the Earl of Sefton, The main road to Aigburth and Garston ran through it, from which access was obtained to the villages that at length sprang up.

The "Pine Apple Tavern," formerly called the "Park Coffee House," which stood at the west side of the road, is about the oldest place of public entertainment in the district, if we except the old "Peacock." The chapel near the Dingle is a venerable structure. It is said to have been at one time used by a Church of England congregation, and also by Dissenters in the time of Cromwell. Thomas Crompton, the celebrated Nonconformist minister, officiated in it, and it was not affected by the Act of Uniformity. From that period it has been occupied by the Protestant Nonconformists, and in its grave-yard many Liverpool worthies are interred, Horrox, the mathematician and astronomer, resided in the Park. His house occupied the site of the Otterspool Railway Station. It was called the Lower Lodge, and was at one time one of the park-keepers residences connected with Toxteth Park. Horrox's celebrated calculation of the transit of Venus has rendered his name renowned in the scientific world. He was born 1610, died 1640.

Without dipping deeply into antiquity, a few words about Toxteth Park may not be altogether uninteresting to the readers of "THE STREETS." It appears that the area of which it consisted was formed by King John, who then enclosed by wooden railings the trees that grew there in great luxuriance and abundance. He afterwards erected round it a stone wall, part of which stood of late years in Parliament-street, as already mentioned. King John enclosed within this wall the manors of Toxtathe (mentioned in "Domesday Book,") with a large portion of the Manor of Esmedune, or Smithum (whence Smithdown-lane), which latter he obtained from John de Smithum. This manor is also recorded in the "Domesday Book." The Toxtathe property the King bought of the Mullineux family. The park consisted altogether of 2,000 acres, being about five miles in circuit. The present

Parliament-street was the northern limit of the park. The river skirted it on the western side, while Otterspool was its southern border.

In the time of Mary, 1588, "the maister of Simmons Wood and keeper of Toxteth Park" received two pounds per annum as his fee, and the park was then abundantly stocked with deer. In 1596, temp Elizabeth, the park was disforrested, and sold to Edmund Smolt and William Aspinall, by the Earl of Derby, who then held it. These persons not being able to complete their purchase, the Earl re-sold it to Sir Richard Mullineux in the reign of James I. From that time the park was put under cultivation. Thus the ancient house of Mullineux became again possessed of the lands that their ancestors formerly held, after an interval of four hundred years. In 1604 no vestige of the forest remained, for the deer were then reported to be all destroyed, the park being cut up into farms and small allotments.

In the last century, Charles William, the first Lord Sefton, endeavoured to improve his property by commencing a new town on his estate, which he called "Harrington," in compliment to his wife, the Lady Isabella, daughter of the second Earl of Harrington. It was one of these Earls of Harrington, who, about 1825, married the celebrated actress Maria Foote, whose charms and histrionic powers were celebrated by painters and song writers. Theodore Hook wrote—

If all the world I were to lose,
  I'd heed it not a farden,
If only there was left to me
  One *Foote* of Covent Garden.

Many of us can remember the aspect of the "South Shore" before the dock walls were carried out to stand the assault of the tidal waves; and many of us have strolled along the sands to the Dingle, rambled over the pleasant meadows that sloped down to the river, or sat at sundown to watch the magnificent setting of the great luminary over the Wirral peninsular.

The Copper Works, which preceded the Herculanæum Pottery, may be said to have been the first properties that trenched upon the picturesque in this vicinity. The latter undertaking was started in 1794 by a potter named Abbey. After working it for some time he sold it in 1796 to a company of proprietors, by which sale he was enabled to retire to Aintree, his native place, where he died in 1801, aged eighty-one years. His death was caused by the rupturing of a blood vessel while singing in the choir of Melling Church, of which he was the leader, being a man of considerable musical abilities. Mr. Abbey was buried in Walton Church-yard.

The new company, which consisted of a number of leading gentlemen of Liverpool and elsewhere, engaged as their foreman and manager a Mr. Mansfield, a thrower from Staffordshire, who engaged a large party of operatives highly skilled in the Ceramic art to come to Liverpool, bringing with them their wives and children. On the 10th December, 1796, having made their way from Burslem by the canal to Runcorn, these operatives, about fifty in number, embarked on board a flat and were brought down to the Herculanæum Pottery, where they were met by a band of music and flags, while a number of persons interested in the undertaking escorted the immigrants through the town and to the Pottery, where they immediately commenced operations. The Herculanæum earthenware was notable at first for a greenish tinge, caused by the minute particles of copper with which the air was impregnated. In 1806 an enlargement of the Pottery was carried out, and additional capital raised. The works were continued until 1833, when the company was dissolved, and the Herculanæum was sold to Mr. Ambrose Lace for £25,000. The show rooms of the Herculanæum Pottery were in a large house nearly at the bottom of Duke-street, which was afterwards converted into a barrack. It is now a warehouse.

The Herculaneum Dock was projected about 1841. It was near the Herculaneum Dock that the amiable young minister, Thomas Spencer, whose tomb in Newington Chapel-yard must be familiar to all who pass along Renshaw-street, was drowned on the 5th August, 1811.

At the close of the last century, and well into the present, the inhabitants of Toxteth Park and other outskirts of Liverpool, were constantly suffering from night robberies. Indeed to such an extent did this occur, that at one time it was proposed to form what we at the present day would term "a Mutual Protection Society" for the purpose of patrolling the district. One proposition was to cause alarm bells to be erected on the roofs of the houses in the Park, so that a signal could be made when assistance was required.

At the south end of the Brunswick Dock, near the shore, as late as 1835, stood a singular erection, known as the "Tall House." This strange, ghostly-looking building was exceedingly high, and narrow in proportion to its height. It was of four stories, and had a sloping roof, It was erected in 1776, by an architect well-known in Liverpool at the time, named Cuthbert Bisbrown. He built it under the sanction of the Earl of Sefton, for the purpose of converting it into a ferry-house. It was then proposed to establish a ferry between that point of the Lancashire shore and Cheshire. It was said, but with what truth cannot now be very well ascertained, that the peculiar shape of the house arose from the intention to set up in it suitable machines for working an endless chain, which was to be stretched over to Rock Ferry, for the purpose of dragging the boats or barges to and fro, containing cattle, vehicles, or passengers, that, it was thought, would extensively make use of the undertaking. But the ferry signally failed, as seems to have done every other attempt to communicate with Cheshire from the south end of the town. The "Tall House" was afterwards applied to a variety of purposes; amongst others, it was opened as a ladies' school.

In 1785 there were no houses in Blundell-street; Norfolk-street terminated at Simpson-street, whence to the shore were fields belonging to Mr. Jackson and Mr. Bolden. At the bottom of Stanhope-street and Norfolk-street there were in 1802, a mill and dam, no house being near; there also was a mill and pond fed by the same stream, known as Mather's dam, which is supposed to have been in use as far back as the time of Sir Edward Moore.

In the middle of the last century the river front was all open shore with large timber and shipbuilding yards, from which, from 1789 to 1792, some of the finest frigates in the navy were launched. A long list of vessels of war could be exhibited which for the most part highly redounded to the credit of the Liverpool shipbuilders, not only for beauty of design, but for strength, speed, and durability. Crosbie-street was called after Mr. Crosbie, who was Bailiff in 1748. He was present at the laying of the foundation of the first stone of the Exchange, and Mayor in 1754, when it was opened, on which occasion he gave a grand ball and supper. Sparling-street was named after Mr. Sparling, who was High Sheriff of Lancashire, in 1785, and Mayor of Liverpool in 1790. He it was that purchased the St. Domingo estate at Everton. At the west end of Tabley-street there were then only a few houses. What is now Wapping was the shore until the King's and Queen's Docks were constructed. The Duke of Bridgewater's Dock, in 1783, was the southernmost dock. The Salthouse Dock was constructed, by provisions of Act of Parliament, in 1734. It was so called on account of its proximity to the salt works in Mersey-street and Hurst-street. There is a curious incident connected with this vicinity, giving the realization of ship launching under difficulty. Previous to the construction of the Southern dock there was a ship being built in a yard, the site of which is now occupied by Ansdell-street or thereabouts. The vessel was so far advanced when the dock commenced that the owners determined to finish her, and get her into the water "somehow," When the water was let into the "South Dock," as the Salthouse Dock was first called, the ship was ready for launching, therefore ways were laid down to the quay over the road-way, and she was started to enter the dock in a way not usual to ships generally. The ways, however, broke between the yard and the water, and the ship stuck fast. However, by immense exertions, on the following day she was again put into motion, and was successfully launched, amid the cheers of crowds of spectators who had assembled to witness the novel sight.

Amongst the ship-building yards of note on the Estuary Bank was Baker and Dawson's. The latter, was, before he joined Baker, the commander of his partner's, and afterwards father-in-law's privateer, the Mentor, twenty-eight guns. In October, 1778, this vessel captured the Carnatic, French East Indiaman. The sale of which realized upwards of £135,000. There was a box of diamonds found on board after the prize entered the Mersey that produced, on being sold, a large sum. Baker was Mayor in 1795, and died during his year of office. Baker and Dawson bought the Mossley Hill estate, and erected thereon the mansion which in joke was called by the wags "Carnatic Hall."

Baker and Dawson in 1778 bought of the Corporation the Manor of Garston. In January, 1791, these gentlemen conveyed their undivided moities to Mrs. Elizabeth Kent, widow of Mr. Kent, of Duke-street.

## STREETS SOUTHWARD.

"The Road to the Park" was the old designation of Park-lane. It was originally a mere horse road that led to Toxteth Park, access being obtained to it by foot passengers, at first across the Ferry at the bottom of Water-lane, or Liverpool-lane, now South Castle-street, and afterwards by the Weir, which was erected to keep up the waters of the Pool river, by the sluices of which, the little haven was kept free from mud. The horseman went across the bridge by Lord-street, and made his way to the Park by winding along the banks of the stream until he entered Park-lane by some near cut that then perhaps existed. That there was a haven here at one time is established by the fact that in 1561, as we are told, a terrific storm damaged it to such an extent as to call forth the energies of the town's people, who, at a public meeting, agreed to repair it at their own cost, by each street sending house by house one labourer daily to work at the repairs. Thus on Mondays the houses in Water-street would send their men, Castle-street theirs on Tuesdays, Dale-street theirs on Wednesdays, and so on till the week was completed. Little positively is known about the first creeping out of the town southwards, but, at the latter end of the seventeenth century, after the country had become settled down into peace and quietness, dwellings then began to appear in that direction.

The construction and opening of the "Old Dock," or "Custom-house Dock," by authority of the Government of 1709, gave a start to the erection of buildings suitable to the wants of the shipping trade, and those employed in it. Just previous to the construction of the Dock, which was quite a new thing in England, and, indeed, was the first water enclosure in this country, there was a scheme afloat to lay out houses upon a settled plan on the site of Park-lane, and thereabouts, which was to have been called the "New Town." The pool was to have been narrowed, and over it a bridge thrown, about opposite to Mersey-street, as a mode of communication; but the dock scheme knocked this plan on the head. The Old Dock was wider at the west end than the east. The former was ninety-five yards in breadth, and the latter eighty yards, the length being 195 yards. Opposite the eastern end the Custom House was erected, being a red brick building, which many of us well remember. It was built by Mr. Sylvester Moorcroft. Previous to its erection great complaints were made of the inefficiency of the customs department, and the inconvenience arising from the absence of a commodious and proper place for public business. There was considerable opposition to the construction of the Old Dock exhibited by the London cheese traders, who did not like to pay dock dues for their vessels loading at Ince and Frodsham, as they did not want to use a dock at Liverpool. This opposition was completely over-ridden by public opinion, which appreciated at once the great utility of an expanse of water enclosure as a harbour for shelter in a river so exposed and dangerous to shipping as the Mersey. The filling up of the Old Dock has been greatly regretted as a want of foresight in the anthorities who consented to it. The Dock Trustees, however, with Mr. Jesse Hartley as their adviser, in conjunction with the Corporation, agreed that the Dock should be filled up. It was first proposed that a market should be erected on the site of it (to supersede that in Cleveland-square) besides the Government offices, which were to be centralised—the Custom House being then in one place, the Post Office in another, and the Excise Office in a third. The market scheme was abandoned, although in the Act of George III. it is mentioned as projected. Through the intervention of Mr. Huskisson, the terms upon which the Government offices were to be built were that the Corporation should provide the site, valued at £90,000; that the Corporation should erect the building; that at the expiration of twenty years it should be ceded to Government upon payment of £150,000, to be paid by annual instalments of £95,000 each. The first stone of the Custom House was laid by Mr. T. Colley Porter, the Mayor, at the north-east corner, 12th August, 1828. The incidental expenses for the ceremony were—Preparations, £5 14s. 0d.; Silver trowel, £4 18s. 0d.; Plate for foundation-stone, £6 6s. 0d. The act empowering the filling up of the Old Dock was obtained in 1811 (51 George III). It is surprising that some spirited townsman did not manfully expose such an obnoxious scheme. The Dock was constructed on the very site which nature seemed to suggest as the most fitting for a dock. It may not occur in our day, or in that of our children, but at some time that great ungainly, ugly, building —the Liverpool Custom House—will be removed, and a dock constructed on its site, which, for utility and convenience, will be preferred to all others as a receptacle for shipping.

In excavating the foundations for the Custom-house and the buildings in Canning-place, numerous remains of a long-past period were discovered in the *debris* of trees, boughs, acorns, hazle-nuts, and stag horns. Mr. Foster's drainage scheme was not out when it was proposed to fill up the Old Dock, which received the contents of nearly all the town sewers, and it was said that in hot weather the effluvium that arose from it with a south-westerly wind blowing, pervaded the whole town. This is one of the reasons ascribed for the willingness of the inhabitants to have the Old Dock filled up.

As building southward progressed, the Clevelands, an influential family in Liverpool, whose benevolence has been proved by numerous benefactions and bequests to its charities, laid out Price-street and Cleveland-square, which was originally called "Price's-square or "New-square." On the 14th March, 1760, Captain Tarleton's Independent Company of Volunteers were reviewed in Cleveland-square, by the Earl of Scarboro'. There were also present companies commanded by Colonel Spencer and Captain Ingram. Colonel Spencer's company was clothed in blue, lappelled and faced with buff. Captain Ingram's had scarlet coats and breeches, lappelled and faced with green, green waistcoats, gold-laced hats, and cue wigs. Captain Tarleton's in blue, with gold-vellum button-holes. Captain Thomas Johnson's Troop of Artillery wore the uniform of the navy, blue and buff with gold-laced hats.

The Prices were the Lords of the Manor of Birkenhead, and were connected with the Clevelands. When the square was first built it consisted of mansions and handsome houses, the style of which may still in some instances be traced. It was planted on each side with trees, and there was an obelisk in its centre. It would be commenced probably about 1735. The merchants and *elite* of Liverpool society resided in these houses, in one of which, in 1775, dwelt Mr. Yates, an African merchant. This gentleman's house was attacked and nearly demolished by the sailors, who were in that year creating frightful disorders in the town on the question of wages, in dispute with their employers. In Pitt-street the Methodist Chapel, in 1756, was on the verge of the town, all beyond being fields. In this building, which was superseded by the present commodious chapel, Wesley, in 1758, preached. He had two services daily for a week, one of which commenced at six o'clock in the morning for the convenience of the working classes, who thronged to hear his charming ministrations. In or about 1831, James Montgomery, the Sheffield poet, author of "The World Before the Flood," addressed a large audience in this chapel on the occasion of a missionary meeting, delighting all by the elegance of his language and the grace of his elocution.

St. Thomas's Church was erected, in 1750. Park-lane was then a narrow little street, the last house in it being at the corner of Greetham-street. The land on which the church stands was given by Mr. Okell, a wealthy gentleman, whose large estate eventually went into the hands of a field labourer, who actually received the announcement of his accession to great wealth spade in hand! Mr. Okell, it was said, when the church-yard was required, charged over three times the value for it. The spire of St. Thomas's Church was originally 216 feet high. It was of very elegant proportions. In York-street at one time was the Pinfold. In Greetham-street was the public "Dye-house Well." The water was in use within the last few years in the yard of a public-house, and may be still.

Lydia Ann-street was so named after the wife of Mr Perry, an eminent man in his day, who was the originator of Fawcett and Preston's Iron foundry. Mrs. Perry, was a Miss Lydia Ann Delacroix. Pothouse-lane (nearly at the bottom of Duke-street), was so called from the Drinkwater potteries carried on there. Mr. James Drinkwater, who was Mayor in 1810, married Miss Leece, the daughter of Mr. Leece, an eminent merehant residing in Water-street, after whom Leece-street takes its name. In the riots of 1775 a party of sailors proceeded to Mr. Leece's residence clamouring for money. Miss Leece, although with only two female servants in the house, went to the door, opened it widely, and asked the leader of the gang in a determined way what he wanted knocking thereat as he did? The man, completely taken aback by the spirited demeanour of the young lady, in very respectful terms solicited, instead of demanded, money, which on being given he drew off his men, making Miss Leece a low bow and a scrape in true sailor fashion. Few houses of the African Merchants so escaped that day.

Duke-street was called formerly "The way to the Quarry," It was then merely a country road, very much cut up by the carts which conveyed the stone down to the town for the construction of the docks and public buildings. In 1785 there were no houses in it on the west side from Kent-street to Great George-street. All the land which these streets skirted on the south-east, and St. James's-street on the west, was the property of Mrs. Hardman, Mrs. Coore, and Mrs. Roughsedge. Colquit-street was the original name of Berry-street. The present Colquit-street was laid out at a much later date. In the large house now occupied by the Royal Institution resided Mr. Parr, who built it for himself. This property was disposed of by Tontine. Mr. Parr, used to boast that he had the handsomest house, wife, and horse in Liverpool. Along the east side of Duke-street, commencing opposite York-street (formerly called George-street), was the "Ladies' Walk," consisting of four rows of trees with walks between. Behind the "Walk" was a ropery. Westward, a fine view of the distant river was obtained with the fields intervening.

When the "Ladies' Walk" was cut up it was converted into a brick field. The clay was said to be the best of any in or out of Liverpool for the purpose of brick-making. Parr-street, called after Mr. Parr, occupies the site of it. In one of the houses in Duke-street, above Slater-street, resided, in 1812, Bellingham, who shot Mr. Spencer Percival in the lobby of the House of Commons. He was a sort of agent or general merchant in Liverpool. He committed the assassination on the 11th May. He was tried, convicted, and sentenced on the 15th, and executed on the 18th of that month. His wife was a dress-maker, and carried on business in Duke-street. She was much commiserated by the ladies of Liverpool, who extensively patronised her after Bellingham's death. Felicia Browne, afterwards Mrs. Hemans, one of the sweetest and tenderest of English Poetesses, was born, in 1793, in a house a little below Colquitt-street. In one of the houses having steps up to the entrance, opposite Cornwallis-street, lodged John Howard, the Philanthrophist, during his stay in Liverpool, and while his work on prisons was passing through the Warrington press. He used to ride on horseback to Warrington to correct his proofs. The Rev. Gilbert Wakefield lodged at the bottom of Duke-street while he officiated as curate at St. Paul's Church.

Kent-street was so called after Mr. Kent, whose large mansion and grounds occupied one side of the street. Mr.

Kent was an extensive shipowner. He built the Kent East-Indiaman, then the largest vessel that had been constructed in the north-west of England. She was 1,000 tons. The ship William was built for him in Sutton's Yard for the Greenland trade. This vessel became the Mariners' Church. Miss Elizabeth Kent married Lord Henry Murray, brother to the Duke of Athol.

At one time or another some of the leading Liverpool merchants have dwelt in Duke-street. Mr. Sparling resided in it, Mr. Watt, Mr. Moses Benson, Mr. Gildart (mayor in 1750), Mr. Gildart, the younger (who was mayor in 1786), Mr. Bolden, Mr. Naylor, Mr. Birch (afterwards Sir Joseph Birch), Mr. Layland (who was mayor in 1798, 1814, and 1820), Colonel Bolton, Mr. James Aspinall, and others.

Great George-street was not built upon until after 1803, and the west side at that time had no houses on it. Great George-square and the streets intersecting it were laid out in 1802, but there were then no houses erected on or about it. The statue of George III., in the London-road, was intended to have been set up in the garden in the centre, as related in the account of London-road.

Great George-street Chapel, or Dr. Raffles' Chapel, as it is generally designated, was destroyed by fire on 19th February, 1840.

In 1802, Washington-street, Alfred-street, and Nile-street were projected, but no houses were then erected thereon. In Rathbone-street (called after the Rathbone family), were some extensive stone quarries. St. James's Market was held in 1823 in front of the present market, the site of which was then a field. Opposite St. James's Church the Cattle Market at one time was held in a farm-yard. Near it stood one of the Lodges of Toxteth Park. It had a court-yard in front, in the centre of which was an old tree, and on this being taken up the roots were found to have spread themselves out horizontally in the most extraordinary way, having encountered the rock beneath, which prevented their downward growth.

Parliament-street ran up as far as the quarry; above St. James's Church was the Spring Garden, a place of Public resort as a tea garden. In Parliament-street at one time stood the ancient boundary wall of Toxteth Park. Previous to its being taken down there were about 100 yards of it remaining. It was supposed to have been erected in the days of King John. At the corners of the quarry were windmills. The great quarry is now St. James's Cemetery, opened in 1829. The stone for the erection of nearly all the public works have been taken from it. It was of great extent and depth. Dr. Houlston, a physican of some note in his day, discovered a ferruginous spring of water in the quarry, which he dignified by the title of the "Liverpool Spa." The spring now flowing in the cemetery is not that about which Dr. Houlston wrote, although it has the same properties, tending to the cure of rheumatic complaints. St. James's Mount was constructed in 1767, during the severe winter of that year and 1768. The then Mayor, Mr. Thomas Johnson, taking pity on the poor out of work, set gangs of people to form this artificial hill. It was originally called "Mount Zion." On it was erected a public-house. A Welsh minister wrote some lines on this subject, to the following effect:—

"The mayor and council in a dreaming fit,
To slight the scripture and to show their wit,
The name of Zion, sacred seat of Heaven,
To this unhallowed common walk have given.
Here on their mount—behold the shrine!
They've dedicated to the God of Wine,
And to excite our admiration more—
See "Bottled Beer" recorded on the door."

It is said that the once well-frequented rookery in this garden was originated by a gentleman who seeing two magpies pairing and building their nest in one of the trees, procured some rook's eggs, which the magpies hatched, and from which sprung a numerous colony.

On the summit of the Mount the first photographic establishment in Liverpool was started. The process of taking likenesses was after the Daguerre mode. A Mr. Spencer was the projector and operator. Sometimes the likenesses were good, but at other times failures. There is a good story told illustrative of a failure. A gentleman whose face being familiar to many in this town, was solicited by the proprietor of the studio to have his visage taken as a "specimen," accordingly he repaired to the mount, and, after waiting for a considerable time for his turn, he was invited into the room, and took a seat for "his counterfeit resemblance" to be obtained. When it was finished it was put into a case and given him to take away to show his friends, previous to its being publicly exhibited. Having been detained so long, he did not wait to examine his portrait, leaving the investigation of it till he had arrived at home. However, his curiosity on reaching Berry-street got the better of him. When he opened the case, he was as much horror-struck at the likeness as was the lion spoken of by Rabelais, on meeting the old woman in the wood. Just at the moment of glancing at his *portrait charmant* an old *quid nunc* friend came up and asked "the news." "The news!" replied the Daguerrotype victim, "Here's a likeness of the man who murdered his wife last Monday." "Bless my life!" exclaimed the *quid nunc,* putting his "glass eyes" on nose and examining the portrait, "Well, if this *is* like him, I should say he is capable of perpetrating any crime that it is possible to commit.

---

## WESTWARD.

As late as 1786 the Liverpool Salt Works stood on the very margin of the river. The approach to them was from Mersey-street, the south end of which terminated in the Salt-house yard. They stood on the south side of a little haven or bay, which was called "the Strand," into which the vessels ran to load with salt, or discharge their cargoes of rock salt, from Northwich and the salt districts, or the coals that were used in the manufacture of the refined salt. The vessels lay high and dry at half tide and ebb, and were liable to damage in stormy weather. The salt works originally stood in quite an isolated situation, there being, when first started in the middle of the seventeenth century, no houses near them. Gradually, Hurst-street, Campbell-street, and Salthouse-lane, clustered round them, and their approach by Mersey-lane became built upon and inhabited. The Liverpool salt was always esteemed for its fineness, purity, brilliance, and absence of colour. It was manufactured from rock salt and river water, in the proportion of fifteen tons of the former to forty-five tons of the latter, to produce thirteen tons of fine salt for the table.

Salt is frequently mentioned in the Bible. It is first introduced to notice in the fate of Lot's wife. In Leviticus ii., v. 13, it is a special command that it shall be used with meat-offerings, "and every oblation of thy meat-offering shalt thou season with salt." "With all thine offerings, thou shalt offer salt." The Greeks used it in their religious ceremonies. Horace frequently mentions it, as well as Virgil, Juvenal, Persius, and other great writers of antiquity. The Romans found the Britons manufacturing salt by pouring the brine on ignited faggots, collecting the salt after the aqueous parts had evaporated. The Roman mode of making salt in pans has never been improved upon, although many attempts, attended with almost constant failures, have been made to produce a greater weight of salt with a smaller weight of coal. The average size of a salt pan is forty feet long, twenty-four feet wide, and about fifteen inches deep. A salt work of average size produces about 250 tons of salt per week. Bay salt is made by slow evaporation at a temperature of 110 degrees. Common or rough salt is formed at a temperature of 175 degrees, and stoved or fine table salt at 220 degrees. The crystals, which are all cubes, from the largest grain to the minutest atom, form at the top of the brine and sink to the bottom of the pans by their own gravity. The Greeks, Jews, and Romans of old appear at all times to have taxed salt, as a source of revenue to the state, as have also modern nations. In Doomsday Book we find that a large sum was obtained by this impost. In the 5th and 6th William and Mary a duty was laid on salt for a term of years; but in the 9th and 10th

William III. it was made perpetual. In the 3rd George II. the duty was taken off; but in December, 1739, Sir Robert Walpole proposed to levy a duty on salt for the king's use, from the 25th of March, for one year. From 1746 to 1806 the duty on salt in England was 12s. per bushel, and in the latter year it was raised to 15s. per bushel. In 1801 Mr. Vansittart devoted great attention to the duty on salt, with a view to its reduction. In 1816 a strong attempt was made to get the tax taken off. In this town the agitation and excitement on the subject were very great, but it was not until 1825 that the tax was swept away. The delight of the nation was intense at the abrogation of the salt duty; and the writer can recollect how much lightened domestic care was when a cessation of continuous caution, "not to be wasteful of the salt," took place. Salt was then worth 18s. per bushel. It is doubtless to the high value of salt that superstitions have been engendered, such as it is said to be "unlucky to spill it," as of course it would be when it was sold at so high a price. The duty on salt, high as it was, hardly repaid its collection, from the constant supervision and watchfulness it required, while its existence opened the door—and pretty widely too—to all sorts of trickery, roguery, and demoralisation in attempting to evade it. When the duty was laid on salt the manufacturers were few in number, from the large capital required to carry on the works and advance the duty. These few manufacturers had the trade therefore in their own hands, and they could regulate not only the supply according to the demand, but also the price. Of late years so little profits have been obtained from salt making in the salt districts, from the numbers of salt-houses at work, that the only profit derivable has been from the carrying of it, and coals in the flats plying on the Weaver River. There are strange stories extant of boats clustering round the salt flats, in the duty time, when they arrived in the open estuary. These boats took away a few tons of salt, to be replaced by the river water. This salt, thus surreptitiously obtained, was landed on the Lancashire or Cheshire coasts, where it was readily sold to customers at a comparatively cheap rate. Immense quantities of salt were then smuggled, and there is no doubt that large fortunes were made while the duty was upon it. The object of shipping the river water was to make weight. Every flat load, previous to leaving the works, was carefully weighed, and the contents registered. On the arrival of the flats in Liverpool, if the weight was deficient the duty had to be paid on the deficiency, and if the weight was over the duty had to be paid upon the surplus. This often happened when the weather was damp, or the flat had made a longer trip than usual, from a storm or rough weather. The salt was then made as dry as possible, and was tightly packed in the flat to exclude moisture as much as possible. There are a few old flatmen still living who could tell an amusing tale or two of the tricks they played with their cargoes either with or without their owners' consent. The opening of the salt trade led to the use of salt in various manufactures and ways, that had been unthought of from its prohibitory price. In India, from the year 1835 to 1845, the salt tax yielded upwards of a million of money annually. In 1868, the quantity of salt shipped from Liverpool amounted to 648,531 tons, which, with the quantity shipped from Runcorn, made a grand total of 820,868 tons against 671,134 tons in 1867. The Liverpool Salt Works were discontinued in 1793, the proprietor, Mr. Blackburne, obtaining an Act of Parliament to remove them to Garston Creek (GEORGE III., CAP. 33). The cause of this removal was the complaints made by the increasing inhabitants of the neighbourhood, of the constant clouds of steam that arose from the pans, and of the dense smoke from the furnaces, which created an intolerable nuisance. When the sailors were attacking the houses of the African Merchants in 1775, a cannon was obtained from the old dock by a party of the rioters. One of these fellows took a horse out of Mr. Blackburne's stable at the Salt Works, and attempted to harness it to a truck on which the cannon had been placed. The leader of the gang, in stooping down to fasten a rope to the truck, offered so fair a mark for a bite, that the horse, evidently having notions of law and order, availed himself of the opportunity of making his mark upon Jack's beam end, which sent hin off roaring, leaving the gun in the possession of the saline Bucephalus. When the Salt Works were given up, Orford-street (called after Orford Hall, near Warrington, the seat of John Blackburne Esq)., was run through them; and in this street the presence of salt was constantly detected. In one of the warehouses erected in it, upon the least change of weather a dampness was perceptible on the walls; the yard of these premises also gave out indications of the presence of salt in surface incrustations, and a well therein was so strongly impregnated with salt as to be utterly useless. The site of the Salt Works was sold at the "Star and Garter," Paradise-street, on the 8th of May, 1798.

The Garston Works within the last two or three years have been sold to the London & North-Western Railway Company, and the whole of the plant has been disposed of, and cleared away to make room for a dock which the railway company propose constructing. On the removal of one of the storing houses, a curious discovery was made of thousands of tons of "Rock Dross" beneath it, which was at first supposed to be merely the rock of the district. It had been there for many years unknown to the present generation, the storing house having been built upon it. This dross was the residuum from the rock salt which had been melted in the tanks or cisterns to strengthen the brine, and had been thrown out as valueless. Within the last few years a use has been found for rock dross, in the manufacture of glass bottles; consequently so great a quantity of a now valuable article produced a large sum unexpectedly. On the south side of the entrance to the Old Dock, there was a long wooden pier on poles, nearly out beyond low water mark. The bank of the river sloped down to the beach without any protection wall. Ships used to be built on the bank where they were launched at spring tides.

Opposite the end of Park-lane, at the close of the last century, there was an isolated block of houses somewhat similar to Middle-row, Holborn, the street surrounding it. In Park-lane were the house and gardens once occupied by Mr. Pownall, who was Mayor of Liverpool in 1768, and who died during his Mayority, as elsewhere stated, arising from cold caught in quelling a riot in the "Devil's Acre," near the Salthouse Dock.

Pownall-street skirted his garden, and was called after him. At one time the tide came up very nearly to Mersey-street, on the west and south side. In 1725, the bay or haven called "the Strand" (which was sold for £20 for 100 acres), had on the north side a field, used as a timber and ship-builder's yard. On the north side of this open ground was the quay of the old dock. Out of this area of the river front was constructed the Salthouse Dock; to the westward of it were the ship-building yards of Messrs. Rathbone, Grayson, Fisher, Earl and others. Mr. Grayson was shot in a duel by Mr. Sparling, of St. Domingo House, Everton, 24th Feb., 1804, at a place called "Knot's Hole," on the Aigburth-road, for which offence Mr. Sparling was tried, with his second, Captain Colquitt, for murder, at Lancaster, on the 4th April of that year, and found not guilty. Previous to the construction of the Salthouse Dock the river line swept round the end of Strand-street, which then terminated at the river's brink. The shore then swept along Sea-brow, an isolated row of houses between Redcross-street and James-street, the site of which is now occupied by Back Goree warehouses. At the close of the last century, the quay on the west side of the George's Dock was called the Goree-causeway. Between the dock and Moor-street end were the fish stones. Lineable with the south side of James-street were three isolated row of buildings, the streets between which were called Sea-brow, Strand-street, and Bird-street. Bird-street consisted of two square blocks of houses, with a street between them, running east and west. Strand-street extended to the old dock. Bird-street extended along the quay of the dry basin. This street stood on the site of the Police-station, very nearly to George's Dock-gate. In the improvements that took place in that neighbourhood all blocks of houses were swept away, and the present line of Strand-street was formed. Nova Scotia was erected on the new-made quay to the westward.

The Custom-house was a long, low building of one storey upon the shore, near the corner of Water-street, having a yard at the back. The river washed the beach before it, then swept up to the tower wall and the Church-yard, fronting the strand of New Quay.

From Chapel-street the shore then trended round by Lancelots-hey, near to Oldhall-street, from which two little streets opened to the water side. From this point the shore was skirted by sandhills northward, on which at one time stood some isolated houses. By the close of the century along all this river front were constructed the Salthouse Dock and all the streets adjacent, the Canning Dock, originally called the Dry Dock from its being unprotected by gates to restrain the water, and the George's Dock, at the end of which was the dry basin. Beyond this was a sort of haven, in which were the public Baths, situate at the end of the Ladies' Walk. The haven terminated with a sort of a pier or jetty, on which was a battery of heavy guns. Beyond this northward was the shore skirted by lands belonging to Messrs. Cross, Plumbe, Williamson, Lord Derby, and others. This portion of the river is now occupied by the Waterloo and Clarence Docks. On the pier, which was called "the Fort," was a building which had been originally intended as a powder magazine; but, being found too damp for the purpose of keeping "their powder dry," the authorities converted it into a bridewell. Mr. Neild visited it in 1803, when he was following the footsteps of the benevolent John Howard. Mr. Nield states that it was under the charge of Robert Walton, who received a guinea a week for his services. There were no "fees" or "garnish" to be paid by the prisoners confined in it, for, poor wretches, they had nothing to pay for. They had neither beds, bedding, nor food of any sort found them, fire only being provided by the Corporation. There was no yard nor any accommodation whatever; the prisoners were huddled together male and female, without distinction. Their friends provided them with food entirely. There was not even straw found for the captives to lie upon. Under ground there were two damp, dark vaults, approached by eight stone steps. One of these vaults was 18 feet by 12, the other was 12 feet by 7½. The light was obtained through iron-barred windows. There were two rooms above these vaults; one was 18 feet by 10, the other 10 feet by 9. There were no grates in the rooms. Adjoining these dreadful chambers were two dark cells, 5 feet square by 6 feet high. Mr. Neild declared this place to be a positive sin and shame to be allowed to exist, and a crying disgrace to the town and humanity.

The Pier Head was at all times a favourite public walk, and like the Prince's Pier and Landing Stages was always a point of attraction to the idler and health seeker.

---

## THE "SILENT HIGHWAY."

The "Silent Highway" was the title given to the silvery Thames in olden times, and such might have been the designation of the Mersey before steam puffed, and roared, and whistled on its turbid bosom, fulfilling the great prophecy of Darwin, that it should

> "Drag the slow barge and urge the loaded car,"

or something to that effect. The Mersey can prate of many a deed of darkness as well as of light, wherein life was lost and saved.

There is a great deal of mystery and speculation relative to the early history of the Mersey estuary. It has been conjectured, with considerable show of reason and probability, that in the time of the Romans, and even beyond the period of their exodus, in the reign of Valentinian, this great arm of the sea did not exist. The stream then, it is supposed, made its way out to sea between Bidston-hill and Wallasey-hill, after receiving the marshy waters of the mosses, in the uplands, previously being joined by the Irk, the Irwell, and other little tributaries that fell into its course. In the Itinerary of Antonine there is no mention made of any estuary or river such as the Mersey; and in the map of Ptolemy only a small ribbon of river is laid down, which by some has been considered to be the Belisama alluded to by historians and ancient topographers. The map of Ptolemy is surprisingly correct in projecting the bays, capes, and headlands of the coast of Britain, while the leading cities are equally accurately defined. For instance, strike a triangle on Ptolemy's map between York, Chester, and Lincoln, and lay one down between these cities in any modern map, and it will be found that there is only a slight inequality or difference in the ancient map, between Chester and York, as compared with the modern one. If the Mersey had poured forth its broad and rushing waters in the Roman days, it would have been noted down as accurately as the Dee, the Ribble, and the Lune. During the Roman occupation of 200 years, when their legions were swarming in this vicinity, building up cities, and forming roads in every direction—roads that after a thousand years, are, in some instances, as good as when first constructed—when they possessed Manchester, Warrington, Runcorn, Chester, and Northwich, and near Shrewsbury reared up a great city, is it likely—is it possible—that the Mersey estuary would have escaped their notice, and not be mentioned by them, if it had been in existence? It is therefore conclusive that in the dark ages of the Anglo-saxons, of which period so little is known, this noble expanse of water must have been formed. In fact there is a tradition extant that, at a remote period, there was a bridge of some sort which connected the two counties, and that immense woods or forests were only divided by a narrow strip of stream, while the geological features of both its banks were identical. It is certainly a curious circumstance that the same description of trees and underwood are discoverable on the Cheshire and Lancashire shores, both in subterranean and submarine situations.

The fisheries of the Mersey were at one period of considerable importance. In Doomsday Book it is stated that the King's tenants in Lancashire were bound "to attend to the King's huntings and fisheries." In all the ancient leases relating to the town of Liverpool, the fisheries are mentioned. The Sovereigns who have had direct and peculiar interest in the county of Lancaster, have granted or leased their fisheries to their dependants; and fish as an article of food was more thought of, and in greater request in olden times than at present, because, from the religious faith of the people, they were constrained to consume fish at particular seasons of the year, and on many particular occasions. About the middle of the last century, so plentiful was salmon in the Mersey, that it could not be consumed in the neighbourhood, and was obliged to be sent away elsewhere to be sold. One local historian states that there were in his time upwards of forty-five different species of fish to be found in the Mersey, from the lordly sturgeon to the humble dab or flounder. At one period herrings were caught in great quantities in and about the Mersey: and it was only abandoned by these fish in consequence (as it was then currently believed) of a fight, which took place at the fish stones, in Chapel-street, in 1756, when blood was shed. To shed blood about fishes is a certain cause, the credulous believe, of their abandoning the locality or neighbourhood where such shedding of blood has taken place. At one time there were extensive curing houses in Wallasey, and several in Liverpool, and fish yards as they were called were established on the banks of the river at Garston.

The Liverpool Corporation, in 1779 purchased the Manor of Garston for £1950, with the intention of carrying out some project for the improvement of the Mersey fisheries. Whatever that scheme might have been, it was not proceeded with, for they sold the manorial rights for £2,387, which afterwards became the property of the great ship-builders, Baker and Dawson, and afterwards of Mrs. Kent, the widow of Richard Kent, the eminent merchant. There are many curious and notable facts relating to the fish supply and also to fisheries. It seems to be a most prominent feature, that in many seaport towns the fish markets are very badly supplied from their waters direct. Many seaboard places are supplied from Liverpool, while Liverpool obtains its principal supply of fish from the Isle of Man, Ireland, Scotland, and the east coast. Indeed, if the fish eaters of the town and its vicinity relied on their supply from what the Liverpool fishermen caught in the Mersey, they would have to pay pretty dearly for all they could place on their tables. Take this as curious. Last year, when salmon was selling at fifteenpence a pound, it was freely hawked in Burnley—not far from the Yorkshire borders—for one shilling, good and lawful weight, and the fish of fine quality, and when mackarel have been selling in Liverpool for threepence each, they have been vended in Sheffield for a penny. The disturbance of the Mersey waters by the innumerable steamships and vessels constantly present on their surface, their pollution by the Manchester dyeworks, the sewage of the places they pass, and the reckless and improvident conduct of the fishermen themselves, have all conduced to destroy the finny tribes that once made these waters their habitation.

Crossing to Cheshire from Liverpool fifty years ago was a very different expedition to what it is at present. In fact, very few people ever thought of paying the Cestrian regions a visit then, and it was only from necessity that such a voyage was undertaken. In the first place there was but little or no accommodation in the vicinity of the ferries. The ferry houses themselves were little better, and in some cases not so good, as road-side inns. Then the hazards of the weather were too heavy to risk a voyage for mere jaunting purposes. The boats plying were either half-decked or open, and were of not more than from five to six tons burden, with accommodation for 10 to 15 passengers at the utmost. It was quite like a voyage to a foreign land to cross to the opposite shore in those days. There were thousands of the inhabitants of Liverpool who, in all the course of their lives, never put foot in Cheshire. At the Old Dock Gut there was a famous boatman named "Denny," whose boats were much in request. He was a remarkably smart fellow, and was very attentive to his female and youthful passengers, making special provision for their comfort. He was a brave fellow to boot, for in his time he had saved the lives of several persons who had been near drowning. On one occasion a man fell into the river; the alarm being raised, Denny put off in his boat to rescue him; the man rose to the surface, but, before a helping hand could be put out, he had disappeared. Denny then took his boat-hook, and, after prodding about for a short time, found a weight at the end of it. On hauling it up, it appeared that he had caught the drowning man by the *os frontis,* and in the corner of the eye. The man was brought on board Denny's boat, and on being taken on shore was with difficulty restored to life. On finding the mode in which he had been saved from inevitable death, he rewarded his brave preserver with unlimited abuse for the damage he had sustained to his face; and he actually threatened Denny with an action at law for his disfigurement. Whereupon Denny declared with a boatman's oath that he would hook no more people out of the river for the future.

To cross the water was a perilous undertaking at that date. Even within thirty years it had its discomforts and horrors, in dirty slow steam-boats, in inconvenient and perilous landing-places, and in uncertain times of departure and arrival. But, even under these adverse circumstances, the passage was made with vast advantages over the former mode of transit. Until the introduction of steam, in 1815, the cost of the passage depended upon any bargain made with a boatman, who would get all he could, from a penny a piece from a lot of schoolboys, to half-a-sovereign from a green and credulous passenger.

Tales are told of people passing half the night on the water striving to make the pierhead, "The Old Dock Gut," "The Potteries," "Knott's Hole," "The Dingle," or anywhere, in fact, and felt at length grateful to land amidst rain, wind, and darkness, by the calm waters of Garston Creek, although a long walk of six miles was entailed. A gradual and vast improvement has taken place of late years in the ferry traffic. The first steamboats were small vessels with one mast, having a square sail. The paddles were of limited size, and the funnel slender and tall. In the *Mercury* of 14th March, 1816, on the application of steam to the Tranmere boats, a correspondent remarks that it is equivalent to "bridging over the Mersey." In 1770 there were only five ferries—namely, at Carlton or Eastham, the Rock, Tranmere, Woodside, and Seacombe. Previous to 1800 there was a long wooden pier running out into the river to the south of the Old Dock entrance.

In adverse weather the passage boats ran alongside of this pier, but it was a very dangerous landing, having no protecting railings. In the beginning of the last century, the ferry-boats ran to the shore opposite St. Nicholas's Church and the bottom of Water-street. Then people had to scramble up to land through the shingle, ooze, and dirt, at low water, or be carried on men's shoulders, or by stepping along a rickety moveable foot platform at the time of the flood. In an open boat, in rough weather, it may be imagined what sort of a voyage half-a-dozen people would endure, most of them proving disagreeable to their fellow-passengers, as well as to themselves, suffering from that aquatic complaint which may be termed "the quarcks." Few persons thought of staying in Cheshire until evening or night, for the uncertainty of the weather made the passage, if not perilous, at any rate full of terrors to landsmen. At Woodside almost the only dwelling was the ferry-house. In 1815 it stood at the top of the rising ground on the left hand side, about the site of the Adelphi Hotel. The landing place was a timber and stone causeway, which ran out at some distance into the river, at all times being wet, slimy, slippery, and dangerous, from its exposed situation and unprotected sides. The causeways to two or three of the present ferries, although a great improvement upon the old ones, can convey, on a windy boisterous night or day, a strong idea, in progressing along them, what the old ferry landing places must have been. Where Gough's Hotel stands was a farm-house. Between it and Tranmere Hotel there were only one or two isolated houses.

At Seacombe there were a few houses, and only a farm or two between it and the Magazines, near which was the little public-house kept by "Mother Red Cap," where, in the last century, the sailors fled from impressment, and where the privateers' men lodged their gains with the landlady, who earned her title by the red cap she always wore. Many curious stories are extant about this old woman and her inn. There is a tradition that the caves at the Red Noses communicated in some way and somewhere with "Mother Red Cap's" house, and it was in their recesses that the hunted sailors, in the war time, used to be put into safe hiding. Those who now composedly, and with the utmost complacency, walk on board the fine ferry steamers of the present day, little imagine what people some thirty years ago had to endure in embarking and debarking from the steamboats of their day.

Reader of "The Streets," step towards the south end of the George's Landing Stage, and look steadfastly at the river wall before you. Do you see under, or in front of the clock-tower of the baths, a steep, narrow set of steps, and do you see another set or flight of narrow steps at the end of the river wall adjoining the Duke's Dock? Well, at one time those steps were the only modes of landing from, or getting on board of, the river steamers, and by those steps had the young and old, the lame, and the infirm, and the lazy, to descend or climb in boisterous or calm weather. In the former, when the old ferry tub ran up, frantically bumping herself against the wall, the unhappy passenger had to watch his or her opportunity to jump on shore or on board, as the case might be, on the rising or falling of the boat. Unless a person was uncommonly active, the chances were that a wave overtook him, and gave his legs a taste of the "briny." It was slow work ascending those terrible steps, for by their steepness, as may be supposed, when many persons were ascending them, the progress of disembarking in single file was no speedy job. Alongside that wall did the public, my dear madam, arrive on *terra firma*; and very glad you may be assured, people were when they found themselves safe under the baths piazza, waiting, may be, for some other members of their party to land, or until one of them, who had fortunately been amongst the first to get on shore, had gone up to Castle-street for a car! No handy omnibuses were there till 9-30 at night, to convey weary travellers to all parts of the town! No strings of neat cars or cabs were then ready to be hired. To stump it was your only remedy, let the night be what it would. Believe me, we are living in very convenient times, if we only look back a little. The voice of the public grew loud, and complained bitterly and lustily of this dangerous landing. Then the gut was made, into which the steamboats glided when they could, and the passengers had the slippery incline to climb. Next came a small landing-stage, to which access was obtained by a moveable platform run out from that yawning cavern to be seen in the river wall near the landing-stages' northern bridge. The round-house, now occupied by the 'Bus Company as an office and waiting-room, was the depository of the machinery by which the stage was lowered or raised. Next came the gigantic flight of stairs near the Seacombe slip, where the Seacombe boats used to accommodate their passengers. To watch any one going down those steps would tell whether such individual was a native or an exotic. The native, if a fair one, would rush down the steep flight of steps like a sea bird, utterly unconscious of danger; while the exotic would hug the side wall, scarcely daring to cast an eye over the depth between the edge of the steps and the water or shore below. In 1847 this small stage was replaced by the present noble landing-stage, the design of Mr. Cubitt. How people escaped without accident in those old days goodness knows, for it appeared to the humble writer of these sketches that the safe landings in stormy weather appeared like miracles, all things considered; for at one time, at low water, the passengers had to be huddled into a rickety old punt, and were transported to shore from the boat in batches, exciting alarm in the minds of the timid, and even some qualms in the hearts of the brave. The Cheshire ferries are now the most convenient, the cheapest, and pleasantest to use in the kingdom. The fare was reduced to a penny from twopence on the 1st of June, 1848. In the Edwards' time it was certainly only twopence, but twopence was then equal in value to our half-crown.

Whether the proposed tunnel or tunnels under the Mersey will depreciate the value of the ferries remains to be seen. It is said by those who have studied the subject that there is sufficient population to keep both over sea and under sea undertakings fully at work and profitable. There is a tradition that in the vicinity of Birkenhead Abbey ruins there is a narrow passage that runs directly under the river, and a person many years ago positively asserted to the writer that he had explored a portion of it when a youth. The writer did not believe it.

Respecting the Wood-side Ferry there are many curious particulars connected with it, which would alone fill a volume. Richard the third, granted the Woodside-ferry "to Richard Cust, for good and faithful service performed and shall perform to Lytherpole, with the boat and profits. Given at Nottingham, 14th September, in the second year of His reign." In the third year of Henry VII. the King took possession of the ferry which had been given to Richard Cust for his life. Henry leased it to him for seven years, at a yearly rent of sixty shillings.

In the reign of Henry 8th, the Woodside Ferry was granted to Ralf Worsley of Worsley, with all the property of the Monks of Birkenhead, valued at £115 13s. 5d.

The last century was a lawless time in its history, for it swarmed with fierce privateer's men, inhuman slavers, reckless merchantmen, and violent men-of-war's men, who all conspired to make the sailor element of the town "thick and slab." In these days of peace we have no conception of the uproar, the violence, the turbulence, as well as the merriment that prevailed when men came home from some short voyage with large sums to receive, the results of their rapacity upon and robbery of their neighbours, that war gave countenance to and justified. These men's hearts were hardened against the cry of humanity. After some great engagement, when men were scarce and the strength of the navy was enervated, the press-gangs stalked through the town, seizing anyone to whom they took a fancy; and though such an one might have been able to show himself to be a simple landsman, or, if a sailor as having protection, if the service was hard pushed but small consideration was used in any case. A man, was a man, and away he went on board the tender. It was no uncommon circumstance in those days for persons to be unaccountably missing, men in really respectable positions in life, who would after a year or two suddenly turn up, having been impressed and sent to a foreign station. The atrocities of the pressgangs we read about, but can scarcely credit. It is said the first step towards their abolition arose from the following circumstance: During the American and French war two men, apparently half seamen half landsmen, were seen strolling along Tower-hill, when they were stopped by a pressgang. The officer commanding it demanded who they were? One produced a free waterman's certificate, which exempted him from impressment, while the other stated himself to be the foreman of the Phœnix fire engine, and showed his warrant. The lieutenant laughed at their documents, and ordered his men to seize the two. In spite of strong remonstrance, they were hurried to Tower-stairs, hustled on board the pressgang cutter, and taken off to a tender lying in the river. Although the officer knew he was committing an illegal act, having given his orders, he determined to carry out his act of oppression. On board the tender, the two friends were almost thrown headlong below, amongst as complete a set of rascals as it was possible to collect together, for sometimes the gaols even were scoured to provide a contingent. Suffering the utmost indignity, these two strangers' ears were assailed by the vilest of language, and they had the greatest difficulty in saving themselves from being plundered. At length they demanded to be taken before the captain of the tender, that their case might be investigated. After considerable delay, insult, and opposition to this demand, they were ushered into the presence of the petty tyrant, who held their fate in his hands. Brutally accosting them, he inquired how they dared to come into his presence, and what they wanted? They demanded their release upon the plea that they were both free from impressment. The captain of the tender, instead of being softened by their firm but respectful behaviour, became doubly insolent and overbearing. He was cautioned by the elder man of the two, to mind what he was about, for they knew who he was, and would make him smart if he treated them unfairly. They were determined, at all odds, to resist any attempt to impress them. The captain of the tender, boiling with wrath at what he considered to be their insolence, ordered the marines in attendance to "bundle them out of his sight." The marines, thereupon, attempted to seize the two men, who at once proved that they were neither of them to be easily mastered. Finding that the marines were giving way, and likely to get the worst of the scuffle, the captain next ordered a reinforcement, when a sergeant, who had come to the rescue of his men, dashed into the fray, and seized the shorter and stouter of the two young men who had, up to this time, resisted successfully all attempts to capture him. In the fierce struggle that ensued, the over jacket or coat that had hitherto been tightly buttoned over the young man's chest, was suddenly torn open, when on the left breast of an under garment was discovered the Star of the Garter! It was the Duke of Clarence, who had, with a post-captain in the navy as his companion, determined personally to become a witness to the scenes of horror that had at length excited public attention. From that day, a reform in the impressment for the navy commenced, until its total abolition took place a few years subsequently.

When the pressgangs came on shore the utmost confusion and dismay took place among the denizens of Bridge-street, Wapping, Little Bird-street, and thereabout. On the 30th May, 1775, upon the arrival of the ship Upton in the river, from Maryland, the Winchelsea man-of-war, then lying at anchor off the town, sent her barge, under the command of a lieutenant, to board her. On the Upton's men finding the barge's intention, they seized their captain and chief officer and fastened them in the cabin. As the Winchelsea's barge ran alongside, the Upton's men swore that the man-of-war's men should not board them, and if they did they would depress their guns and fire upon them. At that time every merchant man was more or less armed, and able to make a stout resistance in case of attack. Seeing matters thus formidable, the Winchelsea's barge sheered off, to put back for a reinforcement. The Upton's men, seeing this, lowered their yawl and pulled to shore. They were, however, followed by the Winchelsea's men, when a fierce encounter took place, shots being fired on both sides, the struggle ending by the yawl being upset. Two of the crew swam ashore, others were captured, and two were drowned. The officer commanding the barge was shot in the cheek, the ball passing clean through his mouth.

On the 7th July, 1759, the Golden Lion, from Greenland, a famous ship of her day, built in Liverpool, on returning to port from the whale fishery, was boarded by two man-of war-boats, crews from the Vengeance, for the purpose of impressing the seamen. The officer in charge of the boats declared he would impress every man on board unless a certain number of them volunteered. The crew of the whaler declared their intention to resist impressment, claiming as whalers their right of freedom therefrom. They would neither suffer themselves to be impressed, nor would they volunteer. Words brought on blows, and a fierce struggle took place. The captain of the Vengeance, perceiving this, ordered his guns to be turned on the Golden Lion, which was lying between the frigate and the town. Some shots were fired, which actually fell in among the houses by the Old Dock, filling the inhabitants with consternation. The whaler's men, however, cleared their deck of the pressgang, hoisted sail, and ran their vessel along the Old Dock pier. The whalers then jumped ashore, and hurried up to the Custom House, where some obtained protection, as allowed by Act of Parliament to them as whalers. The pressgang, recovering from their repulse, started in pursuit of the Greenlandman's crew, some of whom they overtook on their way to the Custom House. A fierce fight ensued, which ended in the capture of Captain Thomson, of the whaler, and five of his men. In the midst of this portion of the fray a woman was wounded. This affair caused great excitement at the time, and created much ill-blood between the man-of-war's men and the townspeople, who resisted the impressment of the whalers, and caused them to be given up.

A punch-bowl presented to the captain of the Golden Lion is deposited in Mayer's Museum. It has on it a spirited view of this fine ship.

On the 12th of February, 1777, a curious circumstance occurred in the river. A ship called the Aurora arrived, laden chiefly with tobacco. She had sailed from America for Nantz, and was manned by Americans, Frenchmen, and four or five Englishmen. On the fifth of April the Englishmen contrived to make prisoners the captain and the rest of the crew, when, putting her head to wind, they brought the Aurora safely into the Mersey, where she was condemned under an Admiralty warrant, and sold by auction in eighty lots, realizing upwards of £30,000, which amount was divided between the gallant seamen who had successfully made the capture.

Something of a similar nature occurred in 1862, when a ship called the Emilie St. Pierre, arrived in the Mersey, commanded by Captain Wilson, who had recaptured her from a Federal American prize crew.

A remarkable occurrence took place in the river in 1778, which strikingly proves the lawlessness of the times. A Liverpool privateer, named the Mersey, having captured a French merchantman called *L'Equité*, brought her in to the Mersey. In taking her up the Sloyne roads the prize ran aground opposite New Ferry, where she was left high and dry by the receding tide. A number of flats were speedily despatched alongside, to lighten her and take out the cargo, when she again floated, While in this position a crowd of Cheshire people assembled on the shore, attracted by the sight of a large ship being so situated, when, stirred by some sudden impulse, or by some preconcerted arrangement, an attack was made on the crew of the ship and the labourers at work. In spite of strong resistance the country people took forcible possession of a great portion of the cargo. Finding their property fast disappearing, the owners made application to the Mayor of Liverpool to assist them in its protection. They applied also to the Colonel of the Leicestershire Militia, then quartered in the town, for a party to guard their vessel; but both civil and military authorities declined interfering, as they considered they had no jurisdiction whatever in another county. The owners of the vessel, thus finding they could get no aid, sent down to her a quantity of fire-arms and ammunition, ordering their people to defend themselves and the cargo at all risks. On the third night of the ship being ashore, another attack was made by the Cheshiremen, who were fired upon. They returned the fire, and after a smart struggle they took possession of the ship, turned out the crew and labourers, completely gutting her, and attempting to set her on fire.

Privateering was no new feature in Liverpool, for in the days of Elizabeth the Earl of Derby's son, Sir Thomas Stanley, fitted up a privateer, which brought him a prize to the Mersey "with great rejoicings." A privateer belonging to some Chester merchants also brought into the Mersey a prize, when the "shipping shot off," we are told, "so noble a peal of guns, so quick and fast one upon another, that the like was never heard in these parts of England and Wales." In later years we find noblemen embarking in the hazardous trade, for in 1778 the Marquis of Granby and Nicholas Ashton owned the Marchioness of Granby, Captain Rogers, of 200 tons, 20 guns, and 130 men; and the same firm owned the Lady Granby, Captain Powell, 45 tons, 10 guns, and 60 men, in which probably the Marquis had a considerable interest.

The prevalence for some time of westerly winds detains numbers of vessels in port. On a change taking place, the view of the Mersey previous to and during high water is magnificent in the extreme. From all the docks are seen issuing vessels of every size and rig, from the stately ship of 2,000 tons or more, to the little fishing or coasting craft.

Like terrestrial objects, there are those on the water that pass away and become forgotten. The old ferry-boats, and the cries of "Woodside, ahoy!"—"Now for Tranmere, and we're off!"—are no longer in existence. The river front of the town is utterly changed; the open fields, sloping to the water's edge, on which large war vessels were built, are now fringed with massive stone walls for miles and miles. Amongst other things that had its day, prospered, and then disappeared, was the "Floating Bath," which was at first moored off the St. George's pier. She afterwards, as the ferry traffic increased, took up her station opposite the Prince's Parade. She was launched from Horner's yard, below the fort, in 1816. In her interior was a capacious swimming bath, or tank, seven feet deep at one end, and three feet at the other. The river water constantly flowed through this receptacle, so that bathers had really a salt water bath, pure and simple. In one part of the vessel there were dressing closets well supplied with towels, and there were two coffee-rooms in which all sorts of refreshments were supplied at moderate prices. On the deck was a promenade, which in summer weather was overshadowed by a large awning. From a flagstaff or mast floated an ensign bearing the words "Floating Bath." Between the bath and the shore a boat was constantly passing, to take off bathers. The admittance was sixpence each person, which included the passage to, and from the bath, and the use of towels. The deck of the baths was the *rendezvous* of some of the noted *quid nuncs* of the town —such as Mr. Egerton Smith, the clever editor of the *Mercury*, Thomas Coglan (the owner), Mr. Woods, Mr. Romer, and others. These worthies discussed, while they smoked their pipes, and quaffed their old ale, the jokes, the griefs, the successes, the calamities, and gossip of the town, while they imparted general and local information to each other, as well as turned over many a knotty point and opinion that was then popular. Scarcely one of these clever men remains. Very often swimming matches were got up *impromptu*, to come off in the open river, and many an exciting scene has been witnessed as, perhaps, when six lusty swimmers plunged in simultaneously, manfully contesting for some little prize subscribed for on the occasion. There were two Hebrew gentlemen who frequented the baths at one time who were admirable swimmers, performing all sorts of antics, jumping into the open river from the upper part of the bath deck, and turning somersaults before entering the water. These young men would remain under water so long as to alarm their friends and spectators, which would only be allayed by seeing them rise to the surface at some far different point than was anticipated. These exhibitions of natation were, however, discontinued when the number of ferry steamers increased. Two days a week, at certain hours, the bath was devoted to the use of the ladies. It was at one period much patronised by fair swimmers. A famous swimming match came off in July, 1827, that excited great interest. The competitors were a Dr. Bedale and a Mr. Mathew Vipond, of Manchester. They swam from the Graving Dock to Runcorn. The doctor beat his opponent by half a mile. The distance was swam in three hours and thirty-five seconds.

Accidents of a deplorable nature have taken place occasionally in the Mersey. In May, 1793, a market boat, when off Stanlow, above Eastham, was upset in a squall, when seventeen people lost their lives. In 1793, a curious accident took place off Seacombe, when the Pelican (privateer), that had only just before been launched, suddenly capsized, filled with water, and sank. There were 200 persons on board, consisting of the shareholders and their friends, partaking of an entertainment in honour of the event of her being launched. Seventy persons were drowned, the rest either swam ashore or were rescued by boats. Amongst the latter was one James Creasey, the pilot, of the ship, who was tried at the Lancaster Assizes for manslaughter, as it was said to have been through his negligence that the accident was caused. He was, however, acquitted. In 1797 ten people were drowned by the sinking of a boat off the Pier-head.

On the 17th November, 1834, two boats, loaded with persons who had been to see a prize fight at Rock Ferry, were upset, and many as fifty of the passengers were drowned. In December of that year a Revenue cutter's boat was upset in a violent gale, when the officer, Mr. Walker, and four of her crew were drowned, as was also Captain Evans, who commanded the Duchess of Clarence, which had just arrived in the river from Canton, being the first vessel that had come to port direct from China.

# EVERTON.

## NORTHWARD.

Of the outskirts of Liverpool, no portion has undergone so great a change in character and appearance as Everton within the last five-and-twenty years. Within the last fifteen years even the process of metamorphosis has gone on until one of the pleasantest suburbs of Liverpool has become as life-teeming, cottage-bearing, and street-streaming as the densest part of Liverpool itself. Hosts of cottages now swarm up the hill sides, scramble over the top, and flood the plain on its summit. Fifty years ago Everton was a courtly place, wherein resided the richest merchants, the most distinguished citizens, and the most fashionable and leading families. Indeed, so high did the inhabitants hold their heads, in consequence of their wealth, stability, and position, that they were termed "Everton nobles." Within the memory of middle-aged people, the whole range of the hill-side extending from the back of Brunswick-road and under Plumpton-terrace, and the rear of Shaw-street, to Everton village, or "Town," as it used to be termed, there was not a house to be seen, while from the north side to Kirkdale all the land was fields and gardens. Very old people recollect how beautiful the view was once from the Beacon Hill, and they have spoken with animation of the lovely prospect they could obtain from Everton-lane, over Mr. Plumpton's breast-high wall, which was skirted by lofty trees, of the distant town, the river, and the Cheshire shore. Plumpton-terrace now occupies the site of the wall, the trees, the brushwood, and the crest of the green fields. To the Beacon-hill came crowds of holiday folks, whenever an "out" was to be obtained; and truly they must have enjoyed a prospect of no common order, embracing, as it did, town, village, plain, pasture, river, and ocean. From the Beacon a view of fully thirty miles round could be obtained, and under certain conditions of light and atmosphere a distance of fifty miles could be compassed. Some few years ago, when building cottage property began, it was said that Everton would never be a chosen site for the people to reside at, in consequence of having the hill to climb. A false prophet has been convicted by the facts of the present day, as there is scarcely an outlet from the town wherein houses have been run up with such marvellous celerity, in such abundance, and so readily occupied, as in Everton.

Everton in 1728 was called "Yerton." It began to be a fashionable locality about the middle of the last century, when mansions of some pretension to elegance and stately appearance began to spring up on the hill top, and on the range above the lower ridge. In Netherfield-road, then called Lower-lane, many very handsome dwellings were erected, with beautiful gardens attached to them. In Everton-crescent resided the Hadwens, Waterhouses, Dovers, Wrights, &c.

Prince Edwin-street, on the south side, exhibits some large houses. Mr. David Hodgson, when Mayor, as late even as 1846, was visited by his Royal Highness the Prince Consort, in his house now standing back on the north side of the street, about fifty yards from the top. In Roscommon-street dwelt many leading people. At one time the Rev. Hugh M'Neile, now the Dean of Ripon, resided in it. Mr. Dobson, once treasurer to the Blue Coat School, also resided in it, and other notable gentlemen. Mr. Ewart dwelt in a large mansion that stood at the corner of Netherfield-road and George's-hill. Mr. C. Horsfall had a large mansion at the end of the road. Mr. Carson, Mr. Dobson, Mr. William Earle, Miss Tarlton, Mr. John Cropper, and Mr. Potter, occupied large houses with gardens running down the hill. The handsome houses towards the north end of Netherfield-road on a terrace were all occupied by leading Liverpool people. Near and on Everton-terrace dwelt the Dysons, Mr. Blackburne, Mr. Hope, and others of note. The Waterhouses had a handsome mansion between the terrace and Church-street erected by Mr. Clarke in 1790, and between their garden wall and kitchen garden was Waterhouse-lane, that had been open fifty years preceding their occupation of the premises. In this house, previous to its being converted into a barrack, resided Mr. M. J. Whitty, proprietor and editor of the *Daily Post* and *Journal*. All these houses and their beautiful gardens have disappeared, streets having been run through them, and numberless small houses thereon erected. The stone houses have given way to the brick houses, and the green houses have been superseded by the red houses. Where the charming matron sat with her daughters and their fair companions on a summer day, under a wide spreading tree, lines of little cottages are now to be seen; matron, girls, trees, and lawn, all have disappeared to be seen "never more." Jefferson-street, Waterhouse-street, Abbey-street, Hibbert-street, Stonewall-street, Copeland-street, and other thoroughfares, now occupy this once delightful and fashionable locality.

On the hill-top on the site of St. George's Church tower, previous to 1803, stood the Everton Beacon. It was blown down in a storm in that year, having been previously, it is said, undermined by a person who regarded it and its visitors as a nuisance. It was a square tower, about twenty-five feet high, and five yards square. It was constructed of the red sandstone of the district. It consisted of a room on the ground floor used as a kitchen, a room above as a sleeping apartment for the guard, and for storing combustibles, while above these was a flat roof for the reception of the Beacon fire. At the north-west corner was a sort of turret, having a recess, for the purpose of sheltering the watchman on duty. The light in the interior was obtained by square-headed windows. A flight of stone steps led to the upper apartment. It is said that the Beacon was erected as far back as 1220, but this is evidently a mistake. It is probable that the tower was erected some time previous to the sailing of the Armada; for the arrival of that formidable flotilla was looked for with as much dread and anxiety by the timid and meek at heart as was the threatened attack of

Thurot—or the promised invasion of the first Bonaparte. It was to a Liverpool man, Master Humfraye Brooke, that Queen Elizabeth was indebted for the first intelligence of the Armada being at sea; for that worthy captain and shipowner, on his voyage from Liverpool to the Canaries, espied the flotilla swarming up one morning on its way to England. On beholding it he forgot all about his voyage, but put ship about, and made all haste to Plymouth, whence he despatched couriers with the news—perhaps went himself—to her Majesty, whose Ministers, sea commanders, and gallant sailors proved themselves quite "equal to the occasion." The Beacon would be the first link in the chain or communication with the south, the east, and the north of the kingdom. By Halton and Beeston Castles to the Wrekin one way, by Billinge or Ashurst and so on to Rivington Pike, and on to Blackburn, Burnley, and Pendle, another way. Thus a burst of flame from Everton would have put at one time all England up in arms. Rupert's men, doubtless, occupied the Beacon, for on digging the foundations of St. George's church, two skeletons were found lying together which it was conjectured were the remains of some Royalist Troopers, by the leather accoutrements found near them. In the troublous times of Charles I, marriages were celebrated by a Justice of the peace in the Beacon; an Act passed in 1660 legalized all these unions, doing away with the necessity for re-solemnising them. On the east wall grew a gooseberry bush and a thorn tree. At one time a watch-finisher or movement-maker occupied the Beacon, while previous to its downfall a cobbler took up his abode in it, eke-ing out a livelihood by keeping goats that browsed on the heather and furze covered hill. After the exodus of the cobbler some gipsies took up their abode in the tower, making short work of the woodwork to ignite their fires. After this the building became dismantled; the cattle feeding on the hill took shelter in it until 1803, when it was demolished as stated.

Previous to 1815 there was a telegraph or semaphore station on the hill, conducted by a Lieutenant Watson. After the battle of Waterloo the station was given up. This telegraph occupied the site of the present schools. In 1762 the land about the Beacon was let to a Mr. Hardwar, for 2s. 6d per annum. He afterwards bought it for a few pounds. In the letting and selling, a path to the Beacon was duly and carefully provided for. Everton Church was erected in 1813-14. The site had long before been determined upon, and the first stone actually laid, but in consequence of a disagreement among the proprietors no steps were taken until the above date. Mr. Atherton, who resided in Lodge-lane, afterwards called St. George's hill, gave the land whereon to erect the edifice, with this stipulation, that no funerals should ever enter by the west gate, that being opposite to his mansion. The galleries of St. George's, Everton, are constructed of iron. The church is celebrated for its magnificent stained windows. That in the east, partly in memory of the Rev. Mr. Buddicomb, the first incumbent, and partly in remembrance of his successor, Mr. Ewbank, is a superb and elaborate specimen of this costly and beautiful art. In 1772, two cottages stood, surrounded by gardens, near the site of the church. These were consumed by fire on one night—supposed to have been the work of incendiaries.

At the corner of Mere-lane, opposite the church, was the entrance to the grounds and handsome mansion of Mr. Myers, which was in its last years occupied as a school by Mr. Brunner. The beautiful row of trees down Mere-lane were the admiration and delight of all residents in the neighbourhood. Into the grounds extended a canal, crossed by two ornamented bridges, from the pool in Breckfield-road North, which at one time was called Hangfield-lane. "St. Domingo Pit" is at present a naked, hideous pond. As late as 1860-1, it used to be a very pretty and picturesque object, when seen with the morning sun upon the pretty trees that skirted its western bank. It certainly did not smell very sweet at times, but the old pool was nevertheless kindly regarded. The Pinfold stands at its northern corner.

Breckfield-road then ran into Beacon-lane, having a wall, with fine old trees on the west side. Three or four handsome mansions with lawns and carriage sweeps up to them were on the east side, the remainder of the road being fields enclosed by hawthorn hedges. This neighbourhood is astonishingly altered within the last two or three years, a new road having been cut from nearly the top of St. Domingo Grove to Sleeper's Hill. Beacon-lane used to be a pretty lane, having a wall on one side overhung with trees, and a copse or thicket on the other, in which was at one time an old and abundant well.

The view from Breckfield-road North to the eastward, at one time, was exceedingly beautiful, comprising all the country lying between the Old Swan Glass Works and Ashurst Beacon. Prescot-road and town were distinctly visible. With a good telescope vehicles and cattle were discernable moving up the hill. Next Knowsley Park and Hall, then Croxteth Park and Hall, Garswood, Bellinge Beacon, Ashurst Beacon, and all the country in front of the range were before the spectator. Black Combe, in Cumberland, once or twice a year, can now be descried from St. Domingo-grove, while the Derbyshire hills can be seen from the top of Mr. Herdman's House. A great portion of Everton has only been brought into cultivation within the last hundred years or so. A shoemaker enclosed a great deal of land in the neighbourhood of Sleeper's-hill. He called his Estate "Cobbler's Close." Mr. Barton bought this property, and called it "Pilgrim," after a privateer of that name owned by Mr. Thomas Birch, in which Mr. Barton had a share, and which privateer captured off Barbadoes a French ship called *La Liberté*, which realised £190,000. The Pilgrim property was next sold to Mr. Atherton, who re-sold it to Mr. Woodhouse. He re-named it Bronté, which name it still retains. He so called it in consequence of his connection as agent for Bronté, Lord Nelson's estate, bestowed upon him by the King of Sicily.

The St. Domingo Estate was so called by Mr. Campbell, who, in 1755 purchased the first lot of land thereabouts from the Halsall family, and frequently adding to it in 1758. He called it by the name it bears in consequence of a privateer which he owned taking a rich prize off St. Domingo. The mansion erected by Mr. Campbell, was a rather eccentric sort of place, resembling very much an ecclesiastical edifice.

Mr. Campbell commanded, in 1745, the "Liverpool Blues," about which a good story is told. The regiment started one November morning about three o'clock to march to Warrington to guard the bridge, and, if need be, destroy it, as the Earl of Cholmondely, the commandant of the district, either from scarcity of workmen or distrust of the many Jacobites in the neighbourhood, felt himself in a position of difficulty. On arriving near Penketh Common, the vanguard of the "Blues" was seen hastily retreating, when the main body came to a halt. The valorous vanguard reported that there was a large body of the enemy ahead, occupying the road and a part of the common. A party of skirmishers was then sent forward, when terrific screams and shouts were heard through the darkness of the night. It was then proposed at a council of war, called on the emergency, that the main body should deploy into the fields and endeavour to take the enemy in flank; however, before the movement could be effected, the skirmishers had come in with each a prisoner in the shape of a goose, whereupon the main body of the gallant "Blues" charged *en masse* and completed the victory their advance guard had commenced; and it was said in Warrington that so many geese were never cooked in one night as there were on the occasion of the arrival of the "Liverpool Blues" in the town.

The next proprietor of St. Domingo was Mr. Crosbie, who purchased it from Mr. Campbell's executors for £3,800, paying down £680 deposit. Mr. Crosbie being unable to complete his bargain, and becoming bankrupt, the estate was put up for sale, unsucessfully, at the "Pontack," in Water-street. Messrs. Gregson, Bridge, and Parke next became the purchasers, at the price Mr. Crosbie was to pay for it, in addition to his forfeit money. They thus obtained it for £4,129. These gentlemen, in 1773, re-sold their purchase to Mr. Sparling, who was mayor of Liverpool in 1790, for £3,470, thus entailing on the three speculators a loss. Mr. Sparling took down the old house, and erected the present handsome mansion. He was one of the "old school," appearing on 'Change in knee breeches, broad-flapped coat, gold-laced waistcoat, broad shoes, with gold buckles, and wearing a three-cornered hat.

Mr. Sparling left a proviso in his will that the St. Domingo estate should be occupied by no other than "a Sparling" by name. Finding it impossible to get a tenant under this condition, the will was set aside, by an Act of Parliament in 1810 to nullify the clause, and enable the executors to sell the property. Mr. Sparling was interred in Walton Church-yard, where he erected in his lifetime a handsome tomb, which he could see from the windows of his mansion. Sparling-street, Everton, is called after him.

On the 24th of February, 1804, Mr. Sparling fought a duel with Mr. Gregson, as mentioned elsewhere.

Mr. Sparling was the projector of the Queen's Dock, which he disposed of to the Dock Trustees in 1783.

In 1811 Mr. Sparling's executors sold the St. Domingo estate for £20,295 to Messrs. Ewart and Litt. Mr. Ewart next purchased Mr. Litt's interest, and on 13th September, 1812, re-sold the estate to the Government, to be converted into barracks. The price was £26,383, subject to 19s. 3d. lord's rent.

Prince William, of Gloucester, resided at St. Domingo house, when Commandant of the district, 1803. The Prince was very affable and made himself exceedingly popular in the neighbourhood. Scandal said that he was often to be seen turning down Gloucester Place of an evening, to visit a fair lady who dwelt therein. St. Domingo Estate was next sold in two lots, one lot, the land, being bought by Mr. Atherton, and the other, the mansion, by Mr. Macgregor. Soon after the purchase had been completed, Mr. Atherton inquired of Mr. Macgregor when he was going to take away his house.—Mr. M. said he did not intend to do so.—"What do you mean to do with it?" "Why I think I shall let it, or perhaps live in it myself."— "Well, but how will you get to it, because I bought all the land round it, and you have no right of way!" Mr. Macgregor found that he was at Mr. Atherton's mercy, and it was said sold him the mansion at a great loss.

After other mutations, St. Domingo house became as at present, St. Edward's College.

It is a rather curious circumstance that two valuable estates adjoining each other should have been the products of two rich privateering adventures.

The quartering of soldiers at Everton has always been loudly protested against by the inhabitants, and always without success. When St. Domingo House was about to be sold and converted into barracks, in 1812, public meetings of the wealthiest and most influential inhabitants took place at the Everton Coffee-house, to protest against the introduction of troops in that quiet neighbourhood. Government was memorialized, but to no effect; the reply being that the arrangements had been all completed, and that no alteration could take place in the destination of the troops intended to be there located.

In 1854, Everton again became a military post, for several regiments succeeded each other in occupying the mansions of Mr. Waterhouse, Mr. Shand, and other gentlemen, the gardens of which adjoined. On the east side of Church-street (now called Heyworth-street, in compliment to the Heyworth family who held much property hereabout, and were amongst the earliest residents in Everton when it was fashionable,) in 1848, an encampment was formed, which caused great annoyance to the inhabitants. The presence of the military on this occasion arose in consequence of anticipated disturbances in the town.

At the end of Netherfield-road, at one time, was a large stone, on which was inscribed "Head Quarters." It was said to have been put there by Mr. Holme as a resting place for pedestrians.

A singular looking house which once stood at the corner of Priory-road, was erected by Mr. Hinde, and was intended as a copy of the beacon. However, from some defect in the foundations, it became necessary not only to prop up the western but the southern side also, to prevent the main building experiencing the fate of its original.

## EVERTON CENTRAL.

The small houses on "the Brow side," one of which is the late Mrs. Cooper's toffee shop, were erected about 1692. The toffee shop has been dispensing its sweet confections for upwards of seventy years. The Barn o' the Hill field was sold to the township in 1770, by Mr. Seacombe for £20. The shambles at the top of the Brow are not of the antiquity that has been ascribed to them. Previous to Mr. Houghton occupying them they were tenanted by Mr. George Hayes, who was also special constable. In 1830, there were only two butchers in all Everton. Near the entrance to Everton-terrace was the mansion of Mr. Staniforth, which is now converted into Ragged Schools. Rupert-lane was at one time merely a rugged cart-rutted sandy road, scarcely passable for vehicles of any description, until repaired by Mr. Harper, who erected, in 1788, the mansion at one time occupied by Mr. Shand, previous to its being converted into barracks. Mr. Harper proposed to lay out about forty pounds on the repairs of the lane, but was met with vigorous opposition by the authorities. He however persisted in improving it, but did so mainly at his own expense. Rupert-terrace was erected in a field across which was a footpath leading into the town road, past the village smithy. Opposite the end house built by Mr. Lowrie, adjoining the Coffee-house, in April, 1818, a desperate affray took place, in which blood was freely shed, and two persons were frightfully wounded. A man named Pendleton, had been robbed by two footpads in Breck-road, and had contrived to follow them to Rupert-lane, where he obtained the assistance of a man named Kelly to attempt to capture them. A struggle took place between the four, when knives were drawn, and the robbed man was left for dead in the road, the thieves escaping. They were, however, afterwards captured and transported. A handsome subscription was got up by the inhabitants, as a testimonial of their respect for the pluck these two had shown. Pendleton received his moiety down. Kelly's was invested in government securities. The roads out of Liverpool at that period were not safe to travel along without being fully armed. The original Everton cage and pinfold stood on about the site of the barrack gate. Mr. Harper caused the removal of the latter to St. Domingo Pit. Everton Coffee-house has been always a favourite meeting-house for the Everton *quid nuncs* and politicians, who, either in its little parlour or long room, settled the affairs of the nation and those of the township to their satisfaction. The house has been licensed as far back as 1770. Nearly opposite to the south side of the Coffee-house, on the site of Eastbourne-street, stood—up to 1845, when it was taken down—a long low one-storied building which was known as "Prince Rupert's Cottage." In it—*so it is said*—the Prince took up his quarters during the siege of Liverpool in 1644. This cottage was constructed of wood, mud, and stone, and was thatched with straw. It contained four rooms, and the kitchen had a tiled floor. Its interior presented the usual appearance of such like country habitations. When the building was demolished an *armoire* or wardrobe was removed from it to the Collegiate Institution, which was said to have been in use at the time of Prince Rupert's sojourn. Behind the cottage was a raised mound, which at one time was used as a bowling-green. The mound has been dignified by the learned as having been constructed by the Prince for the reception of a battery, but of what use it would have been at that distance from the town, far beyond the ball range of the time, can scarcely be understood. It was expected that some interesting discoveries would have been made on the removal of the soil, and the labourers employed in the excavations were specially enjoined to give notice of the slightest object of note that should turn up, to a gentleman resident in the vicinity deeply versed in antiquarian lore, but nothing of value or interest was discovered. Something of deep interest would assuredly have resulted from the soil being removed, had it not been for the unavoidable absence from town of an Everton wag, who had concocted a famous hoax upon those of historic proclivities. An admirably got up old box, which really was of some antiquity, was prepared, in which some capitally stained, coloured, and dilapidated documents, scarcely legible, were to have been placed, containing accounts of the progress of the siege, muster rolls of the men, with sundry accounts and disbursements of the besiegers. This box, with some cannon balls duly oxydized, and some bullets made venerable, were to have been buried one night in such a situation and position as would have been certain to be discovered by the labourers. The mound, however, was entirely removed before the joker's return home, so that the chance of perpetrating a capital hoax was lost.

A great deal of spurious enthusiasm has been kept up on the subject of that ugly cottage, and a sort of morbid reverential feeling has been engendered respecting it. If Prince Rupert did sleep under its roof, all that can be said of it is that it sheltered a daring, reckless, overbearing, indiscreet leader, who was ready to quarrel with anybody at any time, who was a mere freebooter by land, and a pirate by sea; who was baptized in blood, and swam in it from his youth to old age. So highly, however, has the memory of this Prince been estimated, that boxes containing addresses to royalty and nobility have been constructed of the timbers of the cottage, and ornaments and paper knives have been manufactured from its beams. It is said that the Royalists, while at Everton, completely stripped the country round of provisions, for which the poor farmers and cottagers obtained no recompense.

About midway up "the town," as it used to be called, though now it is termed "village," stood, thirty years ago, some old cottages which were said to have been the quarters of the Royalist officers. In one of them, at one time, which previous to its removal was used as a parish office, resided a Mistress Molly Bushell, who was the original possessor of Dr. Gerrard's famous recipe for making a confection that has rendered Everton as well known in connection with it, as Shrewsbury by its cakes, Bologna by its sausages, Strasbourg by its pies, Chelsea by its buns, and Islay by its whiskey. Toffee was recommended at first as a specific for coughs, colds, and catarrhs; and it so speedily became known and patronised by the sweet consuming world that it tended greatly to Molly's mental content and worldly prosperity.

At the top of the town, in a line with Everton-road, then called Everton-lane, stood Everton Cross. It consisted of a round stone pillar about four feet in height, surmounted by a sun-dial, for which a "mayson" in 1774 was paid a shilling for "squaring." This pillar stood on a square pedestal or base of three stone steps. During the sweating sickness of 1651 and the plague of 1665 a market was held round the Cross, and all those who traded at it deposited their money in payment for provisions in bowls of water, to prevent contagion. The Cross became, as Everton increased in population, an intolerable nuisance. It was in everybody's way by day and night, and was the cause of constant collisions by vehicles, especially after dark, when oil lamps only shed flickering rays around, and gas lights were not in use. By day numbers of loafing fellows used to haunt it, and often insulted passers-by. Frequent applications were made to the authorities to remove it, but without success. The Evertonians venerated the Cross, and would not hear of its abolition. At length what the authorities dared not or would not do, private individuals achieved. One dark, stormy night in 1820, two individuals might have been seen propelling two barrows, with muffled wheels, loaded with spade and pickaxe, up to the Cross. They made short work of its dismemberment, for in the course of two or three hours every stone of it was safely locked up in the Roundhouse, and the place where it stood being carefully raked and smoothed over, it appeared as if a Cross had never been there. Not a vestige was left "to prate of its whereabout;" and when some early risers had discovered the absence of their much-loved sundial, column and base, the news of their disappearance spread like wildfire, and in a very short time at least a hundred people were gathered round the spot. The news soon flew down to Liverpool, and actually numbers of persons came up to satisfy themselves of the truth of the report. Vague, undefinable, and marvellous stories were soon afloat, in not a few of which diabolic agency had existence. The perpetrators of "the deed of dreadful note," although chuckling mightily at their performance, dared not breathe a word of their participation in the affair; and it was not until many years afterwards that it was known that the abductor of Everton Cross was the late Mr. William Shaw, the surveyor of the high roads of the township. A view of this cross may be seen in "Herdman's "Ancient Liverpool."

In a large and handsome house that once fronted the "Village" dwelt Mr. John Shaw, who married the widow of Mr. Hallsall, through whom he became possessed of large properties in Everton. His son, Mr. Thomas Shaw, dwelt in it after him. He was called "Squire Shaw," and was the projector of Shaw-street. Only a few houses were erected in Shaw-street, at the north end, in 1827. In 1830, out of the seven houses erected thereon, there were four unoccupied. Part of Shaw-street was originally an immense stone quarry, a portion of which is still to be seen in the garden enclosure, on the northern side of St. Augustine's Church-yard wall, exhibiting the depth of the cutting and the quality of the stone.

Great alterations have latterly taken place in Everton Village —houses have been removed, streets have been formed and boldly widened, especially one running from the town or village end towards Breck-road. Here were once several old houses of the "nobles." There was a cottage on the left hand side bearing a tablet, having inscribed on it "T.H.M., 1688," and was a well-known object of interest. Opposite here dwelt, in 1782, Mr. Hayes, with whom resided a Miss Molly Banks, who rendered herself famous by boldly shooting a burglar with a fowlingpiece, when in the act of entering the house by one of the back windows. The junction of this road with Rupert-lane, Breck-road, and Heyworth-street, was at one time called "Four Lane Ends," and there, about 1680, was buried, with a stake through his middle, a man who had committed suicide after murdering his wife. This custom of interring suicides at four lane ends, arose from the desire to place the self-destroyer as near sanctity as possible, by putting him under ground at the sign of the Cross, while the stake through his middle was intended to keep his body from being carried away by the "foul fiend." Burying at cross roads was done away with by Act of Parliament, passed in 1825.

Breck-road was formerly called "Breck-lane." In 1800 it was entirely unbuilt upon, and was nothing but a sandy, rough country road, leading to Club Moor and Gill Moss. The "Odd House" stood all alone at the corner of Hangfield-lane, between which and the Mere or Pit there was not a single habitation. Thousands of houses are now springing up on both sides of this lane, which has been lately widened and greatly improved. This part of Everton will soon be as densely populated as any other suburb of Liverpool.

## EVERTON, SOUTHWARD.

EVERTON-ROAD was formerly called "Everton-lane," was rough and narrow, with a causeway in the centre.

At the north-west corner of Everton-lane there was a clump of fine old lime trees, which were removed, greatly to the regret of the inhabitants of Everton, when it was found necessary to widen the road. A row of beautiful lime trees skirted Everton-lane all the way to the Baptist Cemetery, and a low breast-high wall divided the meadows from the road. The view of the town of Liverpool was uninterrupted from this locality. The little Baptist's burying ground now covered by a Chapel, was a most interesting locality especially to the Baptist body. In the year 1698, there was at Low-hill, a young Apothecary named Bean, who Latinized his name to "Fabius," from Faber. He appears to have been a young man of much piety and benevolence, and with his sister (Hannah or Mary), did much good in the neighbourhood, in spite of the persecutions of the non-conformists at the time the Fabius's made a stand in their neighbourhood, and obtained in 1700 a licence from Manchester, to hold prayer meetings in their house at Low-hill. They were supplied with a Pastor from Hill-cliffe, in

Cheshire, near Warrington, at which latter place the Baptists mustered in large numbers, having fled to that place in 1662 to avoid the persecution which had been set on foot against them as well as other Nonconformists.

The Hill Cliffe Chapel is a low building situated on a rising ground, and is still in use, having its burial ground behind it, and its minister's house at its side. It is said Cromwell, in August, 1648, attended worship there, one of his soldiers occupying the pulpit. It is a common tradition that the Puritan soldiers, who fell at the battle of Stockton Heath, were interred in this burial ground. The Baptists built also a chapel in Warrington, which enabled them to evade the Act of Conformity, when its provisions were put in force against them, for those who resided in Cheshire attended the chapel in Warrington, while those who dwelt in Warrington went to worship at Hill Cliffe in Cheshire—so that, when a writ was issued against the residents of either Lancashire or Cheshire worshipping contrary to the forms of the Established Church, it could not be proved that they had attended chapel in their own respective counties.

Dr. Fabius, as he was by courtesy it is supposed called, must have been only about eighteen years of age when the license was granted. From his intercourse with the people about, he would have opportunities of inducing them to attend at his house to worship there, being no other place in the neighbourhood; indeed, it is a remarkable circumstance, that until St. George's Church, Everton, was erected, there was not even up to its date, any place of worship in all Everton, and that Church remained alone, until the erection of St. Augustine's. Fabius finding his congregation increase next erected a little wooden Tabernacle or Chapel, close by the wall of the Cemetery on his field, for in the deed of gift he describes "the burial ground" as "adjoining the Chapel field." The Chapel was erected about 1705. In 1707 the Cemetery was given to the Baptists "for ever" by the Fabius's. The earliest date on a tombstone was 1711. Dr. Fabius was interred in the Cemetery, on his tombstone was inscribed "In this Dormitory reposeth the body of Daniel Fabeus, who departed this life, ye 12 April, 1718, aged 37

Little did this good and pious family anticipate that this bit of ground near the Chapel-field would be utterly inadequate to the wants of the Baptist community as a place of interment, and that the community itself should have so much increased, as to be one of the most influential, respectable, and numerous of the Dissenting bodies. The Tabernacle being after a time too small to accommodate the Low-hill Baptists, they moved down to Byrom-street, in 1722.

It is a curious circumstance that the name of Fabius appears to have been spelt in three different ways. On the tombstone it is "Fabeus," in the leases of the common land at Everton taken up in 1715, and in the township records, it is spelt "Fabious," while in the Cemetery deed it is "Fabius" which is probably the way it was intended to be spelt, as this deed was drawn up by Fabius himself. The name of "Mary Fabius" appears as one of the copyholders of the waste lands, which consisted of 115 acres, leased by the lord and trustees of the lady of the manor. This "Mary Fabius" would probably be Daniel's Mother, as Fabius's sister is said to have been named "Hannah." Mary Fabius had allotted to her "one close by Kennyon's (the Odd House, Breck-road), consisting of one acre and thirty perches, and one close at Kirkdale of two acres and ten perches." In July, 1715, the copyholders signed articles to divide fairly the lands contracted for in 1714, to be leased for 1,000 years, paying "twenty shillings per acre, money down, and one shilling per acre annual rent." Daniel Fabius was one of the copyholders. It seems a case of strange ignorance of their existence, or neglect of their memory, that not even a single street has been named after them in this locality.

Nearly on the site of the Fabious' house Mr. Gregson's villa was erected. It is to this gentleman that the peculiar shape hereabout of Everton-road is attributable. Finding that he had erected his villa too near the highway, he persuaded the authorities, in 1780, to divert the road, so that he might not be incommoded by the dust. At the gate of Mr. Gregson's villa there was a famous well. A very good view of it may be seen as a sign in front of the public-house at the corner of Low-hill.

This well was a regular gossiping place, for the old women and girls of the neighbourhood who went to it to fetch water for family use. The top was protected by an iron railing. The approach to the water was by steps. The overflow ran down the hill at the back of the houses in Brunswick-road, on the north side, and is still flowing it is believed. The little stream divided West Derby from Everton.

Plumpton-terrace was erected in 1827. It was then considered the handsomest row of houses about Liverpool. The Plumpton family has always held much land in and about Everton. Mr. Samuel Plumpton was one of the copyholders under the agreement of 1715. It is a singular circumstance that the Plumpton property has been inherited for four generations by an only child. The commodious houses on the terrace are gradually disappearing; at the south end several have been converted into shops. Everton-road has of late years greatly deteriorated. Shops, cottage property, and small terrace houses have sprung up on the sites of the old mansions. Gleave-street takes its name from Dr. Gleave, an Everton physician. Cresswell-street is called after Mr. Cresswell, member for Liverpool in 1837, 1841, and 1842.

When we contemplate the myriads of houses that have sprung up in this vicinity, it is scarcely credible that old people can talk about "their country walks to Everton" in their philandering days. The route of this "country walk" was along Fairclough-lane, then called "Love-lane," which was skirted by trees and hedges that enclosed fields and market gardens, extending towards Prescot-street; then along Low-hill, obtaining an uninterrupted view of the town down the slope of the hill, and a prospect eastward of the fine open country towards Old Swan and West Derby. Then they tell how they were treated by, or did treat, their sweethearts with cakes at the "Half Way House" in Everton-lane, or toffee at Molly Bushell's. Next strolling along Higher-lane, (Heyworth-street) to the Beacon Hill, they there beheld a glorious sunset and a magnificent prospect till the moon arose, when, by her light, they wandered along "Lower-Lane" to Richmond Meadows, which they crossed on their way back to town!

At the eastern side of Everton-road, about the site of Wren-street, dwelt in a handsome mansion, erected in 1790 by Mrs. Bridge, the Stathams (father and son), who were town-clerks of Liverpool from 1807 to 1832. After them resided in it the Rev. Archdeacon Brooks, senior Rector of Liverpool, who died in 1855, and whose fine effigy, in marble, may be seen in St. George's Hall. Once, on being asked whether the Necropolis which adjoined his garden, was not detrimental to his health or comfort, the Rector replied, no—" he had always found the inhabitants very quiet neighbours." On the south of Gleave-street stood the once famous " Half Way House," at one time known as " Boyds." After it lost its license the house was converted into a cake shop, above alluded to, and was renowned for its confectionery. Dr. Gleave purchased the house and erected a mansion on it, the garden of which adjoined the late Rector's residence.

In November, 1812, an affray took place, opposite the end of Mill-lane, characteristic of the time. As already stated, the outskirts of Liverpool were at the commencement of the century infested by highwaymen, who either went about in bands or singly, to rob foot passengers, stop coachmen, and even horsemen. " Stand and deliver" were expected words to be heard by those who were compelled to be out on the roads after nightfall; nor did the empty-pursed wayfarer always sing before the robber, for if he proved not worth plundering he was often maltreated in revenge for the disappointment he had occasioned by his poverty. To such a pitch had a gang haunting Everton arrived, that the Liverpool authorities determined on breaking it up. It need hardly be told that then there were no " Roberts" in blue to fly to a belated wayfarer's assistance, for police-constables at that period attired themselves in any way their finances or tastes suggested. The famous Bow-street runner, old Townsend, the guardian angel of the Georges' Third and Fourth, wore a broad-brimmed white hat, blue coat with brass buttons, drab breeches, and top-boots! A constable, therefore, could not be recognised at that time from a " civilian," as sometimes we hear ordinary people termed by " officers of police," much to Mr. Raffles' great disgust. To encounter this particular gang five constables engaged, on the night in question, a coach, with four horses, at Edge-hill, and ordered the driver, Robert Chambers, who afterwards kept the Castle Inn, Scotland-road, to proceed leisurely along Vernon Hall-lane, Low-hill, and Everton-lane. On reaching Mill-lane five fellows sprang out of an ambuscade and stopped the coach. Opening the door, they ordered those in it to alight. This one of the constables did, and suffered himself to be searched, as agreed upon with his companions. The others then sprang out, when a battle royal took place. Pistols were discharged on both sides. One of the constables was severely wounded, while two of the thieves were winged; the others making their escape over Mr. Plumpton's wall, took to their heels down the hill, closely followed by two of the constables at a racing pace. These, however, did not capture their game until they had arrived at the bottom, in Folly-lane. All these fellows were tried at Lancaster in 1813, found guilty, and executed.

St. Chrysostom's Schools, in Mill-lane, were opened in 1837, in connection with St. George's Church, Everton (then the only place of public worship in the district), under the supervision of the Rev. R. P. Buddicom. They were erected to supply the educational and religious wants of the poorer classes in this part of the township, there being no other schools but those in Everton Valley. This district's schools were originally held in one or two houses in Hygeia-street, where boys and girls were taught together. Through Mr. Ewbank's exertions the present schools in Mill-lane were erected, at the cost of Mr. William Smith, who resided in Church-street, opposite the Priory. The lower room was licensed for Sunday services, which were conducted by the Rev. Incumbent or his Curates. The Rev. Mr. Ewbank, succeeded Mr. Buddicom on the removal of the latter to St. Bees as principal. When the Rev. John Macnaught became curate at St. George's in 1849, Mr. Ewbank placed the district and schools under his supervision, so continuing until 1854, when they were formally made over to the members and congregation of St. Chrysostom's Church, to which Mr. Macnaught had been inducted. The schools continued, for some years, to be managed by the incumbent of St. Chrysostom's and a committee of gentlemen with great success. On Mr. Macnaught's resignation they continued for a short time under the supervision of the present incumbent, the Rev. T. Cowan, Mr. Macnaught's successor; but shortly after his appointment he intimated that he declined acting in conjunction with the committee which had been in office so many years. From this period these schools have been carried on, independently of any clerical supervision, with much satisfaction to the parents of the children educated there, and great credit to these connected with them. There are at present between six and seven hundred children in these schools.

Where the Necropolis wall stands there used to be a high hedge with a dry ditch. Mill-lane was hedged on each side, and was so narrow, that two carts could not pass. To enable them to do so, one cart had to go into a field while the other went on. It originally terminated in a stile-road running by the end of the Strawberry Gardens, into Boundary-lane. On the site of the ground on which St. Chrysostom's Church and the Reservoir stand, it was proposed, in 1827, to erect a magnificent square with gardens in the centre. Sixty-yard streets were to radiate from the square, having handsome mansions erected in them. The Reservoir was erected in 1853. The stone of which it is constructed was taken from a delf by the side of Whitefield-lane; it was conveyed along a little railway, laid down across the field, to the Reservoir. It is said that the whole mass of stone of which the Reservoir is composed was drawn by one and the same horse.

The distance of Audley-street to the Rivington lakes is 27 miles. The water arrives through immense iron pipes. The reservoir will contain six and a half millions of gallons. The tank at the top of the tower contains a quarter of a million gallons. The tower is 150 feet high, and 257 feet in circumference. This and other receptacles, erected after the designs of the late Mr. Duncan, the water engineer, are monuments of his great constructive abilities. The arches in the interior are 38 feet high. The walls are at least five feet in thickness, the stones being laid in concrete and packed with asphaltum. The floor of the reservoir is bricked in strong concrete, and is coated thickly with asphaltum. The engines first employed in lifting the water to the tank were of 28 horse-power. The contractors for the stone work of this building were the Messrs. Holme. The iron was cast at the Haigh Foundry. The clerk of the works was the late Mr. William Stubbs, a young man of great promise.

St. Chrysostom's Church was erected by subscription in 1853, for the Rev. John Macnaught, who had been curate to the Rev. Mr. Ewbank, St. George's, Everton. Mr. Macnaught's peculiar views on "Inspiration" and the "Infallibility of the Scriptures" drew down upon him the bitterest animosity of his clerical brethren. He made a bold stand in support of his opinions, preaching them freely and without fear of consequences; drawing round him, in the then lonely church in the fields, a numerous and influential congregation, whom he certainly taught to think. Assuredly, in no congregation in Liverpool could have been seen so many thoughtful faces, as might have been looked upon within the walls of St. Chrysostom's. The fame of Mr. Macnaught's oratorical powers drew numbers of strangers to hear him, who went away impressed with the idea that if he really were unsound in his theology, he was a man of extraordinary abilities. A more devotedly attached congregation no man ever possessed than did this young clergyman, and no man ever possessed greater powers of obtaining friends amongst the laity. His broad and liberal views; his honestly delivered opinions; his bitter dislike to all sorts of humbuggery or trickery; his total abstinence from comment and deterioration of any other denomination of Christians who might not agree with him or he with them; his fervid and impassioned delivery; his well-rounded periods; his sometimes torrents of words; his aptitude in illustration; his remarkably simple and happy way of explaining great Scriptural difficulties, altogether developed charms which few could resist, and many who went to hear him prejudiced against him, left his church his sincere and profound admirers. The resignation of his incumbency in 1861 plunged his friends in deep regret, and filled them, as it did the whole town, with astonishment. In the pulpit Mr. Macnaught on all occasions exhibited perfect self-possession, and did not scruple to correct his congregation, even individually, when they deserved it. On one occasion, noticing two young ladies busily engaged in conversation during the service, he quietly stopped reading and recommended the fair chatterers to defer their communications until they had reached home. On another occasion Mr. Macnaught, alluding to mysteries, assured his hearers that the most complicated of mysteries often proved to be most simple of solution. This observation occurred on a snowy day in winter. Just as the rev. gentleman had arrived at this portion of his discourse a terrific crash was heard, which startled the entire congregation "There," said Mr. Macnaught, "that noise is a mystery that has filled many of you with wonder and consternation. But it is no mystery, my friends,—it is only the snow falling from the roof of the church." In one of his sermons he drew so vivid a picture of the dark side of Hades that his auditors held their breath while they listened to the fate of the wicked, and the frightful torments they had to undergo. The phrase of "hearing a pin drop," might easily have been exemplified, for the most intense silence reigned throughout the church. When he had arrived at the climax of his description, and the imaginations of his congregation had evidently become highly excited, the rev. gentleman suddenly stopped, when, leaning his arms on his pulpit desk, he said quietly and colloquially *more suo*. "There's no such place!" The effect of these words was extraordinary, for the breath suppressed found vent, and it was plain that the weight and terror on many minds had been removed by this assurance that "there was no such place."

In St. Chrysostom's Church, are some very beautiful stained windows put up, as memorials of the sleeping relatives of the members of the Rev. J. Macnaught's congregation. The superb east window is to the memory of the late Mrs. F. J. Eyton; that in the west of Miss Shallcross. There is a pretty window to the south of the Chancel put up by the Rev. John Macnaught, in memory of his eldest daughter. The present organ, by Willis, of London, is of great power and of fine tone. It was purchased by Mr. Macnaught's congregation instead of the original one erected which was not satisfactory.

A few scattered memoranda about Everton may not be uninteresting. The rental of Everton in 1671 was £55; in 1769, £2,209; in 1815, £9,981; in 1829, £30,139; in 1869, £240,000. From 1805 to 1816, there was a sort of mock election held for the choice of Mayor. The Mayor was elected for his position and standing in "the Town." The election took place at the Everton Coffee-house, where the "Corporation" held its sittings. In Everton-terrace, in a little cottage to which access was obtained through a wicket and by two stone steps, lodged for some time De Quincey, the opium-eater, one of the most charming of British essayists. He, during his stay in Liverpool, was in some way connected with the firm of Meritt and Wright, booksellers, Castle-street, who published in 1769, a book entitled "Liverpool testimonial to the departed genius of Robert Burns, the Scottish Bard." The list of subscribers to the Work is introduced by the following paragraph:—"We whose names are hereunto subscribed, calling to mind the delight we have received from the immortal works of this great but unfortunate genius, offer the sums affixed after our names towards the support of his family, as a proof of the sympathy we feel in the affliction of the living, and of the honour we pay to the memory of the dead."—The amounts vary from ten shillings to ten pounds. The name of Dr. Currie, (who published, according to Charles Lamb, a very silly biography of the poet,) is amongst the subscribers. Messrs. William Roscoe, W. Neilson, W. Rathbone, John Gladstone, W. Ewart, Sheppard, Willis, Earle, Drs. Solomon and McCartney have their names down for various sums.

At the top of Rupert-lane, adjoining Japha's Vaults, there stood a few years ago a handsome house, in a garden, enclosed by iron railings, which was built by Mr. Harper as a dwelling for his parents. It was afterwards a ladies' school. Mr. John Kilshaw, town councillor, also resided in it, and, previous to its removal, Mr. McGee, attorney. The adjoining house in Rupert-lane, which was originally Mr. Harper's stables, was converted into a dwelling about 1812, by Dr. Brandreth, who married Mr. Harper's youngest daughter. That lodgings were cheap at one time in Everton is presumable when we find the Rev. R. P. Buddicomb's father told his friends that he lodged with "the Andertons in the Town, occupying a well-furnished bed-room and sitting-room, and paying as rent 2s. 6d. per week!" Grecian-terrace and York-terrace were erected by Mr. Atherton in 1828. They do not seem to have turned out a very flourishing speculation at first starting, for in 1830, in the former, out of seven houses three were unoccupied; while in the latter the whole seven were empty. In 1800 there was not a single house to be seen eastward of the village, all being pasture fields or arable land. To show the value of property forty years ago, compared with what it was 145 years ago, the following statement will be found correct. The close of land at the corner of Mere-lane and Hangfield-lane (now Breckfield-road North) was purchased in 1724, with two other closes of land, by Mr. Ellison's ancestors, for £84 10s, on leasehold for 1,000 years, at 1s. per acre quit rent. Mr. Ellison sold this land by Mere-lane (on which Springfield is built) for £3,000. Whitefield house was erected in 1810 by Mr. Bailey, a tailor and draper in Liverpool. Whitefield-lane was, not long ago, a mere sandy thoroughfare, having no houses along it, except a small cottage near the reservoir stone quarry. Everywhere about it were fields and gardens, within the last twelve years. In January, 1833, a frightful murder took place at Mr. Okell's, in Breck-lane. After robbing the house, a man named Thomas murdered the servant girl, under circumstances of peculiar atrocity. Thomas was hung at Lancaster in the month of March following.

Some curious entries occur in the town records. 1736, the cock of the dial repaired; 1744, spent on six journeys to Prescott, to meet the Commissioners about Papists, 6s.; for cleaning the town arms, 2s. 10d.; paid at three times for searching every papist in town, 1s. 10d.; 1746, paid Croft for the town musket; 1749, all persons taking sand from the lanes to be charged 2s. 6d. per load; 1759, paid £8 13s. 10d.

for paving Loggerhead-lane (now Everton-crescent); paid Dr. Livesley for setting Alice Knowles' leg, 42s.; paid for a coffin for Witch Nancy's child, 1s. 6d.; 1763, land in Netherfield-road let to R. Lunt for £3 3s. per annum; land in Netherfield-lane rented to Joshua Rose for £4; the Brow from the Coffee-house westward to be lowered and brought three inches to the yard; 1785, the Cross repaired, 1s. paid for same; 1787, the Bridewell to be erected (this is the round house on Barn-o'-Hill field, opposite the Toffee-shop;) £21 paid by the inhabitants of the Township to Joshua Rose, for the pump at the top of Roscommon-street; 1785, Mr. Harper agrees to give and take land opposite the Coffce-house, to improve the road; 1803, a mole catcher employed at £10 10s. per annum; in 1807 the mole catcher to be dismissed; 1817, ordered to be paid £17 14s. 9d. expenses of prosecuting four footpads.

The Manor of Everton is held by the Marquis of Salisbury, and it is in this way that the family became posessed of it:—In 1717, Mr. Isaac Green, a solicitor of considerable eminence in Liverpool, whose wife was heiress of Sir Gilbert Ireland, purchased the rights, privileges, and emoluments of the Manor of Everton, with those of the Manors of West Derby and Wavertree. In 1749 at his death, 5th July, his posessions became the property of his daughters co-heiresses: one became Mrs. Blackburne of Hale, and the other Mrs. Bamber Gascoyne of Childwall. Everton fell to the lot of Mrs. Gascoyne, wife of the M. P., for Barking, by whom she had two sons. The Manors of West Derby, Everton, and Wavertree, descended to Mr. Bamber Gascoyne, (many years member for Liverpool, his brother was Gen. Gascoyne.) Mr. Gascoyne's death took place May 8th, 1797. At the death of the younger Gascoyne, 16th January, 1864, the Manors were inherited by his daughter, who married the Marquis of Salisbury.

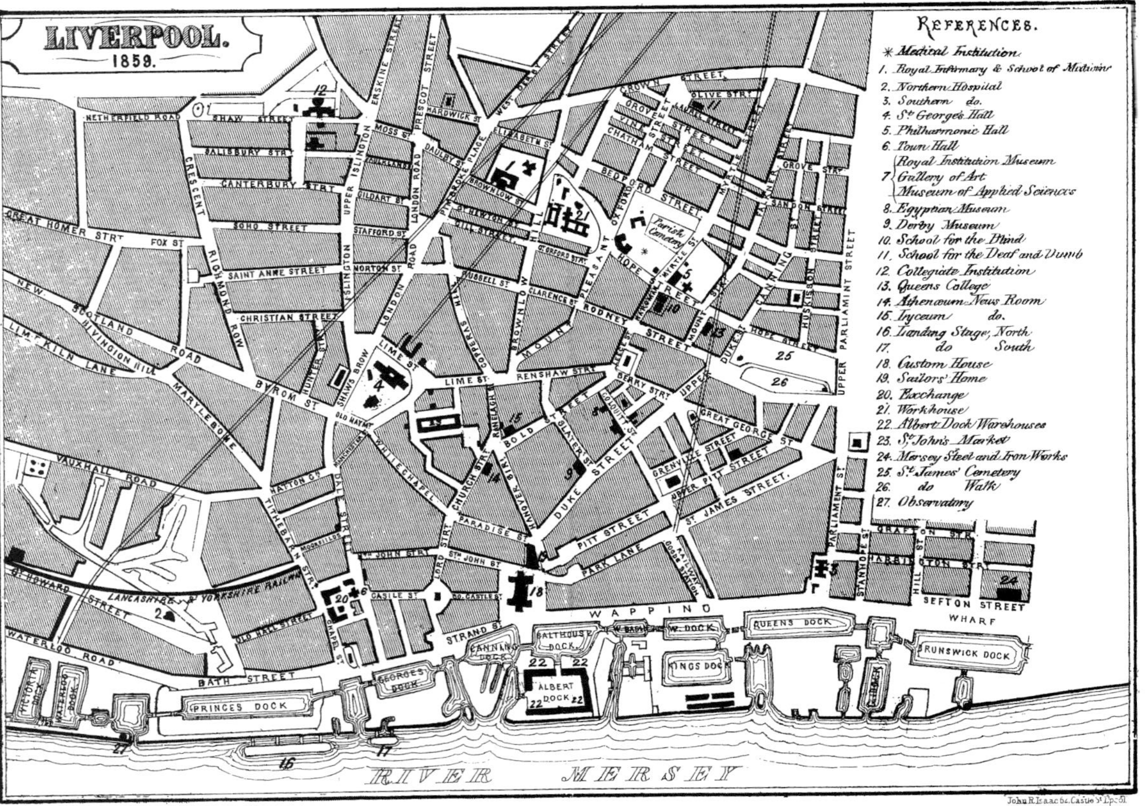


Liverpool. 1859.

Chapel Street. 1865.

Water Street. 1860.

Oldhall Street. 1866.

Tithebarn Street. 1856.

Dale Street. 1790.

Dale Street. 1865.

Scotland Road. 1869.

Castle Street. 1862.

Castle Street. 1786.

Lord Street. 1867.

Lord Street. 1810.

Church Street. 1867.

Bold Street. 1856.

Ranelagh Street. 1872.

Lime Street. c. 1835.

London Road. 1733.

Shaw's Brow. 1854.

William Brown Street and Byrom Street. 1870

Brunswick Road. 1869.

West Derby Road. 1867.

Pembroke Place. 1862.

Seymour Street. 1870.

Judge's House, St. Anne's Street. Undated.

St.Thomas' Church, Park Lane. 1855.

Liverpool from Birkenhead Ferry. c. 1830.

Everton Village. 1828.

Everton Brow. 1860.

# INDEX

Page numbers in bold type indicate major references. *'B/w ill.'* and *'col. ill.'* followed by page numbers in italics refer to illustrations.

## A


Abbey, Richard, potter, 171
Abbey Street, 207
Aber Street, 113
Abercromby Square, 79, 148
Academy of Art, 37, 74–75
Ackers, Mr, merchant, 163
Adam, son of Ranulf, of Letherpull, 27
Addison Street, *formerly* Sickman's Lane or Deadman's Lane, 42, 44
Adelphi Hotel, 82, 83, 84, 194
Adelphi Theatre, formerly the Circus, Queen's Theatre, Victoria Theatre, 167-8
Aigburth, 12, 161, 169
Aigburth Road, 187
Aintree, 171
Albany Buildings, Old Hall Street, *b/w ill. 4*
Albert Dock, 162
Albert, Prince, 162, 168, 206
Alexander, Robert, editor of the *Liverpool Standard*, 61–63
Alexandra Drive, *formerly* Parkfield, 150
Alexandra Theatre, Lime Street, *later* Empire Theatre, *col. ill. 5*
Alfred Street, 180
All Saints' Church, 50–51
Almond, Mr, landowner, 30
almshouses, 59, 77, 91
Altcar, 44
Amoryson, John, of Wigan, 5
Ancient Chapel of Toxteth, 81

Anderson, Hugh, minister of Ancient Chapel of Toxteth, 81
Anderson, Thomas Darnley, 114
Anderton family, 229
*Angel and Crown*, inn, Dale Street, 38
Angus, Charles, 163–64
Ansdell Street, 173
Anson Street, 96
Anthony Jones & Co, 68
Apprentices' Library, 69
Argyle Street, 69, 70
Armada, 207, 208
Arnold, Mr, Blind School pupil, 95
Artillery Volunteer Corps, headquarters, Mason Street, 131, 142
Artillery Volunteer Corps, storehouse, Mason Street, 131, 145
Ashlin, Capes, treasurer to Health Committee, 112
Ashton family, shipowners, 125
Ashton, Nicholas, shipowner, 202
Ashton Street, 125
Ashurst Beacon, 208, 210
Aspenwall, Roscoe and Lace, solicitors, 68
Aspinall, Sergeant, 30
Aspinall, Sir James, Mayor of Liverpool (1834-35), 109, 152–53, 180
Aspinall, William, 170
Astley, Mr, theatre owner, 167
asylums
- Asylum for the Blind, 94-96
- Deaf and Dumb Asylum, 146
- Licensed Victuallers' Asylum, St Anne's Street, 114
- Licensed Victuallers' Asylum, West Derby Road, 113, 114-15
- Lunatic Asylum, Brownlow Hill, 157

Lunatic Asylum, Lime Street, 90, 91
Athenaeum, 74, 75, 77
Athenaeum Newsroom, 74, 75
Atherton, James, 209, 210, 212, 229
Atherton, Revd. William, rector of St Peter's Church, 72
Atherton Street, 53, 70, 125
Atholl, Duke of, 180
Atkins, John, proprietor of Zoological Gardens, 120
Atkins, Mrs, 120
Atkins, Thomas, proprietor of Zoological Gardens, 116–19
Audley Street, 97, 225
*Aurora*, ship, 200–201
Avery, Grace, cookmaid, 153
Ayndoe, Thomas, Mayor of Liverpool (1655-56), 21

**B**

Bachelor Street, *formerly* Bachelor's Weint, 29
Bachelor's Weint *see* Bachelor Street
Back Goree, 20, 187
Back Lane *see* Lime Street
Back Lime Street, 88, 89
Back Mason Street, 145
Bailey Brothers, iron warehouses, Water Street, 12-13
Bailey, Mr, M.P. for Liverpool, 12
Bailey, Thomas, tailor and draper, 229
Bainbridge, Dr, author of *Fly Fisher's Guide*, 166
Baker and Dawson's, shipbuilders, 174, 191
Baker, Peter, Mayor of Liverpool (1795-96), 174
Balm of Gilead, 123–24
Bamber Street, 129
Banister, Revd. Robert, minister of All Saints, 50
Bank of England, 56, 75
Bank of Liverpool, 11
Bank Street *see* Water Street
banks
  Bank of England, 56, 75
  Bank of Liverpool, 11
  Barned's Bank, 67, 77
  Hadwen's Bank, Church Street, 165
  Heywood's Bank, 56, 124
  Mercantile and Exchange Bank, 56
  National Bank, 56
  North and South Wales Bank, 60
  North Western Bank, Dale Street, 3
  Roscoe's Bank, 55
  Royal Bank, Dale Street, 38
  Union Bank, Brunswick Street, 54
Banks, Molly, 218
Banks, Mr, 167
Bannister, Mr, 73
Baptist chapels *see* chapels
Baptists, 219–21
Barker, Revd., incumbent of St Mary' Edge Hill, 138
Barn o' the Hill field, 214, 230
Barned's Bank, 67, 77
Barnes, Zachariah, potter, 100
Barnet, Mr, Jacobite, 97
Barrow, Jane, 108
Barton family, 94
Barton, Irlam and Higginson, East an West India Merchants, 21
Basnett family, 71
Basnett Street, 73, 159
Bates Hotel, coaching house, 68
Bates, Mr, grocer, Tithebarn Street, 3
Bath Street, 10, 22, 23
baths
  Dwerryhouse's Bath, 23
  Floating Bath, 202-03
  Liverpool Baths, 22-23, 188
  Pier Head Baths, *b/w ill. 26*

Sadler's Bathing Establishment, Hanover Street, 76
Beacon Hill, Everton, 205–6, 222
Beacon Lane, 209–10
Beacon *see* Everton Beacon
Beacon's Gutter, 24, 109
Bean, Daniel *see* Fabius, Dr Daniel
*Bear,* public house, 120
Beau Street, 79
Bedale, Dr, 203
Beeston Castle, 208
Bellinge Beacon, 210
Bellingham, John, 179
Bellingham, Mrs John, dressmaker, 179
Belmont Road, 110, 113
Ben Jonson Street, 44
Bennett, Alderman, 90
Benn's Gardens Chapel, 26
Benson, Moses, merchant, 180
Berry Street, *formerly* Colquitt Street, 58, 78, 179, 182
Bevington Bush, 44
Bevington Hill, 25, 28, 30, 44, 45
Bevington Lane, 42, 44
Bickersteth, Mr, surgeon, 151, 152
Bidston Hill, 189
Bidstone Lighthouse, 49
Billinge, 208
Binns' Collection, Free Public Library, 81
Birch, Colonel Thomas, Governor of the Castle and Tower of Liverpool, 15, 57
Birch, Sir Joseph, 180
Birch, Thomas, shipowner, 210
Birchfield, 104
Bird Street, 187
Birkenhead, 11, 75, 177, 197
Birkenhead Abbey, 196
Birkenhead Ferry, view from slipway, *b/w ill. 26*
Birkett's warehouses, Lancelot's Hey, 9
Bisbrown, Cuthbert, architect, 172
Bishop of Chester, 50, 51
Bishop West *see* West, Montgomery
Bixteth family, 31
Bixteth, Thomas, Mayor of Liverpool (1635-36 and 1642-43), 31
Bixteth Street, 31
Black Combe, Cumberland, 210
*Black Horse*, High Street, 108
Blackburn, 208
Blackburne, John, of Orford Hall, Warrington, 186
Blackburne, Mr, 148, 206
Blackburne, Mr, proprietor of Liverpool Salt Works, 185
Blackburne, Mrs Thomas, of Hale, *formerly* Miss Green, 230
Blackburne House, 148
Blackburne Place, 148
Blackstock, Miss, 30
*Blackwood's Magazine*, 149
Blind Asylum, 94-96
Blind School, 94-96, 129, 150
Blome, Richard, 36
Blondin, 119
Bloore, Richard, 8
Blue Bell Inn, 94, 160
Bluecoat Hospital, 71, 129
Bluecoat School, 7, 69, 108, 164–65, 206
Blundell, Bryan, 127
Blundell family, of Ince, 20
Blundell, Revd., incumbent of St Anne's Church, 163
Blundell Street, 172
Boaler Street, 121
Boaz, Mr, 6
Boke, Joe, sexton, 70

Bold family, 76
Bold Street, *b/w ill. 14*, 50, 60, **76–78**, 79, 128
Bolden, Mr, merchant, 172, 180
Bolton, Colonel John, 77, 128–29, 159-60, 180
Bolton Street, 86, 131, 137
Bonaparte, Napoleon, 70, 208
Bonke Street *see* Water Street
Bootle, 21, 89
Bootle Sands, 127
Borough Gaol, Great Howard Street, 24
Borough Gaol, Water Street, 17
Bostock Street, 47
Botanic Garden, Edge Lane, 146
Botanic Garden, Myrtle Street, 146
Botanic Gardens, Great Homer Street, 91
Bote House, 70
Boult, Joseph, 125
boundaries, of borough of Liverpool, 108-09
Boundary Lane, 121, 225
Boundary Road, 109
Boundary Street, 123
Bourne Street, 113, 121
*Boyds see Half Way House*
Brade, Hannah, 104–5
Braham, John, 78
Brancker, Sir Thomas, Mayor of Liverpool (1830-31), 151
Brandreth, Dr Joseph, 151
Brandreth, Dr J.P., 229
Brandreth, Mrs J.P., 229
Breck Lane *see* Breck Road
Breck Road *formerly* Breck Lane, 31, 214, 218, 219, 229
Breckfield Road, 209
Breckfield Road North, *formerly* Hangfield Lane, 209, 210, 219, 229
Bretherton, Bartholomew, coach proprietor, 87, 88
bridewells
  Everton, 230
  the Fort, 188-89
  Prescot Street, 107
  Vauxhall, 30
Bridge, Mr, 211
Bridge, Mrs, 223
Bridge Street, 199
Bridport Street, 96
Briscoe, John, draper, 21
Briscoe's Buildings, 21
British Association, 89
Broadneaux, Colonel Robert, 9
Brocklebank, Mr, grocer, Church Stre 73
Bromfield, Mr, 154
Bronté, property, 210
the Brook, 69
Brooke, Humfraye, 208
Brooks, Joseph, merchant, 74
Brooks, Major Edward, 78, 128–29, 1
Brooks, Mr, 77
Brooks, Venerable Archdeacon Jonathan, senior Rector of Liverpo 74, 223
Brooks' Alley, 74
Brougham, Henry, Lord, 53
Brougham Terrace, 113
Browne, Felicia, later Mrs Hemans, 1 179
Browne, Mr, actor, 168
Brownloe, Lawrence, 125
Brownlow Hill, *formerly* the Way to Wavertree, 79, 81, 82, 83, 84, 123 157
Brownlow Hill Lane, 148, 157
Brownlow Street, 123, 125
Brunner, Mr, schoolmaster, 209
Brunswick Dock, 20, 172

Brunswick Place *see* Brunswick Road
Brunswick Road, *formerly* Brunswick Place, Folly Lane, Mill Lane, *b/w ills. 20, 21*, 104, **105–12**, 113, 205, 222
Brunswick Street, 54, 56, 57, 58
Brydges, Admiral George, first Baron Rodney, 149
Buddicomb, Revd. R. P., 209, 224, 229
*Bull and Punch Bowl*, inn, Dale Street, 38
Bull Hotel, Dale Street, 36
*Bull*, public house, Warbrick Moor, 31
Bullock, Mrs William, 70
Bullock's Museum, 70
Bulmer, Mr, curate, 84
Burgess family, 160
burial grounds *see* cemeteries, churchyards
Burnley, 191, 208
Burns, Margaret, 163–64
Burns, Patrick, 18
Burns, Peter, 84
Burns, Robert, poet, 228
Burslem, 171
Bury, Baron, 97
Bus Company office, 196
Bushell, Molly, shopkeeper, Everton Toffee Shop, 216–17, 222
Bushell, William, roper, 57
Button, John, Liverpool burgess, 68
Button Street, 68
Byrom, Octavius, 39
Byrom Street, *formerly* Dog Kennel Lane, Townsend Lane, *b/w ill. 19*, 36, **39–44**, 155, 221

**C**

Cable Street, 34, 53, 66, 70
Caird Street, 113
Cambridge Street, 149
Camden Street, 96
Campbell, George, Mayor of Liverpool (1763-64), 210–11
Campbell Street, *formerly* Pot House Lane, 183
canals, 22, 25, 49, 171, 209
Canning, George, MP for Liverpool, 53, 150
Canning Dock, *formerly* Dry Dock, 188
Canning Place, 176
Canning Street, 147
Cardwell, Edward, MP for Liverpool, 151
Cardwell, Revd., of St Paul's Church, the *Pier Head Parson,* 150–51
Carlton, 193
Carmichael, Captain John, 127, 159–60
*Carnatic*, French East Indiaman, 174
Carnatic Hall, 174
Carpenter, Revd. H., incumbent of Emmanuel Church, West Derby Road, 115
Carron Iron Warehouse, 58
Carson, Dr James, 84, 156, 164
Carson, John, 206
Cash, Mrs, 74
Castle Ditch, 60
Castle Hill, 60
*Castle Inn*, Scotland Road, 224
Castle (of Liverpool), 15, 58, **60–61**, 64, 65, 85
Castle Street, *b/w ills. 9, 10*, 25, **52–63**, 69, 128, 175, 195, 228
Causey Lane *see* Everton Crescent
Caxton Printing Office, 86
Cazneau, B., 49
Cazneau Street, 49, 79
cemeteries (*see also* churchyards)
Baptist cemetery, Everton, 110, 219, 220–21

Hill Cliffe Baptist Chapel burial ground, Cheshire, 220
Jews' cemetery, Cumberland Street, 35
Jews' cemetery, Oakes Street, 125
Necropolis, *b/w ill. 21*, 106, **110-12**, 113, 116, 223, 225
Quaker cemetery, Hackin's Hey, 28
St James's cemetery, 181
St John's cemetery, 58, 90
Wesleyan graveyard, Plumbe Street, 26
Central Station, *b/w ill. 15*
Chadwick's map of Liverpool (1725), 79
Chaffers, Edward, potter, 100
Chaffer's stone-yard, 19
Chambers, Robert, 224
Chambre, Sir Allan, 163
Chantry, Mr, sculptor, 75
Chapel of Our Lady and St Nicholas *see* St Nicholas' church
Chapel of St Mary, Edmund Street, 25
Chapel Place, 33, 107
Chapel Street, *b/w ills.. 2, 5,* **4–10**, 55, 59, 86, 151, 188, 191
chapels (*see also* churches)
Ancient Chapel of Toxteth, 81
Baptist Chapel, Bootle, 89
Baptist Chapel, Byrom Street, 40, 221
Baptist Chapel, Gerard Street, 41
Baptist Chapel, Hope Street, 89
Baptist Chapel, Myrtle Street, 89
Baptist Chapel, Rose Street, 89
Baptist Chapel, Warrington, 220
Benn's Gardens Chapel, 26
Bethesda Chapel, Hotham Street, 158
Chapel of St Mary, Edmund Street, 25
Dissenters' Chapel, Cockspur Street, 32-33
Dissenters Chapel, Whitechapel, 71
Dr Raffles' Chapel (Great George Street Chapel), 180
Dr Thom's Chapel, Bold Street, 78, 153
Fabius Baptist Chapel, Low Hill, 40, 219, 220–21
Hill Cliffe Baptist Chapel, Cheshire, 220
Hope Hall, 149
in Sir Thomas's Buildings, Dale Street, 35
in Tower of Liverpool, 18
Methodist chapel, Pitt Street, 177
near the Dingle, 169
Newington Chapel, 81
of Blind Asylum, 95
Old Scotch Secession Meeting House, Gloucester Street, 35
Quaker Meeting House, Hackins Hey, 28
Russell Street, 158
Salem Chapel, Russell Street, 158–5
Sandemanian Chapel, Cumberland Street, 35
Sandemanian Chapel, Gill Street, 12
St Joseph's Roman Catholic Chapel, Grosvenor Street, 49
Unitarian Chapel, 148
Wesleyan Chapel, Moss Street, 125
Wesleyan Chapel, Plumbe Street, 2
Chase, Revd. Philander, Bishop of Ohi 50
Chatmoss, 55
Chaucer Street, 44
Cheapside, *formerly* Dig Lane, Dog an Duck Lane, 29, 30, 35
Cheese and Linen Halls, Chester, 166
Cheetham Brow, 129

Cheetham Green *see* Mount Vernon Green
Cheetham's Hill *see* Edge Hill
Cheshire, 29, 32, 40, 45, 121,125, 172, 184, 190, 201, 205, 220
Cheshire ferries, 10-11, 192-6
Chester, 11, 12, 15, 166, 190, 202
Chester, Bishop of, 147
Childwall Street, 107
Cholmondely, Earl of, 211
Chorley family, 57
Chorley Street, 57
Christ Church, Hunter Street, 49, 76, 103, 162
Christian, Phillip, potter, 100, 103
Christian Street, 103, 105, 167
Christie, John, 95
Church Alley, 73
Church Lane, *b/w ill. 13*, 86
Church Street, *b/w ill. 13*, 67, **69–76**, 77, 79, 155, 156, 159, 165, 207, 224
Church Street, Everton *see* Heyworth Street
churches (*see also* chapels)
  All Saints' Church, 50–51
  Christ Church, Hunter Street, 76, 103, 162
  Emmanuel Church, West Derby Road, 114, 115
  Mariner's Church (ship *William*), 180
  Melling Church, 171
  New Jerusalem Church, Russell Street, 159
  Scotch Church, Oldham Street, 33
  Scotch Church, Rodney Street,153
  St Andrew's Church, Heathfield Street, 81
  St Anne's Church, 49, 163, 166
  St Anthony's Church, 47
  St Augustine's Church, Everton, 220
  St Catherine's Church, Russell Street, 158
  St Chrysostom's Church, 114, 224–28
  St Clements' Church, Russell Street, 159
  St George's Church, Derby Square, *b/w ill. 26*, 60, 61, 67
  St George's Church, Everton, 49, 207, 208, 209, 220, 224, 226
  St Helen's Church, Sefton, 8
  St James's Church, Park Road, 180
  St James's Church, West Derby, 51
  St John the Evangelist, Hope Hall, 149
  St John's Church, *b/w ill. 16*, 90, 95
  St Jude's Church, 48, 139
  St Luke's Church, Bold Street, 78
  St Mark's Church, 147
  St Martin's Church, 48–49
  St Mary's Church, Edge Hill, 49, 130, 138
  St Mary's Church, Walton, 6, 8, 52
  St Matthew's Church, 48
  St Michael's Church, 48–49
  St Nicholas' Church, *b/w ills. 2,* 26, **6-9**, 10, 15, 53, 72, 194
  St Paul's Church, *b/w ill. 26,* 26, 150, 179
  St Peter's Church, *b/w ill. 13,* 71, 72
  St Simon's Church, 35
  St Stephen's Church, Byrom Street, *b/w ill. 19*, 41
  St Thomas's Church, Park Lane, *b/w ill. 25*, 132, 178
churchyards (*see also* cemeteries)
  Newington chapelyard, 171
  Scotch Church, 153
  St Anthony's, 48
  St Augustine's, 218
  St Mary's, Walton, 6, 171, 212

St Nicholas', 6, 8, 16, 151, 187
St Peter's, 17, 72
the Circus *see* Adelphi Theatre
Circus Street, 167
Civil War, 15–16, 21, 36, 91, 208, 215–16, 220
Clarence Dock, 10, 23, 188
Clarence, Duke of, 154, 199
Clarendon Rooms, 67
Clark, Mr, barrister, 163
Clarke, William, 22, 55, 207
Clay, Robert, wholesale chemist, 77
Clayton family, 57, 71
Clayton, Sarah, 45, 72
Clayton, William, Mayor (1689-90) and MP for Liverpool, 57, 72
Clayton Square, 71, 90
Clayton's Alley, 11
Cleveland family, 177
Cleveland Square, *formerly* New Square, Price's Square, 176, 177
Club Moor, 219
Cobbler's Close, 210
Cockle, Sergeant, 163
Cockspur Street, 32, 33
Coglan, Thomas, owner of *Liverpool Mercury*, 111, 203
Coke, Thomas Williams, of Holkham, first Earl of Leicester, 154
College Lane, 75, 76, 165
Collegiate Institution, 215
Collingwood, Mr, Jacobite, 97
Collingwood Street, 45
Colquitt, Captain, 187
Colquitt, John, 75
Colquitt Street, 75, 179 *see also* Berry Street
*the Comet,* publication, 48
Commerce Court, 65
Committee of Taste, 150
Common Shore *see* Paradise Street
Commutation Row, 93, 94
Compton House, 72, 73
Comus Street, 43
concert halls
Lord Nelson Street, 85
Philharmonic Hall, 148
Concert Street, 77, 78
Conor, Revd. J. R., incumbent of St Simon's, 35
Cook and Townshend's shops, 40
Cook Street, 56
Cooper, Mrs, owner of Everton Toffee Shop, 214
Cooper, Sir Astley, 151
Cooper's ironmongery warehouse, London Road, 94
Cooper's Row, 40
Coore, Mrs, 179
Copeland Street, 207
Cope's, London Road, 95
Copper Works, 170-71
Copperas Hill, *formerly* Elliot Hill, 69, 79, 81, 82, 83, 84, 96, 100, 126, 15[illegible]
Copperas Works, 81
Cork, Earl of, 57
Corless, Henry, council man, 65
Corn Exchange, 57, 58
Corn Market, Brunswick Street, 58
Cornwallis Street, 179
Corporation *see* Liverpool Corporatio[illegible]
Cosgrove, Thomas, 30
County Court, Liverpool, 89
Cowan, Revd. T., incumbent of St Chrysostom's, 225
Cowper, William, poet, 26
Coxwell, Mr, balloonist, 119
Crabtree Lane *see* Falkner Street
Cranage Hall, Cheshire, 125
Creasey, James, pilot of Pelican, privateer, 204
the Crescent, 61, 67

Cresswell, Justice, MP for Liverpool, 222
Cresswell Street, 222

criminals
Bellingham, John, 179
Dowling and Burns, 18
Harnett family, 46-47
highwaymen, 31, 223-24
Moore family, 31
Mulvey family, 31
robbers, 72, 214-15, 218, 229
Wakefield, Edward Gibbon, 121-22
Croft, Mr, 229
Crompton, Thomas, Nonconformist minister, 169
Cromwell, Oliver, 169, 220
Crookenden, Mr, minister of Salem Chapel, 159
Cropper, James, 79
Cropper, John, 206
Cropper Street, 79
Crosbie, James, Mayor of Liverpool (1753-54 and 1765-66), 81, 147, 173, 211
Crosbie Street, 173
*Cross Keys*, inn, Dale Street, 38
Cross, Mr, landowner, 30, 188
Crosse family, 36, 42
Crosse Hall, 36
Crosse, Humphrey, incumbent of St Nicholas' Church, 7
Crosse, John, 7
Crosse, Sir John, 36
crosses
Everton Cross, 217-18, 230
High Cross, 21, 33, 56
Scotland Road, 47
St Patrick's Cross, 29, 45
White Cross, 5, 19
Crown Street, 88, 125, 126, 148
Croxteth, 14
Croxteth Hall, 210
Croxteth Park, 210
Cubitt, Mr, designer of landing stage, 196
Cumberland, Duke of, 35
Cumberland, 135, 210
Cumberland Street, 35
Cunliffe, Sir Foster, Mayor of Liverpool (1716-17, 1729-30 and 1735-36), 30, 147
Cunliffe Street, 29
Currie, Dr James, 75, 228
Currie, William Wallace, Mayor of Liverpool (1836), 152
Cushman, Miss, actress, 168
Cust, Richard, 197
Custom House, 161, 175, 176, 187, 200
Custom House Dock *see* Old Dock

**D**

D'Altera, Joseph, 150
Daish, William H., architect, 114–15
Dale Street, *b/w ills. 6, 7, 10,* 29, **33–39**, 42, 53, 55, 65, 69, 74, 99, 100, 175
Dalefield, 27
Dalton, Revd. William, incumbent of St Jude's Church, 48
Dannett, Revd. Henry, minister of St John' Church, 95
Dansey, Mr, landowner, 123
Dansie, Mr, merchant, 69, 71
Dansie Street, 123
Daulby, Misses, 121
Daulby, Mr, landowner, 123, 125
Daulby Street, 98, 125, 129
Davies, Miss, later Mrs Wakefield, 121, 122
Davies Street, *b/w ill. 7*
Dawson, James, 155

Dawson, Pudsey, Mayor of Liverpool (1799-1800), 94, 150, 174
de Mora, John, 27
De Quincey, Thomas, 19, 228
de Smithum, John, 169
de Stanley, or Staney, John, 10
de Walley, Alexander, 33
de Walley, Matthew, 33
de Walton, Richard, 33
Deadman's Lane *see* Addison Street
Deaf and Dumb Asylum, 146
Dee, river, 190
Delacroix, Lydia Ann, later Mrs George Perry, 178
Denison, John, 47
Dennison, Mr, churchwarden, 151
Denny, boatman, 192–93
Derby, Earls of *see* Stanley family
Derby Chapel, 76
Derby Hotel, 116
Derby Museum, 19
Derbyshire, 210
Derrick, Mr, 57
Devil's Acre, 32, 186
Dig Lane *see* Cheapside
Dingle, 43, 150, 169, 170, 193
Dismore, Mr, shop-keeper, 77
Dispensary, 37, 74, 129
Dissenters' Chapel ,Cockspur Street, 32-33
Dobb, Mr, 166
Dobson, Richard, treasurer of Bluecoat School, 206
Dock Trustees, 176, 212
docks
  Albert Dock, 162
  Brunswick Dock, 20, 172
  Canning Dock, *formerly* Dry Dock, 188
  Clarence Dock, 10, 23, 188
  Custom House Dock *see* Old Dock
  Dry Dock *see* Canning Dock
  Duke of Bridgwater's Dock, 173, 1
  George's Dock, *col. ill. 1*, *cover ill.* 10, 46, 187, 188
  Graving Dock, 203
  Herculanaeum Dock, 171
  King's Dock, 173
  Old Dock, *formerly* Custom House Dock, 61, 75, **175-76**, 186, 193, 200
  Prince's Dock, 10, 23
  Queen's Dock, 173, 212
  Salthouse Dock, 8, 32, 173, 186, 187, 188
  Waterloo Dock, 188
Dodgson's shop, the Crescent, 61
Dog and Duck Lane *see* Cheapside
*Dog and Duck*, tavern, 29
Dog Kennel Lane *see* Byrom Street
Domeri, Monsieur, prisoner, 24
Domesday Book, 6, 169, 183, 190
Domus beatoe Marie *see* Town Hall
Donison, Mr, builder, 109
Donison Street *see* Phythian Street
Doran's Lane, *b/w ill. 11*
Dover family, 206
Dowling, Sylvester, 18
Downe Street, 43
Dr Pulford's day academy and boardi school, Norton Street, 160
Dr Raffles' Chapel (Great George St Chapel), 180
Dr Thom's Chapel, Bold Street, 78, 1
Drinkwater, James, Mayor of Liverp (1810-11), 78, 178
Drinkwater, Sir George, Mayor of Liverpool (1829-30), 78, 87, 151
Drinkwater potteries, 178
Drummond, Mr, Jacobite, 97
Drury Lane, *formerly* Entwhistle Stre 11, 57

Drury Lane Theatre, 57
Dry Bridge, Fenwick Street, 58
Dry Dock *see* Canning Dock
Dryden Street, 44, 45, 47
*Duchess of Clarence*, ship, 204
duels
between Bolton and Brooks, 126-29
between Carmichael and Brooks, 160
between Grayson and Sparling, 187
Duffin, Mr, 153
Dugdale, Mr, carrier and publican, 9
Duke of Bridgwater's Dock, 173, 195
Duke Street, *formerly* the Way to the Quarry, 22, 25, 26, 58, 78, 171, 174, **178-80**
Dunbar, Sir George, colonial broker, 155
Duncan, Mr, water engineer, 225
Duncan Street *see* Hotham Street
Durandu, Mr, proprietor of Zoological Gardens, 120
Dutton Street, 19
Dwerryhouse's Bath, 23
Dye-House Well, Greetham Street, 178
Dyson family, 206

**E**

Earl, Mr, shipbuilder, 187
Earle, Colonel, 128, 159
Earle, Mr, 228
Earle, William, 206
Earps warehouse, Lord Street, 68
Eastbourne Street, 215
Eastham, 193, 204
Eccleston, Kitty, 45
Edge Hill, *formerly* Cheetham's Hill, 129, **130–46**, 156, 224
Edge Lane, 92
Edge Lane Road *see* Pembroke Place
Edmund Street, *formerly* Mill House Lane, 25, 26
Eldon Place, 31

Elizabeth I, Queen,
Liverpool in reign of, 5, 15, 42, 56, 170, 202, 208
Ellenborough Street, 45
Elliot Hill *see* Copperas Hill
Elliot Street, 89, 90
Ellison, Mr, 229
Ellison, Mrs, *formerly* Harvey, Miss, 82
Elm Street, 129
*Emilie St Pierre*, ship, 201
Emly Street, 110
Emmanuel Church, West Derby Road, 114, 115
Empire Street, 121
Engineers' headquarters, Mason Street, 131
English Civil War *see* Civil War
Entwhistle family, 57
Entwhistle Street *see* Drury Lane
Erskine Street, 107
Esmedune, manor of *see* Toxteth Park
Evans and Co., drapers, London Road, 99
Evans, Captain, commander of *Duchess of Clarence*, 204
Everton, *b/w ill. 27*, 24, 43, 109, 113, 187, **205-30**
Everton Beacon, 206, 207–09
Everton bridewell, 230
Everton Brow, *b/w ill. 28*, 230
Everton Coffee House, 213, 214, 215, 228, 230
Everton Crescent, *formerly* Causey Lane, Loggerhead Lane, *b/w ill. 28*, 167, 206
Everton Cross, 217–18, 230
Everton Hill, 48
Everton Lane *see* Everton Road

Everton Road, formerly Everton Lane, *b/w ill. 21*, 110, 205, 217, 219, 221, 222, 223, 224
Everton Terrace, 206–7, 214, 228
Everton Toffee Shop, 214, 216-17, 222, 230
Everton Valley, 86, 224
Ewart and Rutson, brokers, 162–63
Ewart, Joseph, 84
Ewart, Mr, 206, 212
Ewart, Myers, & Co, Exchange Court, 155
Ewart, W., 228
Ewart, William, 47, 84, 162–63
Ewart, William, broker, 155
Ewbank, Revd., 224, 226
Exchange, 33, 45, 56, 98, 164
Exchange Building, 19
Exchange Buildings, 54, 55, 56
Exchange Court, 155
Exchange Room, 56
Exchange Street East *see* High Street
Excise Office, 75, 176
Eye and Ear Infirmary, 156
Eyes' map of Liverpool (1768), 69, 83
Eyre, Mr Justice, 97
Eyton, Mrs F. J., 227

**F**

Fabius Baptist Chapel, Low Hill, 40, 219, 220–21
Fabius, Dr Daniel, 219–21
Fabius, Hannah (or Mary), sister of Dr Daniel Fabius, 219, 221
Fabius, Mary, mother of Dr Daniel Fabius, 221
Fairclough Lane, 222
Fairhurst, Mr, 162
fairs, 53, 102, 166
Falkner, Edward, High Sheriff of Liverpool (1788), 24
Falkner family, 24
Falkner, Mr, 147–48

Falkner Square, 24, 79, 147
Falkner Street, *formerly* Crabtree Lane, 147
Falkner Terrace, 24
Falkner's Folly *see* Falkner Terrace
Fall Well, 90
Falvey, Mr, publican of *Throstle's Nest*, 47, 48
Farrer, Miss, Quaker schoolmistress, 28
Fawcett and Preston's Iron Foundry, 178
Fells, Captain, 72
Fenwick, Dorothy, *later* Lady Moore, 58
Fenwick, Sir William, of Meldon Hall, 58
Fenwick Court, 57
Fenwick Street, 11, 55, 58, 60
ferries, 11, 70-71,172, **192–97**
*Ferry House*, tavern, 16
Fever Hospital, Brownlow Hill, 40, 15
Fielding, Mr, market gardener and nurseryman, 125
Fielding's nursery, 125, 128
Finch Street, 160
Finch, Mr, 48
Finney Lane, 70
Fire Station, Hatton Garden, 36
fish markets
Chapel Street, 10, 191
the Goree, 10
Great Charlotte Street, 80
James Street, 10
Moor Street, 61
Redcross Street, 10
St John's Market, 10
fish stones *see* fish markets
Fisher, Mr, shipbuilder, 187

Fisher, Revd., pastor of Gerard Street
Baptist chapel, 41
fisheries, 190–92
*Fishing Smack,* public house, 9
Flashes, pond, 29
Flitcroft, Seth, 56
Floating Bath, 202–03
Folly Fair, 94, 96, 102
Folly Gardens, 103
Folly Lane, 102, 103, 104, 105, 224 *see also* Brunswick Road
Folly Tavern, 103
Fontenoy Street, 30, 36, 39, 40
Foote, Maria*, later* Countess of Harrington, 170
Formby, 5, 10, 32
Formby, Margery, 65
Forrest's glass warehouses, 88
Forshaw, H., proprietor of *Black Horse* and *Rainbow*, High Street, 108
Forster, William, headmaster of Bluecoat School, 165
the Fort, 188
Foster, Dr, plant collector, 146
Foster, John, 176
Four Lane Ends, Everton, 218
Fox Street, *formerly* Trinket Street, 166
Frazer Street, 105, 160
Frederick Street, 35
Free Public Library, 81, 103
French Prison *see* Borough Gaol, Great Howard Street
Friends' Institute, 104
Frodsham, Thomas, incumbent of St Nicholas' Church, 7
Frog Lane *see* Whitechapel
Furness, Mrs, confectioner, Church Alley, 73

**G**

Gadsby, Revd. John, of Manchester, 50
Gallows Field, 40
Gallows Mill, *b/w ill. 17*, 97, 102
*Gallows Mill*, public house, 93, 96
gardens
  Botanic Garden, Edge Lane, 146
  Botanic Garden, Myrtle Street, 146
  Botanic Gardens, Great Homer Street, 91
  Folly Gardens, 103
  Great George Square Garden, 98
  Ranelagh Gardens, 82-83, 103
  Spring Garden, 180-81
  Strawberry Gardens, 225
  Tower gardens, 16
Garston, 169, 174, 191
Garston Creek, 185, 193
Garston Salt Works, 185, 186
Garswood, 210
Gas Company, 36
Gascoigne, General, 132
Gascoyne family, 129
Gascoyne, Bamber, the elder, MP for Barking, 230
Gascoyne, Bamber, the younger, MP for Liverpool, 230
Gascoyne, General, 230
Gascoyne, Mrs Bamber, of Childwall, *formerly* Miss Green, 230
Gateacre, 41
Gaunt, John of, Duke of Lancaster, 7
Gay Street, 43
Gaythread, William, merchant, 11
*Gentleman's Magazine*, 70
George III, King
  statue, 97–98, 180
*George*, inn, 38
George Street, *b/w ill. 4, see also*York Street
George's Dock, *col. ill. 1*, *cover ill.*, 10, 46, 187, 188
George's Hill, 206

George's Landing Stage, 195
Gerard Street, 41, 42, 105
Gerrard, Dr, maker of recipe for Everton toffee, 216
Gibbon, Mr, 163
Gibbon's Bakery, Fenwick Street, 60
Gibson, John, sculptor, 74
Gibson, Mr, landlord of *Folly Tavern,* 103
*Gibson's Coffee House*, tavern, 103
Gildart, James, the elder, Mayor of Liverpool (1750-51), 180
Gildart, James, the younger, Mayor of Liverpool (1786-87), 180
Gildart, Mr, 45, 156
Gildart, Mrs, 160
Gildart, Richard, Mayor (1714-15, 1731-32, 1736-37) and MP for Liverpool, 45
Gildart Street, 105
Gildart's Gardens, 45
Gilead House, Kensington, 109, 123
Gill, Mr, landowner, 123
Gill Moss, 219
Gill Street, *b/w ill. 22*, 123
Gill Street Market, 102, 123
Gladstone, John, 228
Gladstone, Robert, 150
Gladstone, Sir John, 150
glass works, Glasshouse Weint, 29
Glasshouse Weint, 29
Gleave, Dr, 222, 223
Gleave Street, 222, 223
Glegg, Joshua, Mayor of Liverpool (1748-49), 54
Gloucester Place, 107, 108, 212
Gloucester Street, 35, 69, 79, 85, 99, 109
*Golden Fleece*, inn, Dale Street, 37, 38, 82
*Golden Lion*, inn, Dale Street, 37
*Golden Lion*, whaler, 199–200
Goldsmith Street, 121
Golightly family, 84
Goold's outfitters, London Road, 99
Gore, John, 77
the Goree, 10, 20
Goree Causeway, 187
Goree Piazzas, *col. ill. 1*
Goree warehouses, 19
*Gore's Advertiser*, 61, 83
*Gore's Directory* (1774), 38
Gorse Field, 40
the Gorsey, 40
Gothic Hall, Marble Street, 74
Gough's Hotel, 194
Gouldie, Dr, 151
Government Offices, Canning Place, 176
Gradwell Street, 75
Graham, Mrs, 18
Graham, Sir James, 135
Granby, Marquis of, 202
Grant family, 153
Graving Dock, 203
Grayson, Edward, shipbuilder, 187
Great Charlotte Street, 79, 80
Great Comyn, 79
Great Crosshall Street, *formerly* New Crossehall Street, 42
Great George Square, 180
Great George Square Garden, 98
Great George Street, 111, 116, 131, 1 178, 180
Great George Street Chapel (Dr Raffl Chapel), 180
Great Heath, 36, 39, 64, 65
Great Homer Street, 48, 91, 166
Great Howard Street, 24, 25
Great Nelson Street, 45
Great Newton Street, 96, 123
Great Oxford Street, 45

Greaves, Molyneux and Co., brokers, 84
Grecian Terrace, 229
Green family, 230
Green, Guy, 101
Green, Isaac, solicitor, 230
Green, Mr, balloonist, 119
*Green Man Still*, 94
Greenfield, Edge Hill, 130
Greenshields family, 112
Greenside, *b/w ill. 20*
Greetham Street, 178
Gregory, John, chaplain, 11
Gregson, Matthew, author of *Gregson's Fragments*, 74, 164
Gregson, Mr, 211, 212, 221
Grinfield Street, 129, 131, 140
Groom's Stationers, Lord Street, 68
Grosvenor Street, 49
Grove Street, 147, 148, 156

**H**

Hacking, John, 28
Hacking's House, 29
Hackins Hey, 28
Hadwen family, 206
Hadwen, Joseph, 165–66
Hadwen, Misses, 165
Haigh and Co., builder, 98
Halcyon Cottage, Low Hill, 108
*Half Way House*, Everton Lane, 222, 223
Hall Lane, 129
Hallsall, Mr, 218
Halsall family, 210
Halton Castle, 208
Hammerton, Mr, 151
Hammond, Mr, actor, 75
Hammond, W.J., 168
Hangfield Lane *see* Breckfield Road North
Hanover Street, *formerly* King Street, 66-67, 71, 75, 76, 165
Hardman, Mrs, 150, 179
Hardman Street, 95, 150, 151
Hardwar, Mr, 209
Hardwick Street, 126
Harford Street, 154
Hargreaves, Mr, builder, 129
Harnett family, 46–47
Harnett, Julia, 46–47
Harnett, Mr, chandler, Richmond Row, 46
Harper, Miss, *later* Mrs Brandreth, 229
Harper, Mr, 107, 214
Harper, William, Mayor of Liverpool (1804-05), 215, 228–29, 230
Harper Street, 107
Harrington, Earls of, 170
Harrington, new town, 170
Harrington Street, *formerly* Castle Hey, 66, 101
Harris, Mr, second to Colonel Bolton, 128
Harrison, Miss, of Cranage Hall, Cheshire, later Mrs Thomas Oakes, 125
Harrison, Mr, owner of *Rats' Castle*, 107
Hartley, Jesse, engineer, 87, 176
Harvey family, 82
Harvey, Miss, *later* Mrs Ellison, 82
Harvey, Mr, 55
Hatton Garden, 29, 30, 36
Hatton, Mr, 29
Hausburg, Mr, 73
Hay Market, 54, 91, 101
Hayes, George, 214
Hayes, Mr, 218
Heathcote, Sir William, 8
Heathfield Street, 80, 81
Hellewell's premises, Rose Street, 89

Hemans, Mrs, *formerly* Browne, Felicia, 167, 179
Henderson, Cornelius, artist, 131, 137, 143
Henderson, Mr, first incumbent of St Paul's, 26
Herculaneum Dock, 171
Herculaneum Pottery, 170–71
Herdman, Mr, 210
Herdman's *Ancient Liverpool*, 101, 218
Hesketh, John, 38
Hesketh, William, Mayor of Liverpool (1783-84), 5
Heywood family, 153
Heywood's Bank, 56, 124
Heyworth family, 213
Heyworth Street *formerly* Church Street, Higher Lane, 213, 218, 222
Hibbert Street, 207
High Cross, 21, 33, 56
High Cross Market, 56
High Street, *formerly* Jugglar Street, 11, 54, 61, 108, 145
Higher Lane *see* Heyworth Street
Hilbre Island, 81
Hillcliffe, Cheshire, 219–20
Hillcoat, Revd. Dr, incumbent of St Matthew's Church, 48
Hime and Son, Church Street, 73
Hime, Edward, 73
Hime, Humphrey, 73
Hime's Music Warehouse, 73
Hinde, John, 213
*Hindes,* public house, 8
Hobb's hatter's shop, London Road, 94
Hockenhall Alley, *formerly* Molyneux Weint, 29, 34, 35
Hockenhall family, of Cheshire, 29
Hodgson, David, Mayor of Liverpool (1845-46), 206
Hodgson, Mr, auctioneer, 75
Holborn, 186
Holloway, Mr, proprietor of Sanspareil Theatre, 80
Holme, Mr, 213
Holroyd, Mr, barrister, 163
Hook, Theodore, 170
Hope Hall, 149, 154
Hope Street, 91, 95, 110, 147, 148, 149
Hope, Martha, sister of William, 110
Hope, Mr, 206
Hope, William, merchant, 110, 148
Horatio Street, 45
Horner, Revd. Mr, 84
Horner's yard, 202
Horrox, Jeremiah, mathematician and astronomer, 169
Horsfall, C., 206
hospitals
  Bluecoat Hospital, 71, 129
  Eye and Ear Infirmary, 156
  Fever Hospital, Brownlow Hill, 40, 157
  Infirmary, Shaw's Brow, 58, 85, 91 109, 129
  Northern Hospital, 19
  Seamen's Hospitals, Shaw's Brow,
hotels *see also* public houses
  Adelphi Hotel, 82, 83, 84, 194
  Bates Hotel, 68
  Bull Hotel, Dale Street, 36
  Derby Hotel, 116
  Gough's Hotel, 194
  Queen's Hotel, 90
  Stork Hotel, 90
  Temperance Hotel, 72
  Tranmere Hotel, 194
  Washington Hotel, 90
  Waterloo Hotel, 77
Hotham Street, 82, 94, 95, 96, 158
Houghton, John, 36, 49-50, 162
Houghton, Mr, 214

Houlston, Dr, 5, 181
House of Correction, Brownlow Hill, 40, 157–58
Howard, John, philanthropist, 16-17, 179, 188
Howard, Mr, 156
Howard, Ralph, 6
Hoylake, 12, 32
Huddlestone, Mr, benefactor of Bluecoat School, 165
Hughes, Mr, 84, 158
Hughes, Richard, Mayor of Liverpool (1756-57), 81
Hughes' pawnbroker's shop, 96
hulks, off Rock Ferry, *col. ill. 3*
Hull, Revd. Edward, chaplain to Blind Asylum, 131, 137, 142
Hunter, Jonathan *see* Jonathan Hunter's house, Water Street
Hunter, Mr, Jacobite, 97
Hunter, Mr, tobacco merchant, 155
Hunter Street, 43, 76, 103, 155
Hurd, Joshua, incumbent of St Nicholas' Church, 7
Hurst Street, 173, 183
Huskisson, William, MP for Liverpool, 53, 87, 151, 176
Hyde, Mr, 87
Hygeia Street, 121, 224

**I**

Ince, 175
Ince Blundell, 20
Infirmary, Shaw's Brow, 58, 85, 91, 109, 129
Ingram, Captain, 177
inns *see* public houses
Ireland, 30, 84, 191
Ireland, Sir Gilbert, 230
Irk, river, 189
Irwell, river, 189
Isle of Man, 13, 191
Islington, **99–105**, 160
Islington Flags, 100
Islington Terrace, 100, 103-04

**J**

Jackson, Mr, 172
Jacobites, 97
James, G.P.R., 19
James, Mr, railway engineer, 87
James, Mrs, landowner, 30
James, Roger, 58
James Street, 23, 58, 187
Japha's Vaults, Rupert's Lane, 228
Jefferson Street, 207
Jevons, Mr, iron merchant, 77
Jews' cemetery, Cumberland Street, 35
Jews' cemetery, Oakes Street, 125
Joe Boke's House, Church Street, 70
John, King, 169, 181
John Street, 37, 66, 72, 74, 168
John the Irischman, rebuilt Tower of Liverpool, 13
Johnson, Captain Thomas, 177
Johnson, Revd., Baptist minister of St Stephen's, 41
Johnson, Sir Thomas, 34, 41
Johnson, Thomas, 7
Johnson, Thomas, Mayor of Liverpool (1695), 34
Johnson, Thomas, Mayor of Liverpool (1766-67), 181
Johnson Street, 30
Johnson's, chemists, Church Street, 165
Johnson's timber yard, London Road, 99
Joliffe, Mr, toll-taker, 43
Jonathan Hunter's house, Water Street, 11
Jones, Revd. Thomas, originator of St Mark's Church, 147

Judge's House, St Anne Street, *b/w ill. 24*, 162
Jugglar Street *see* High Street
Juvenal Street, 44

**K**

Kelly, Mr, 214
Kennyon's, Breck Road, 221
Kent East Indiaman, 180
Kent, Elizabeth, later Lady Murray, 180
Kent, Mrs Elizabeth, 174, 191
Kent, Richard, merchant and shipowner, 147, 174, 179–80, 191
Kent Street, 178, 179
Kenyon College, Gambier, 50
Key Street, 31
Kilshaw, Councillor, 121
Kilshaw, John, town councillor, 228
Kilshaw, Mr, 109
Kilshaw Street, 121
Kind's Bazaar, 70
*King of Edge Hill see* Williamson, Joseph
King Street, 66–67
King Street Lane, 70
*King's Arms*, inn, 56
King's Dock, 173
Kirkdale, 28, 45, 205, 221
Kirkdale Prison, 49
Kirkdale Road, 44, 45, 166
Knight Street, 150
Knot's Hole, Aigburth Road, 187, 193
Knowles, Alice, 230
Knowsley, 14, 16
Knowsley Hall, 210
Knowsley Park, 210

**L**

*L'Equité*, French merchantman, 201
*La Liberté*, ship, 210
Lace, Ambrose, 171
Lace, Joshua, 75
Ladies' Charity, 129
Ladies' Walk, Duke Street, 22, 179
Ladies' Walk, Old Hall Street, 22, 24, 27, 188
*Lady Granby*, ship, 202
Lady Marie Haule *see* Town Hall
Lamb, Charles, 228
Lambert, Daniel, 153
Lancashire and Yorkshire Railway, 32
Lancashire and Yorkshire Railway Company, 31, 48
Lancashire Militia, 127
Lancelot's Hey, 9, 25, 188
Lassells, Mr, dancing master, 163
Lathom, Sir Thomas, of Lathom, 13
Lavan Street, 113
Lawrence, Charles, 84
Lawrence, George Hall, 84
Lawrence, Henry, Commissioner in Bankruptcy, 151
Lawton Street, *b/w ill. 15*, 79
Layland, Thomas, Mayor of Liverpool (1798-99, 1814-15 and 1820-21), 18
le Clerk, Adam, 10
le Clerk, William, 10
le Mercer, Robert, 27
Leather Lane, 28
Leece, Eleanor, *later* Mrs Drinkwater, 78, 178
Leece, William, merchant, 78, 178
Leece Street, 77, 78, 150, 178
Leeds - Liverpool Canal, 22, 25
Leeds Street, 26, 27
*Legs of Man*, 96
Leicester, Earl of, 154
Leicestershire Militia, Colonel of, 201
Leigh family, 8
Leigh, John, 59
Leigh, Wilkinson, and Kerrison, 99

Leland, John, 14
Lewin, Dr, 163
Lewin's school, 148
libraries
Apprentices' Library, 69
Free Public Library, 81, 103
Liverpool Library, John Street, 72
Lyceum Library, 77, 162
Medical Library, 75, 162
Roscoe's library, 154
St Peter's Church, 72
Licensed Victuallers' Association, 115
Licensed Victuallers' Asylum, St Anne's Street, 114
Licensed Victuallers' Asylum, West Derby Road, 113, 114-15
Lime Street, *formerly* Back Lane, Limekiln Lane, *b/w ill. 16, col. ill. 5*, 45, 79, **85-91**
Lime Street Station, 85, 86
Limekiln Lane *see* Lime Street
limekilns, 80, 85
Linen Hall, 166
Liscard, 157
Lister, Revd., of Baptist Chapel, Rose Street, 89
Literary Society, 71
Litt, Mr, 212
Little Bird Street, 199
Little Woolton Street, 126
Littledale, Thomas, Mayor of Liverpool, (1851-52), 114
Liver Drapery, 75
Liver Theatre, 75
Liverpool and Manchester Railway, 86
*Liverpool Arms Inn*, Castle Street, 56
Liverpool Baths, 22-23
Liverpool Blues, 211
Liverpool Castle *see* Castle (of Liverpool)
*Liverpool Chronicle*, 67, 81
Liverpool Corporation
entertainment by, 15
gifts to, 14, 16, 65
payments by, 7, 17, 43, 188
property of, 16, 23, 59, 60, 64-65, 78, 88, 91, 97, 102, 125, 143, 157, 174, 176, 191
transactions of, 81, 91, 153, 156, 176
Liverpool County Court, 89
*Liverpool Daily Post*, offices, Lord Street, 65, 67
Liverpool Fire and Life Buildings, Dale Street, 38
Liverpool Gas Company, 119
Liverpool Humane Society, 5
Liverpool Hunt, 132
Liverpool Hunt Club, 43
*Liverpool Journal*, offices, Lord Street, 65, 67
Liverpool Lane *see* South Castle Street
Liverpool Library, John Street, 72
Liverpool Light Horse, 80
*Liverpool Mercury*, 69, 90, 154, 193, 203
Liverpool Salt Works, 182–86
Liverpool Spa, mineral spring, 5, 181
*Liverpool Standard*, 61–63, 140
Liverpool telegraph, 6
*Liverpool Times*, 61
Liverpool Town Council, 111
Livesley, Dr, 230
Lodge Lane *see* St George's Hill
Lodges, Toxteth Park, 169, 180
Loggerhead Lane *see* Everton Crescent.
*Loggerheads Revived*, public house, Richmond Row, 167
London, 26, 38, 87, 92, 122, 147, 154, 175
London and North-Western Railway Company, 186

London and North-Western Railway Station *see* Lime Street Station
London Road, *formerly* the Way to Warrington, *b/w ills. 17, 23, col. ill.4,* 82, **91–99**, 102, 104, 123, 126, 159, 160, 180
Longbotham, Mr, engineer of Leeds - Liverpool Canal, 25
Lord Molyneux Street, 69
Lord Nelson Street, 79, 85, 96
Lord Street, *formerly* Lord's Lane, Molyneux Lane, *b/w ills. 11, 12,* **64–68**, 69, 77, 92
Lord's Lane *see* Lord Street
Love Lane, 66, 67, 126, 128, 222
Low Hill, *b/w ill. 21*, 41, 93, 107, 108, 219, 221, 222, 224
Low Hill Baptists, 221
Low Hill Cemetery *see* Necropolis
Low Hill Workhouse, 107
Lowe, Mary, *later* Mrs William Meadows, 52
Lower Baker Street, 110
Lower Castle Street, 54
Lower Lane, *see* Netherfield Road
Lower Lodge, Toxteth Park, 169
Lowndes, Mr, first judge of Liverpool County Court, 89
Lowrie, Mr, 214
Lowther family, 151
Lucas's Repository, 80
Lumber Street, 31
Lunardi, Vincenzo, balloonist, 76
Lunatic Asylum, Brownlow Hill, 157
Lunatic Asylum, Lime Street 90, 91
Lune, river, 190
Lunt, R., 230
Lyceum Library, 77, 162
Lyceum News Room, 77
Lydia Anne Street, 178
Lynedoch Street, 115
Lyons, Mr, keeper of the Borough Gaol, Water Street, 17
Lyons, Mrs, 17
Lyons, Revd. John, 51

**M**

Macadam, 155-56
Macclesfield, Earl of, 60
Macfie's sugar house, Bachelor's Weint, 29
Macgregor, Mr, 212
Machell, Mr, owner of roperies, 77
Macnaught, Revd. John, 224–25, 226–28
Maddocks, Mr, landowner, 148
Maguire Street, 31
Maiden's Green, 26, 27
Manchester, 97, 122, 190, 192, 203
Mander and Allender, shop, Castle Street, 54
Manesty, John, merchant, 26
Manesty Lane, 26, 69, 165
Manifold, Dr, 151
Mansfield, Mr, potter, 171
Mansfield Street, *b/w ill.24*
maps, 103, 190
  Chadwick's (1725), 79
  Eyes' (1768), 69, 83
  for British Medical Association meeting (1859), *b/w ill. 1*
  Ptolemy's, 189, 190
Marble Street, 71, 74
March, Evan, council man, 65
*Marchioness of Granby*, ship, 202
Marine Society, 129
Mariner's Church (ship *William*), 180
markets (*see also* fish markets)
  cattle market, Chapel Street, 86
  cattle market, Lime Street, 85
  cattle market, St James's Place, 86
  Church Lane, 86

Gill Street, 102, 123
High Cross Market, 56
Lime Street, 86
Netherfield Road, 86
Old Islington Market, 102
Old Swan, 86
Potato Market, 60
Pownall Square, 32
Richmond Row Market, 43
St George's Market, 61, 67
St James's Market, 180
St John's Market, 10, 58, 80
St Martin's Market, 43, 45
White Cross Market, 5
Wholesale Vegetable Market, 103
Marsh, Richard, 30
Marshall, Mr, 80
*Marshall's Moving Panorama*, 80
Martindale's Hill *see* Mount Pleasant
Marybone, *formerly* the Way to Ormskirk, 30, 31, 44
Maryland Street, 151, 155
Mason, Edward, 130
Mason, Miss, 130–31, 140
Mason Street, *col. ill. 2*, 130–46
Mather's Dam, 127, 172
Mathews, Dr, 50
Matthews Brothers', printers, 70
Maury, James, American Consul in Liverpool, 152
Maury, Lieutenant, 152
May Lane, 154
Mayer's Museum, 100, 200
Mayman, Mr, publican, 120
Mayors of Liverpool
Aspinall, Sir James (Mayor in 1834-35), 109, 152–53, 180
Ayndoe, Thomas (Mayor in 1655-56), 21
Baker, Peter (Mayor in 1795-96), 174
Bixteth, Thomas (Mayor in 1635-36 and 1642-43), 31
Brancker, Sir Thomas (Mayor in 1830-31), 151
Campbell, George (Mayor in 1763-64), 210–11
Clayton, William (Mayor in 1689-90), 57, 72
Crosbie, James (Mayor in 1753-54 and 1765-66), 81, 147, 211, 173
Cunliffe, Sir Foster (Mayor in 1716-17, 1729-30 and 1735-36), 30, 147
Currie, William Wallace (Mayor in 1836), 152
Dawson, Pudsey (Mayor in 1799-1800), 94, 150, 174
Drinkwater, James (Mayor in 1810-11), 78, 178
Drinkwater, Sir George (Mayor in 1829-30), 78, 87, 151
Gildart, James, the elder (Mayor in 1750-51), 180
Gildart, James, the younger (Mayor in 1786-87), 180
Gildart, Richard (Mayor in 1714-15, 1731-32, 1736-37)), 45
Glegg, Joshua (Mayor in 1748-49), 54
Harper, William (Mayor in 1804-05), 215, 228-29, 230
Hesketh, William, (Mayor in 1783-84), 5
Hodgson, David (Mayor in 1845-46), 206
Hughes, Richard (Mayor in 1756-57), 81
Johnson, Thomas (Mayor in 1695), 34
Johnson, Thomas (Mayor in 1766-67), 181

Layland, Thomas (Mayor in 1798-99, 1814-15 and 1820-21), 180
Littledale, Thomas (Mayor in 1851-52), 114
Nicholson, William (Mayor in 1813-14), 164, 167
Porter, Thomas Colley (Mayor in 1827-28), 161–62, 176
Pownall, William (Mayor in 1767-68), 32, 187
Robinson, Nicholas (Mayor in 1828-29), 161
Sandbach, Samuel (Mayor in 1831-32), 161, 162
Seckerston, Ralph (Mayor in 1550-51), 15
Shaw, John (Mayor in 1794-95 and 1800-01), 99–100
Sparling, John (Mayor in 1790-91), 173, 211-12
Spencer, Lawrence (Mayor in 1759-60), 5
Stanley, James, Lord Strange, seventh Earl of Derby (Mayor in 1625-26), 15
Stanley, James, tenth Earl of Derby (Mayor in 1734-35), 16
Stanley, William, sixth Earl of Derby (Mayor in 1603-04), 170
Williamson, John (Mayor in 1761-62), 9
Wright, John (Mayor in 1816-17), 163
McCartney, Dr, 155, 228
McConkey, Revd. Andrew, minister of All Saints, 51
McDowall, Mr, 112
McGee, Mr, attorney, 228
McNeile, Revd. Hugh, Dean of Ripon, 206
Meadow Street, 51
Meadows, William, 51–52
Medical Library, 75
Medley, Revd. Samuel, Baptist ministe[r], 41
Meldon Hall, 58
Melling Church, 171
Members of Parliament *see* MPs for Liverpool
*Mentor*, privateer, 174
Mercantile and Exchange Bank, 56
Merchants' Coffee House, Old Churchyard, 75, 76
the Mere, Everton *see* St Domingo Pit
Mere Lane, 209, 229
Mere Stones, Everton boundary stones, 109
Meritt and Wright, booksellers, Castle Street, 228
Mersey *see* River Mersey
Mersey Bowmen, archery ground, 49
Mersey Lane, 183
Mersey Street, 173, 175, 182, 187
Mersey tunnels, 196
*Mersey*, privateer, 201
Methodist chapels *see* chapels
Middle Row, Holborn, 186
Mile End, 45
Mile House, 24, 45
Mile Lane, 24
Miles, Mr, 87, 88
Mill House Lane *see* Edmund Street
Mill Lane, *b/w ill. 18*, 92, 102, 105, 10[illegible] 113, 223, 224, 225 *see also* Brunswick Road
Mill Place, *b/w ill. 18*
*Mill*, public house, 96
*Mill Stone and Castle*, inn, Dale Stree[t], 38
Milne Street *see* Old Hall Street
Milners' Fire Proof Safe Warehouse, 6[illegible]
Milners' Safe Works, 69

Milton Street, 42, 44
Mint, 46
Mitchell Place, 89
Molly Bushell's Toffee Shop, Everton, 216-17, 222
Molyneux, Anthony, broker, 84
Molyneux family, 8, 14, 65, 82, 169–70
  Molyneux, Sir Richard (of Agincourt), 13, 14
  Molyneux, Sir William, 28
  Molyneux, Sir Richard, bart., 170
  Molyneux, Lord Caryl, third Viscount, 64
  Molyneux, Charles William, first Earl of Sefton, 169, 170, 172
  Molyneux, Lady Isabella, Countess of Sefton, *formerly* Lady Harrington, 170
  Molyneux, William Philip, second Earl of Sefton, 87, 124
Molyneux Lane *see* Lord Street
Molyneux's warehouses, Lancelot's Hey, 9
Montague, Baron, 97
Montgomery, James, poet, 177
Monument Place, 123
Moor Fields *see* Moorfields
Moor Place, 123
Moor Street, 10, 27, 57, 59, 61, 187 *see also* Tithebarn Street
Moorcroft, Sylvester, 175
Moore family, 21, 27, 31
Moore, Sir Edward, 9, 21, 28, 29, 36, 56, 57, 58, 126, 172
Moorfields, 29
Moorfields School, 7
Mordyke Fort, 6
Mordyke House, 5
Mornington Terrace, 147
Morrias, Thomas, proprietor of *Pontacks*, Water Street, 108
Moss Lake, 148
Moss Lake Fields, 64, 86, 126, 148
Moss Street, 104, 125
Mosslake Brook, 126, 156
Mossley Hill, 125, 174
*Mother Red Cap's house*, Seacombe, public house, 194
Mount Pleasant, *formerly* Martindale's Hill, 69, 80, 149, 151, 152, 154, 155, 156
Mount Street, 151
Mount Vernon, 129
Mount Vernon Green, *formerly* Cheetham Green, 129
Mount Vernon Hall, 129
Mount Vernon Street, 129
Mount Zion *see* St James's Mount
MPs for Liverpool
  Bailey, Lawrence, 12
  Canning, George, 53, 150
  Cardwell, Edward, 151
  Clayton, William, 57, 72
  Cresswell, Justice, 222
  Gascoyne, Bamber, the younger, 230
  Gildart, Richard, 45
  Huskisson, William, 53, 87, 151, 176
Mullineux family *see* Molyneux family
Mullineux, James, 129
Mulock, Dinah, later Mrs Craik, authoress of *John Halifax, gentleman*, 71
Mulock, Thomas, 71
Mulvey family, 31
Muncaster, Mr, bookseller and stationer, 73
Municipal Buildings, Dale Street, *b/w ill. 7*
Municipal Reform Bill, 108
Murphy, Mrs, 97
Murray, Lord Henry, brother to Duke of Atholl, 180

Murray, Rear Admiral, 153
museums
Bullock's Museum, 70
Derby Museum, 19
Mayer's Museum, 100, 200
Seaman's Museum, 116
music halls
Bold Street, 50, 153
Concert Street, 78
Mutual Protection Society, 172
Myers, William, 209
Myrtle Street, 88, 89, 146

**N**

National Bank, 56
Naylor, Mr, merchant, 180
Necropolis, *b/w ill. 21*, 106, **110-12**, 113, 116, 223, 225
Neil, Hugh, founder of Eye and Ear Infirmary, 156
Neild, James, philanthropist, 17, 40, 157–58, 188–89
Neilson, W., 228
Nelson, Horatio, Admiral Lord, 45, 210
Netherfield Lane, 230
Netherfield Road, *formerly* Lower Lane, 86, 206, 213, 222, 230
New Crossehall Street *see* Great Crosshall Street
New Exchange, 19
New Ferry, 201
New Jerusalem Church, Russell Street, 159
New Quay, 6, 10, 187
New Scotland Road *see* Scotland Road
New Square *see* Cleveland Square
New Town, 175
Newington, 77
Newington Bridge, 77, 128
Newington Chapel, 81
Newington chapelyard, 171
Newton, Revd. John, hymn-writer, 26
Nicholson, William, Mayor of Liverpo (1813-14), 164, 167
Nile Street, 180
Nixon and Thew, Castle Street, 55
Norfolk Street, 172
Norman, Robert, 156
Norman Street, 98
North and South Wales Bank, 60
North Crescent, 61
North John Street, *formerly* John Stree 66
North Shore, 43
North Street, 30
North Western Bank, Dale Street, 39
Northern Hospital, 19
Northwich, 182, 190
Norton Street, 94, 99, 160
Nova Scotia, 187

**O**

Oakes, Thomas, chemist, 125
Oakes Street, 125
Observatory, 148
*Odd House*, Breck Road, 31, 219, 221
Oddfellows' Hall, St Anne Street, 114
Ogwen Street, 113
Okell, Mr, landowner, 178
Okell, Mr, 229
*Old Angel*, inn, Dale Street, 38
Old Churchyard, 75
Old Dock, *formerly* Custom House Dock, 61, 75, **175–76**, 186, 193, 2
Old Dock Gut, 192, 193
Old Forum, Marble Street, 71
Old Hall, 21-22
Old Hall Street, *formerly* Milne Street Peppard Street, *b/w ill. 4*, **20–27**, 1
Old Haymarket, 36, 91, 100
Old Islington Market, 102
Old Ropery, 57, 58, 59

Old Scotch Secession Meeting House, Gloucester Street, 35
Old Sessions House, *b/w ill. 2*
*Old Style House*, tavern, 8
Old Swan, 86, 222
Old Swan Glass Works, 210
Oldham Street, 33
Olive Street, 91
*Olney Hymns* (Newton and Cowper), 26
Orford Hall, near Warrington, 186
Orford Street, 186
Ormond Street, *b/w ill. 4*
Ormskirk, 30, 37, 38, 92, 95
Otterspool, 170
Otterspool Railway Station, 169
Overton, Mr, merchant, 163
Oxford Street, 148, 156

**P**

Paddington, 129, 130
Paradise Street, *formerly* Common Shore, *b/w ill. 13*, 69, 70, 71, 86, 186
Parish of Liverpool, 72
Park, Mr, first treasurer, Liverpool County Court, 89
Park Coffee House *see Pine Apple Tavern*
Park Lane, *formerly* the Road to the Park, *b/w ill. 25*, 174, 175, 178, 186
Parke, Mr, 211
Parker Street, 74
Parker, Mr, proprietor of Shaw's Brow well, 101
Parkfield *see* Alexandra Drive
Parkinson, J. and J., carriers, 38
Parks, Dr, 77, 128
Parliament Fields, 126
Parliament Street, 23, 147, 169, 170, 180–81
Parr Street, 58, 133, 179
Parr, Mr, 75, 158, 179
Patrick's Cross, 45
Paul's Square, 25
*Peacock*, public house, 169
Pearse, Thomas, 156
Pearson, Miss, 84
Pearson, Mr, minister of St Catherine's Church, Russell Street, 158
Pease family, 87
Peck, Watson, 112
*Pelican*, privateer, 204
Pellew Street, 96
Pemberton's Alley, 11
Pembroke Place, *formerly* Edge Lane Road and Wavertree Road, *b/w ill.22*, 123–30
Pembroke Road *see* West Derby Street
Pembroke Street, *b/w ill. 22*
Pendle Hill, 208
Pendleton, Mr, 214
Penketh Common, 211
Pennington family, potters, 100
Pennington, James, 100
Pennington, John, the elder, 100
Pennington, John, the younger, 100
Pennington, Seth, 100
Peppard Street *see* Old Hall Street
Percival, Spencer, Prime Minister, 179
Percival, William, council man, 65
Perry, George, foundry manager, 178
Perry, Lydia Ann, *formerly* Delacroix, Lydia Ann, 178
Peters' Lane, *formerly* Peter Street, 165
Phenwych Street *see* Fenwick Street
Phibbs, Captain, landowner in Ireland, 84
Phibbs, Mrs, *formerly* Miss Renshaw, 84
Philharmonic Hall, 148
Phithian, John, 109
Phoenix fire engine, 198
Phoenix Fire Office, 155

Phoenix Street *see* Fenwick Street
photographic studio, St James's Mount, 181-82
Phythian family, of Lancashire, 109
Phythian, Mr, publican, 109
Phythian Street, 107, 108, 109, 113
Picton, Sir James, architect, 12
pier, 188
Pier Head, 189, 204
Pier Head Baths, *b/w ill. 26*
*Pier Head Parson see* Cardwell, Revd.
Pilgrim House, 76
*Pilgrim*, privateer, 210
Pilgrim, property, 210
*Pine Apple Tavern*, 169
Pinfold, Everton, 209
Pinfold Lane, 27, 30
Pinfold, York Street, 178
Pitt Street, 177
Platt, Mr, organist to Blind Chapel, 95
Plumbe, Mr, landowner, 188
Plumbe Street, 26, 48
Plumpton family, 222
Plumpton, James, 116
Plumpton, Mr, 107, 110, 114, 205, 224
Plumpton, Samuel, 222
Plumpton Terrace, 205, 222
Plumpton's Hollow, 116
Podmore, John, 100
Police Offices, Hatton Garden, 36
police station, George's Dock, 187
*Polly Tittle's*, public house, 98
*Pontacks*, Water Street, 75, 108, 211
Pool Lane *see* South Castle Street
Pool of Liverpool, 36, 61, 64, 65, 69, 79, 92, 175
Pool river, 36, 39, 68, 69
Pooley's foundry, Old Haymarket, 100
Porter, Thomas Colley, Mayor of Liverpool (1827-28), 161–62, 176
Post Office, 74, 176
Post Office Place, 74, 75
Potato Market, 60
Pothouse Lane, *later* Campbell Street, 178, 183
Potter, William, 206
potteries, **99–101**, 193
  Barnes' potteries, 100
  Chaffers' potteries, 100
  Christian's potteries, 100
  Drinkwater potteries, 178
  Herculaneum Pottery, 170-71
  Pennington's potteries, 100
  Shaw's potteries, 99-100
pound, Pinfold Lane, 30
Powder House, 157
Powderhouse Fields, 156
Powell, Captain, of *Lady Granby*, 202
Powell, Mr, solicitor to the Mint, 47
Pownall Square Market, 32
Pownall Street, 187
Pownall, William, Mayor of Liverpool (1767-68), 32, 187
Preeson's Row, 60
Prescot, 37, 39, 44, 92, 210, 229
Prescot Lane *see* Prescot Street
Prescot Road, 92
Prescot Street, 94, 107, 129, 222
pressgangs, 82, 197-200
Preston, 29, 37, 45, 52, 97
Price family, lords of the manor of Birkenhead, 177
Price Street, 177
Price's provision shop, Old Haymarket, 100
Price's Square *see* Cleveland Square
Prince Edwin Street, 206
Prince of Wales Theatre, 72
Prince Regent, *later* George IV, 132, 154
Prince, Revd., schoolmaster, 163
Prince Rupert's Cottage, 215–16

Prince’s Dock, 10, 23
Prince’s Parade, 202
Prince’s Pier and Landing Stages, 189
Prince’s Street, 37, 74
Prior, Mr, proprietor of school, 123
Prior, Mrs, proprietor of school, 123
Prior's schools, Pembroke Place, 123
Priory, Church Street, 224
Priory Road, 213
Prison Weint, *b/w ill. 3*, 16, 18
prisons, 188–89
  Borough Gaol, Great Howard Street, 24
  Borough Gaol, Water Street, 17
  Everton cage, 215
  House of Correction, Brownlow Hill, 40, 157–58
  hulks, off Rock Ferry, *col. ill. 3*
  Kirkdale Prison, 49
  Mordyke House, 6
  Powder House, 157
privateering, 61, 66, 73, 174, 197, 201, 202, 210
Promoli, Mr, shopkeeper, Church Street, 73
Ptolemy's map, 189, 190
public houses (*see* also hotels)
  *Angel and Crown*, Dale Street, 38
  *Bear*, 120
  *Black Horse*, High Street, 108
  *Blue Bell Inn*, 94, 160
  *Bull and Punch Bowl*, Dale Street, 38
  *Bull*, Warbrick Moor, 31
  *Castle Inn*, Scotland Road, 224
  *Cross Keys*, Dale Street, 38
  *Ferry House*, 16
  *Fishing Smack*, Chapel Street, 9
  *Folly Tavern*, 103
  *Gallows Mill*, 93, 96
  *George*, Dale Street, 38
  *Gibson's Coffee House*, Folly Gardens, 103
  *Golden Fleece*, Dale Street, 37, 38, 82
  *Golden Lion*, Dale Street, 37
  *Green Man Still*, 94
  Greetham Street, 178
  *Half Way House*, Everton Lane, 222, 223
  *Hindes*, 8
  *King's Arms,* Castle Street, 56
  *King's Arms,* Water Street, 56
  *Legs of Man*, 96
  *Liverpool Arms Inn*, Castle Street, 56
  *Loggerheads Revived*, Richmond Row, 167
  Low Hill, 221
  *Mill Stone and Castle*, Dale Street, 38
  *Mother Red Cap's house*, Seacombe, 194
  *Odd House,* Breck Road, 31, 219, 221
  *Old Style House*, 8
  *Peacock*, 169
  *Pine Apple Tavern*, 169
  *Polly Tittle's*, 98
  *Pontacks*, Water Street, 75, 108, 211
  *Rainbow*, High Street, 108
  *Red Lion*, inn, Dale Street, 38
  *Salmon*, Chapel Street, 9
  *Saracen's Head*, Dale Street, 38, 93, 135
  St James's Mount, 181
  *Star and Garter*, Paradise Street, 186
  *Talbot*, Water Street, 11, 93
  *Throstle's Nest*, Scotland Road, 47-48
  *White Dog*, Church Street, 73
  *White House Tavern*, 82-83
  *Windmill Inn,* London Road, *col. ill.4*

*Wishing Gate*, 23
*Wool Pack*, Dale Street, 38
Public Library, 81, 103
Public Offices, Dale Street, 36'
Public Walk, 81
Pudsey Street, 94, 96
Pugh, Revd. R.L., curate of St Nicholas', 7
Pulford, Dr, 160
Pump Field, Bold Street, 78
Pumpfields, Vauxhall Road, 30

**Q**

Quadrant, 89
Quaker's Alley, 28
Quakers' Meeting House, Hackins Hey, 28
*Quakers' Road see* Stockton and Darlington Railway
Quakers' School, London Road, 82
Quakers' School, Quaker's Alley, 28
the Quarry, 5, 178
Queen Anne Street, 50, 165, 166
Queen Insurance Buildings, Dale Street, 38
Queen Street, 21
Queen's Dock, 173, 212
Queen's Hall, 78, 153
Queen's Hotel, 90
Queen's Square, 79
Queen's Theatre *see* Adelphi Theatre

**R**

Radcliffe, Sir Richard, Sheriff of Lancashire, 13
Radley, James, 84
Raffles, Revd. Dr Thomas, pastor of Great George Street Chapel, 110–11, 131, 223
Ragged Schools, Everton, 214
railway stations
Central, *b/w ill. 15*
Lime Street, 85, 86, 91
Otterspool, 169
Tithebarn Street, 48
*Rainbow*, High Street, 108
Raincock, Fletcher, councillor, 151
Raine, Mr, barrister, 163
Rainford Gardens, 68
Rake Lane *see* West Derby Road
Ralph, Mr, pastor, Bethesda Chapel, Hotham Street, 158
Ranelagh Gardens, 82-83, 103
Ranelagh Place, *b/w ill. 15*, 79, 84, 15
Ranelagh Street, *formerly* the Way to Manchester, *b/w ill. 15*, 58, **78–84**
Rathbone family, 28, 180
Rathbone, Hughes, and Duncan, 84
Rathbone, Mr, shipbuilder, 187
Rathbone, Penelope, 28
Rathbone, W. D., 74, 228
Rathbone, William, philanthropist, 84
Rathbone Street, 55, 180
*Rats' Castle*, 107
Ray and Miles' bedding warehouse, Hotham Street, 95
Raymond, Mr, actor, 75
Red Dick, 82
*Red Lion*, inn. Dale Street, 38
Red Noses, caves, 194
Redcross Street, *originally* Tarleton's New Street, 10, 58, 61, 187
Renshaw, Miss, later Mrs Phibbs, 84
Renshaw, Rector, 155
Renshaw Street, 58, 79, 80, 171
reservoir, 225–26
Revenue Buildings, 64, 74
Reynolds, Sir Joshua, 74
Ribble, river, 190
Richard of Mapelduram, 27

Richardson, Mr, landowner, 157
Richmond family, 101, 167
Richmond, Revd. H. rector of Liverpool, 26
Richmond, Revd. Leigh, author, 25–26
Richmond Fair, 166
Richmond Meadows, 167, 222
Richmond Row, 25, 43, 44, 45, 46, 164, 165, 166, 167
Richmond Row Market, 43
Rigby, Peter, 102
Rigby's Buildings, Dale Street, 38, 39
Riley, Mr, 29
Riley's Gardens, 29
riots
  of 1759, 25
  of 1775, 53, 178, 185-6
River Mersey, *col. ill. 3,* 21, 22, 64, 175, 186, **189–204**
Rivington lakes, 225
Rivington Pike, 208
Rivington water, 99
Road and Railway Omnibus Company, 94
the Road to the Park, *see* Park Lane
*Rob Roy*, coach, 38
Robinson, Nicholas, Mayor of Liverpool (1828-29), 161
Robinson, Peggy (*later* Mrs Meadows), 51
Rock Ferry, *col. ill. 3,* 172, 193, 204
Rock Point, 49
Rocky Lane *see* West Derby Road
Rodney Street, **147–53**, 154, 155, 156, 161
Rodney, Admiral George Brydges, first Baron, 149
Roe Street, 10
Roger, son of Elkinwald, 27
Rogers, Captain of *Marchioness of Granby*, 202
Roman Catholic churches *see* chapels
Romer, Mr, 203
roperies, 79, 80, 85, 147, 179
  Machell's roperies, 77
  Phythian Street, 113
  Staniforth's roperies, 76, 77
Roscoe, William, 74, 75, 146, 228
  bank, 55, 155
  birthplace, 148
  legal business, 37, 68, 73
  popularity, 56, 154-55
  proposed Exchange building, 55-56
  residences, 73, 104, 148, 154
  sale of works of art and library, 154
Roscoe's Bank, 55
Roscommon Street, 206, 230
Rose, Joshua, 44, 230
Rose Hill, 18, 44, 79
Rose Place, *b/w ill. 8*, 44, 49, 51
Rose Street, 89
Rose Vale, 44, 48
Roskell, Robert, watchmaker, 155
Roughsedge, Mrs, landowner, 179
Roughsedge, Revd., rector of St Nicholas', 7
Roundhouse, 217
Routledge's shop, London Road, 99
Rowe, Mr, 90
Rowe, Thomas, 56
Royal Bank Buildings, Dale Street, 38
Royal Institution, Colquitt Street, 75, 162, 179
Royal Insurance Offices, 39
Royal Road *or* King's Highway, 27
Runcorn, 171, 185, 190, 203
Rupert, Prince, 15, 21, 36, 65, 91, 208, 215, 216
Rupert Lane, 214, 218, 228
Rupert Terrace, 214
Rupert's Drop, 97
Rushton, Edward, 71, 95, 151

Russell Street, 50, 156, 158, 159
Rutson, William,broker, 155, 162-63
Rutter, Dr John, founder of Athenaeum, 75, 162
Ryley, Samuel William, the Itinerant, 55, 71

**S**

Sadler, John, engraver, 101
Sadler, Mr, balloonist, 76
Sadler's Bathing Establishment, Hanover Street, 76
Sailors' Home, 162
Salem Chapel, Russell Street, 158–59
Salisbury, Marquis of, 230
Salisbury Street, 105
*Salmon*, public house, Chapel Street, 9
salt works *see* Liverpool Salt Works
Salthouse Dock, 8, 32, 173, 186, 187, 188
Salthouse Lane, 183
Sandbach, Samuel, Mayor of Liverpool (1831-32), 161, 162
Sandemanian Chapel, Cumberland Street, 35
Sandemanian Chapel, Gill Street, 123
Sandwich, Lord, 122
Sanspareil Theatre, 80
*Saracen's Head*, coaching house, Dale Street, 38, 93, 135
Saunders, Joseph, 87
Sawney Pope Street, 42, 44
Scanlion, James, 8
Scarborough, Earl of, 177
Scarlatt, Mr, later Lord Abinger, barrister, 163
Scarsbrick, Mr, 101
Schlink Street, proposed name for Rodney Street, 149
Schomberg Street, 113
School for the Blind, 94-96, 129, 150
School for Deaf and Dumb, 129
School Lane, *formerly* Ware Street, 69, 71, 73, 165
schools
  Blind School, 94-96, 129, 150
  Bluecoat School, 7, 69, 108, 164–65, 206
  Bolton Street, 86
  Daulby's ladies school, 121
  Dr Pulford's day academy and boarding school, Norton Street, 160
  ladies' school, Rupert Lane, 228
  Lewin's school, 148
  Mill Lane, 224
  Miss Mason's school for poor girls, 130–31
  Moorfields School, 7
  Mr Brunner's school, Everton, 209
  Prior's schools, Pembroke Place, 12
  Quakers' School, London Road, 82
  Quakers' School, Quaker's Alley, 2
  Ragged Schools, Everton, 214
  School for Deaf and Dumb, 129
  St Anne's Industrial Schools, Mason Street, 131
  St Bees, 224
  St Chrysostom's Schools, Mill Lane, 224–25
  St Jude's, 107, 108
  St Simon's, 95
Scotch Church, Oldham Street, 33
Scotch Church, Rodney Street, 153
Scotland Place, *b/w ill. 8*, 43
Scotland Road, *formerly* New Scotland Road, *b/w ill. 8,* 25, 30, **44–52**, 16 224
Scott, Dr, lecturer, 151
Sea Brow, 187
Seacombe, 193, 194, 196, 204
Seacombe, Mr, 214

Seaman's Museum, 116
Seamen's Home, 168
Seamen's Hospitals, Shaw's Brow, 91
Seckerston, Ralph, Mayor of Liverpool (1550-51), 15
Seel Street, 75
Seel, Thomas, merchant, 75
Sefton, Earls of *see* Molyneux family
Seymour Street, *b/w ill. 23*, 96, 159
Shafter, Mr, fisherman, 9
Shallcross, Miss, 227
Shand, Mr, 213, 214
Shaw, John, 218
Shaw, John, Mayor of Liverpool (1794-95 and 1800-01), 99–100
Shaw, Mr, 79
Shaw, Mr,potter, 36
Shaw, Thomas (Squire Shaw), 218
Shaw, William, surveyor of roads, 218
Shaw Street, *b/w ill. 20*, 205, 218
Shaw's Brow, *later* William Brown Street, *b/w ill. 18*, 25, 36, 39, 91, **99-102** *see also* William Brown Street
Sheil Park, 121
Shelhorne Street *see* Skelhorne Street
Shepherd, Revd. Dr William, minister of Unitarian Chapel, Gateacre, 33, 41, 71, 95
Sheppard, Mr, 228
Shimmin Street, 131
ships
*Aurora,* 200-01
*Carnatic,* French East Indiaman, 174
*Duchess of Clarence,* 204
*Emilie St Pierre,* 201
*Golden Lion,* whaler, 200
hulks, off Rock Ferry, *col. ill. 3*
Kent East Indiaman, 180
*La Liberte,* 210
*L'Equite,* French merchantman, 201
*Lady Granby,* 202
*Marchioness of Granby,* 202
*Mentor,* privateer, 174
*Mersey,* privateer, 201
*Pelican,* privateer, 204
*Pilgrim,* privateer, 210
*Upton,* 199
*Vengeance,* 200
*Winchelsea,* man-of-war, 199
Shrigley Park, Cheshire, 121
Shuter, Mr, manager of Drury Lane Theatre, 57
Sicily, King of, 210
Sick Man's Lane *see* Addison Street
siege of Liverpool, 6, 35, 39, 65, 215–16
Silkhouse Lane, *b/w ill. 5*
Silver Street, 81
Simmons Wood, 170
Simpson Street, 172
Sir Thomas's Buildings, Dale Street, 34, 35
Skelhorne Street, 58, 85
Slater Street, 179
slave trade, 26, 197
Sleeper's Hill, 210
Smith, Egerton, founder and editor of *Liverpool Mercury*, 71, 74, 111, 151, 203
Smith, William, 224
Smithdown Lane, 126, 129, 130, 140, 142, 145–46, 147, 156, 169
Smithum, manor of *see* Toxteth Park
Smolt, Edmund, 170
Soho Street, 50, 167
Solomon, Dr Samuel, inventor of 'Balm of Gilead', 123–25, 228
Solomon's Place *see* Brownlow Street
Sommerton, Mr, publican, 23
Sorge, Mr, tobacconist, 96

South Castle Street, *formerly* Liverpool Lane, Pool Lane, Water Lane, 61, 86, 125
South Dock *see* Salthouse Dock
South Hunter Street, 155
South John Street, *formerly* Love Lane, Trafford's Weint, 66, 70
South Shore, 170
Southport, 12
Sparling, John, Mayor of Liverpool (1790-91), 173, 180, 211-12
Sparling, Lieutenant William, 187
Sparling Street, 173, 212
Spencer, Colonel, 177
Spencer, Lawrence, Mayor of Liverpool (1759-60), 5
Spencer, Mr, photographer, 181
Spencer, Revd. Thomas, 33, 171
Spring Garden, tea garden, 180–81
Springfield, 163, 165
Springfield Street, 166
St Andrew's Church, Heathfield Street, 81
St Anne Street, *b/w ill. 24*, 79, 100, 104, 114, 153, 154, 160–68
St Anne's Church, 49, 163, 166
St Anne's Industrial Schools, Mason Street, 131
St Anthony's Church, 47
St Anthony's Churchyard, 48
St Anthony's Place, 45
St Augustine's Church, Everton, 220
St Augustine's Churchyard, 218
St Bees School, 224
St Catherine's Church, Russell Street, 158
St Chrysostom's Church, 114, 224-28
St Chrysostom's Schools, Mill Lane, 224–25
St Clements' Church, Russell Street, 159
St Domingo Estate, Everton, 173, 210-11
St Domingo Grove, 210
St Domingo House, Everton, 187, 212-13
St Domingo Pit, 109, 209, 215, 219
St Edward's College, Everton, 212
St George's Church, Derby Square, *b/w ill. 26*, 60, 61, 67
St George's Church, Everton, 49, 207, 208, 220, 224, 226
St George's Crescent, *b/w ill. 9*
St George's Hall, *b/w ill. 19*, 91, 223
St George's Hill, *formerly* Lodge Lane, 209
St George's Insurance Company, 20
St George's Market, 61, 67
St George's Pier, 202
St Helen's Church, Sefton, 8
St James's Cemetery, 181
St James's Church, Park Road, 180
St James's Church, West Derby, 51
St James's Hall, 89
St James's Market, 180
St James's Mount, *originally* Mount Zion, 181
St James's Place, 86
St James's Road, 147
St James's Street, 43, 179
St John the Evangelist Church, Hope Hall, 149
St John's Cemetery, 58, 90
St John's Church, *b/w ill. 16*, 90, 95
St John's Lane, 79, 90
St John's Market, 10, 58, 80
St John's Village, 101
St John's Yard, 90
St Joseph's Roman Catholic Chapel, Grosvenor Street, 49
St Jude's Church, 48, 139
St Jude's Schools, 107, 108

St Luke's Church, Bold Street, 78
St Mark's Church, 147
St Martin's Church, 48–49
St Martin's Market, 43, 45
St Mary's Church, Edge Hill, 49, 130, 138
St Mary's Church, Walton, 6, 8, 52
St Mary's Lane, 149
St Matthew's Church, 48
St Michael's Church, 48–49
St Nicholas' Church, *b/w ills. 2, 26*, **6–9**, 10, 15, 53, 72, 194
St Nicholas' Churchyard, 6, 8, 16, 151, 187
St Patrick's Cross, 29, 45
St Paul's Church, *b/w ill. 26,* 26, 150, 179
St Peter's Church, *b/w ill. 13,* 71, 72
St Peter's Churchyard, 17, 72
St Simon's Church, 35
St Simon's Schools, 95
St Stephen's Church, Byrom Street, *b/w ill. 19*, 41
St Thomas's Church, Park Lane, *b/w ill. 25*, 132, 178
St Vincent Street, *b/w ill. 23*, 96
Stafford Street, 93, 96, 97, 98, 99
Stanhope Street, 172
Staniforth, Mr, 214
Staniforth, Mr, owner of roperies, 76, 77
Stanley family, **13-16**, 22, 30, 188
  Stanley, Sir John, 13
  Stanley, Lord Thomas, 13
  Stanley, Edward, third Earl of Derby, 14
  Stanley, Sir Thomas, son of third Earl, 202
  Stanley, Henry, fourth Earl of Derby, 14-15
  Stanley, William, sixth Earl of Derby Mayor of Liverpool (1603-04), 170
  Stanley, James, Lord Strange, seventh Earl of Derby, Mayor (1625-26) and MP for Liverpool, 15
  Stanley, James, tenth Earl of Derby, Mayor of Liverpool (1707-08 and 1734-35), 16
  Stanley, Edward, eleventh Earl of Derby, 91
  Stanley, Edward, twelfth Earl of Derby, 87, 102
  Stanley, Edward, thirteenth Earl of Derby, 117
Stanley Street, 35, 53
Stanlow, 204
*Star and Garter*, Paradise Street, 186
Startup and Brown, medicine sellers, 90
Statham family, 223
Statham, Mr, registrar of Liverpool County Court, 89
Statham, William, Town Clerk of Liverpool, 67
Steers family, 75
Steers, Thomas, engineer of Old Dock, 75
Stephen's Lane *see* Stephen's Weint
Stephen's Weint, 28
Stevenson, Robert, 139
Stithe, Revd. Robert, rector of St Nicholas' Church, 72
Stockton and Darlington Railway, *known as* Quakers' Road, 87
Stockton Heath, battle of, 220
stone quarries, 107, 130, 180–81
Stonewall Street, 207
Stoniers' glass warehouse, Lord Street, 68
Stork Hotel, 90
Stowell Brown, Revd. Hugh, 89
the Strand, 182, 187

Strand Street, 187
Strawberry Gardens, 225
Stretton, Revd. Thomas, minister of St Catherine's Russell Street, 158–59
Stringfellow's nursery, 108
*Style House,* tavern, 8
Survey of Toxteth Park, 125
Sutton's Yard, 180
Swain, Mr, Wesleyan missionary, 112
synagogues
  Cumberland Street, 35
  Frederick Street, 35

**T**

Tabley Street, 173
*Talbot,* coaching house, Water Street, 11, 93
Tall House, 172
*Tally-ho*, coach, 38
Tarleton family, 71, 72
Tarleton, Captain, 177
Tarleton, Colonel, 61
Tarleton, Edward, council man, 65
Tarleton's New Street, *see* Redcross Street
Tarlton, Miss, 206
Tate, Elizabeth *see* Williamson, Mrs Joseph
Tate, Thomas Moss, tobacco merchant, 132
Taylor, Mr,bookseller, Paradise Street, 70
telegraph, 6
telegraph station, Beacon Hill, 208-09
Temperance Hotel, 72
Tempest, Colonel, 129
Tempest family, 29
Tempest Hey, 28, 29
Temple Bar, 60
Temple, Dale Street, 38
Temple Lane, 34
Temple of Jupiter Panhellenus, Aegina, 95
tennis courts, 29, 49, 50, 72
Tetlow, Parson, 163
Teutonic Hall, 89
Theatre Royal, Williamson Square, 75, 103, 168
theatres
  Adelphi Theatre, *formerly* the Circu Queen's Theatre, Victoria Theatr 167–68
  Alexandra Theatre, Lime Street, *lat* Empire Theatre, *col. ill. 5*
  Drury Lane Theatre, 57
  Liver Theatre, 75
  Prince of Wales Theatre, 72
  Sanspareil Theatre, 80
  Theatre Royal, Williamson Square, 75, 103, 168
Thom, Dr David, minister of Scotch Church, 78, 111, 153
Thomas, Mr, 229
Thomas Street, 70
Thomson, Captain, of *Golden Lion*, 2
Thornley, Mr, tailor, Lord Street, 77
*Throstle's Nest*, tavern, 47-48
Thurot, Though, 7, 208
Tinne, Mr, 162
Tipping, Mr, 129
Tithebarn Lane *see* Tithebarn Street
Tithebarn Street, *formerly* Moor Stree Tithebarn Lane, *b/w ill. 5*, **27–33**, 48
Tobin family, 153
Tobin's cooperage, 77
Toffee Shop, Everton, 214, 216-17, 2 230
toll-houses, 43
Tolson, Mr, 109
Tontine Building, Lord Street, 77

Tooke, Mr, shopkeeper, Church Street, 73
Topping, Mr, barrister, 163
Tower Buildings, 6, 12
Tower Gaol, 16-18
Tower Garden, 16, 19
Tower Hill, 198
Tower of Liverpool, 12, **13-19**, 40, 187
Tower Stairs, 198
Town Hall, Dale Street, *b/w ills. 6, 10 26*, 11, 53, 54, 55
Towns-end, 99
Townsend bridge, 39
Townsend House, 39, 40
Townsend Lane *see* Byrom Street
Townsend Mill, 102
Toxteth, manor of, 169
Toxteth Park, 14, 81, **168–74**, 181
  Lodges, 169, 180
  Survey, 125
Trafford Lane, 66
Trafford's Weint, 66, 67, 71
Traill, Dr Thomas Stewart, 162
Tranmere, 193, 202
Tranmere Hotel, 194
Trinity Place, 163
Trinket Street *see* Fox Street
Trollope Street *see* Pellew Street
Trowbridge Street, 96
Trueman Street, 30
tunnels, 19
  Mersey tunnels, 196
  Williamson's tunnels, *col. ill. 2,* 130-31, 136, **138-46**
Turner, Miss, heiress, 121–22
Turner, Mr, of Shrigley Park, Cheshire, 121
Turner, Mrs, 121
Turner, Revd. Henry, minister of All Saints, 50
Tuton, Mr, 88, 89, 90


**U**


Underhill, Samuel, 156
Union Bank, Brunswick Street, 54
Union Newsroom, 75
Union Street, *b/w ill. 9*, 21, 22
Upper Baker Street, 113
Upper Duke Street, 147, 150
Upper Mason Street, 130
*Upton*, ship, 199
Utting, Cecilia, 33


**V**


Vane Street, 110
Vansittart, Mr, 184
Vause, Revd. Dr, incumbent of Christ Church, 162
Vauxhall bridewell, 30
Vauxhall Road, 27, 30, 33, 74, 78
*Vengeance*, ship, 200
Vernon Hall Lane, 224
Vernon Street, 29
Victoria Theatre *see* Adelphi Theatre
Vipond, Mathew, 203
Virgil Street, 44, 45, 46
Virginia Street, 25
Vivian Street, 109


**W**


Wakefield, Edward Gibbon, 121–22
Wakefield, Revd. Gilbert, curate of St Paul's Church, 26, 179
Walker, Mr, revenue cutter, 204
Walker Street, 110, 113
Wallasey, 191
Wallasey Hill, 189
Walpole, Sir Robert, 184
Walsingham, Sir Francis, 15
Walton, 28, 72
Walton, Robert, 188
Wapping, 20, 52, 173, 199

Warbrick Charities, 59
Warbrick Moor, 31, 59
Warbrick, Richard, 59
Warbrick's Charity, 59
Ware Street *see* School Lane
Warren, Samuel , Q.C., author of *Diary of a Physician*, 149
Warrington, 19, 26, 38, 92, 131, 179, 186, 190, 211, 220
Warrington Academy, 26
Warrington Close, 157
Washington Hotel, 90
Washington Street, 116, 180
Waste Lands Commission, 131
Water Lane *see* South Castle Street
Water Street, *formerly* Bank Street, Bonke Street, *b/w ill.* 3, **10–20**, 55, 56, 57, 58, 69, 75, 108, 175, 178, 187, 194, 211
Waterhouse family, 206, 207
Waterhouse, Mr, 213
Waterhouse Lane, 207
Waterhouse Street, 207
Watering Pond, 29
Waterloo, battle of, 56, 208
Waterloo Dock, 188
Waterloo Hotel, 77
Waters, Madame, 7
Waterworth's Fields, 85, 86
Watson, Dr George C., 140
Watson, Lieutenant, 208
Watson's cabinet maker's, London Road, 98
Watt, Mr, merchant, 180
Wavertree, 65, 79
Wavertree, manor of, 230
Wavertree Nook, 92
Wavertree Road *see* Pembroke Place
the Way to Manchester *see* Ranelagh Street
the Way to Ormskirk *see* Marybone
the Way to the Quarry *see* Duke Street
the Way to Warrington *see* London Road
the Way to Wavertree *see* Brownlow Hill
Weaver River, 184
*Weekly Advertiser*, 101
Wellington Monument, *b/w ill. 19*, 102
Wellington Street, 45
Wellington Terrace, 113, 114
wells, 77, 221–22
Dye-House Well, Greetham Street, 178
Fall Well, 90
Shaw's Brow, 101
Wesley, John, 177
Wesleyan chapels *see* chapels
West Derby, 12, 13, 51, 65, 104, 106, 113, 114, 120, 222
West Derby, manor of, 230
West Derby Road, *formerly* Rake Lane Rocky Lane, *b/w ill. 21*, 105, 109, 110, **113–22**
West Derby Street, *formerly* Pembroke Road, 129
West India Association of Liverpool, 127
West, Montgomery, (Bishop West), 50
Westmacott, Mr, sculptor, 98
Westmorland Place, 45
White Cross, 5, 19
White Cross Market, 5
*White Dog*, tavern, Church Street, 73
*White House Tavern*, 82, 83, 103
White Mill Street, 81
Whitechapel, *formerly* Frog Lane, *b/w ill. 11*, 34, 36, 66, 70, 71, 97
Whitefield House, 229
Whitefield Lane, 225, 229
Whitfield, James, council man, 65

Whitty, M. J., proprietor and editor of the *Liverpool Daily Post* and *Journal,* 207
Wholesale Vegetable Market, 103
Whyte, Mrs, 112
Wigan, 5, 22, 55, 97
William Brown Street, *formerly* Shaw's Brow, *b/w ill. 19*, 99–102 *see also* Shaw's Brow
William of Gloucester, Prince, 147, 212
*William*, ship, later Mariner's Church, 180
Williamson family, 56–57, 71
Williamson, John, Mayor of Liverpool (1761-62), 9
Williamson, Joseph, 'King of Edge Hill', 131–46 *see also* tunnels : Williamson's tunnels
Williamson, Mr, 30, 72, 188
Williamson, Mrs Joseph, *formerly* Miss Tate, 132, 138
Williamson, Richard, 56–57
Williamson Square, 57, 71, 72, 103
Williamson Street, 72
*Williamson's Advertiser*, 27, 37, 57, 61, 72, 73, 82, 95
Williamson's Fields, 72
Willis, Mr, 228
Willis, of London, organ manufacturers, 228
Willmer's Buildings, 69
Wilmer, Edward, 69
Wilson, Captain, of *Emilie St Pierre*, 201
Wilson, Mary, 111-12
*Winchelsea,* man-of-war, 199
*Windmill Inn,* London Road, *col. ill. 4*
windmills, 36, 81, 82, 95, 97, 102, 154
Wirral peninsular, 170
*Wishing Gate*, public house, 23
Wolstenholme Square, 132
Wood Street, 76
Woodhouse, Samuel, 210
Woods, Mr, 203
Woodside, 193, 194, 197, 202
*Wool Pack*, inn, Dale Street, 38
Woolfield, Mr, 73
Woolpack ramparts, 21
Woolton, 65
workhouses, 71, 148
  Brownlow Hill, 157
  College Lane, 76
  Low Hill, 107
Worsley, Ralf, of Worsley, 197
Wray Castle, Windermere, 155
Wrekin, 208
Wren Street, 223
Wren, Mr, 67
Wright family, 206
Wright, John, Mayor of Liverpool, (1816-17), 163
Wright, Mr, builder of Liverpool Baths, 22
Wright, Mr, painter, 74
Wyke, John, watchmaker, 36-37, 74
Wyke's Court, 36, 37

**Y**

Yates, Mr, merchant, 177
York Street *formerly* George Street, 178, 179
York Terrace, 229

**Z**

Zoological Gardens, 113, 114, **116–21**

<u>List of Subscribers to the 2002 edition</u>

Abbott, Edna
Abernethy, Ian
Ablewhite, Rita
Adams, Geoffrey
Adamson, Lyn, and Family
Alcock, Graham
Alcock, John
Alecock, Cynthia
Alecock, Edward
Alexander, Mrs E
Allan, Helen Ford
Allaton, David Edward
Allen, Arthur J
Andrews, Alan W
Andrews, M
Antrobus, Cllr Dave
Ardrey Family
Armitage, John
Ashcroft, Mrs E A
Ashcroft, Neil
Ashton, Annie
Ashton, James David
Aspinall, Bev
Athenaeum, Liverpool
Atherton. Sue
Bailey, F G
Baker, Mrs A
Balshaw, Lisa & Mark
Bancroft, George
Banks, Kenneth John
Bannon, J J
Barklem, George
Barlow, Lyn
Barnes, Peter J
Baron, Ray
Batson, Jean
Bawden, Diana
Bebington Family History Society
Belchem, Prof J C
Bell, Barry

Bennett, Wendy & Ian
Bennett, Mrs A M
Bennett, Mrs J
Bernard, Stephen F
Berry, C
Berthelsen, Bertel
Bessant, Roger and Loraine
Betteridge, Clive
Bettison, Norman, Esq., QPM, Chief Constable, Merseyside Police
Bickerton, Mrs Sandra
Billison, John Anthony
Billows, J
Bingham, Elizabeth M
Binks, Sheila
Binnie, Philippa
Birch, Ms E M
Bird, James
Birtill, Paul
Bishton, Patricia
Blackman, Mrs E
Blair, Paul
Blanchard, Edward
Blease, Andrew James
Blennarhassett, Paul and Jill
Bloxham, Mrs Irene
Boardman, Dr Frank
Boardman, Mark & Joyce
Boardman, Terry & Margaret
Boggs, Pamela Elizabeth
Bolger, Mrs S
Bonney, Mr James
Boswell, W E & D T
Bottley, Len
Bowen, Robert E
Bowler, B
Brady, Debbie
Brannigan, Miss A
Brellisford, Mr G G
Brennen, M M
Brent, Mrs V C
Brett, Bernard
Brian, Michael E
Brinkman, Maureen

Briody, Terence
Briody, Thomas & Margaret
Broad, C P
Brocken, Christine A
Brogden, Anne W
Brooks, Barbara & Tony
Brooks, Mr Walter
Brookside PRU
Brown, Anita
Brown, Dot & Dave, & Family
Brown, John Stowell
Brown, Ted
Browne, John Wills
Browning, Barbara M
Burden, Barbara
Burgess, Elizabeth, nee Thomas
Burgess, Janet L
Burgess, Tommy
Burman, Lionel
Burnip, Janet
Burnip, Tony
Burns, Mr J E
Burquest, A F
Burton, Kenneth V
Burton, Mrs Louise, nee Young
Butler, Andrew and Marjorie
Butler, Frances
Butler, Gordon J
Butterworth, Michael
Buxton, Alfred
Bynon Family
Byrne, Bernadette
Byrne, Denis V
Byrne, Mr Peter
Byrne, Yvonne
Cadman Stewart, Mrs V E
Cadman, Edward Joseph
Cahill, Peter
Callaghan, G R
Callender, Mr B R
Campbell, Ian J F
Campbell, Martha Maria
Campbell, Michael

Canavan, Brian
Canty, Tom
Carder-Hall Family
Carey, June
Carr, Edward
Carrick, Mrs Susan
Carter, Alan S
Cartin, Peter
Carus, Elizabeth Valerie
Casey, Alan
Cass, Maria
Cato, Joyce
Catt, Jeremy
Cattell, John
Cave, W A
Cawley, John C
Chaffers, Ada & George
Chapman, A E
Chapman, Ian M
Cherry, Joe
Chesters, Lhind
Christie, Stuart
Clark, Elaine
Clark, Margaret
Clark, Peter
Clark, Shirley
Clarke, Christina
Clein, Cllr Jan
Clein, Eddie
Clements, Dorothy Jean
Clements, Monica, nee Sterry
Cliff, Vivienne
Cliffe, Alison & Patrick
Cliffe, B
Cliffe, Richard & Tek Lee
Clifford, Mrs M E
Clougher, Muriel
Clubmoor Youth Centre
Clugston, Mark
Cockrell, Brian & Irene
Coghlan, Brian
Cohen, Rhona
Coleman, Paul

Colley, Mr M
Collier, Charles
Conlan, Mrs Ruth
Connell, Elizabeth
Connley, Carol & Brandon
Cook, K C, OBE, FCA
Cooke, Anne
Cooper, Alan T P
Copeland, Pauline A
Copeman, Mark
Corkish, J A
Cotton, Professor Brian
Cottrill, William(Bill)
Couche, Mary
Court, Gary A
Cowman, A
Cox, Alastair S
Crabb, Samuel Albert
Cragg, Margaret J
Cragg, Mrs Maureen
Craske, Bruce
Crawford, Marie and Ray
Cregeen, W A
Crimes, Ralph
Crockford, Mr John B
Crompton, Gordon
Cropper, Michelle Elizabeth
Crosby, T J
Crossey, Paul
Culling, H, FSG & Culling, J
Cunningham, Mrs M A
Curtis, Jean
Dale, Ian J
Dale, John
Davidson, A S
Davies, Doreen & Leon
Davies, Stanley
Davis, J B
Davis, Mrs Gwen
Delahunty, Patrick
Delaney, G
Demellweek, Joseph James Ivey
Devitt, Stephen

Dewhurst, Barbara
Dewhurst, Ronnie C
Dickins, Alan
Dickson, Charles R
Dolman, Francis Henry
Donnellan, Sheila
Doran, Frank, and Family, Liverpool
Douglas, William
Dovedale Junior School
Dowler, Dorothy
Downey, Angela
Downey, Gladys
Downey, Roy
Doyle, James
Drury, Marjorie
Duckworth, Steve (2.28)
Dudley, Stephen
Duggan, Mona
Dunbar, Ann Unsworth
Dunn, Mr M McLeod
Durkin, E
Durose, G A
Dutton, Mrs Linda
Dykes, Colin
Earnshaw, Peter
Earnshaw, Rosemary
Eastwood, Tanya J
Eaves, Ann
Eaves, Robert
Edwards, Eric Arthur
Edwards, Jeffrey
Edwards, Nigel
Edwards, Steve
Ellingham, Ronald
Elliott, Kenneth
Ellis, Nigel
Ellis, Rodney (In memory of)
Emery, Rosalind
Emery, W A (Bill)
Enston, J H
Entwistle, John
Evans, Dorothy Mary
Evans, George

Evans, Tony
Evans, Trevor R
Evans, Winifred
Everett, Mrs Cherie E, MBE
Evetts, Naomi
Fairbrother, Victor E
Fairfax, Margaret
Fairhurst John
Falconer, E
Farrar, Mr Russel
Farrell, Kenneth
Farthing, Doreen Mildred
Fawcett-Smith, Archie
Feelgood Factory
Fellows, Sheila
Fennah, Robert Mark
Ferns, Arthur Dominic
Ferns, John Patrick Michael
Fischer, Mrs E G R
Flack, John A
Fleetwood, Kenneth
Fleming-Yates, Mrs J
Fletcher, Duncan
Fletcher, Mrs & Mrs F E
Floyd, Sydney
Forrest, F T
Forshaw, Roy
Forster, Eric
Forster-Dean, Peter
Fortune Jones, Valerie & Tony
Foster, P J
Fothergill, E
Fowler, Ray
Fraser, Ian
Fraser, Marjorie W
Frayling, Nicholas, The Very Reverend, Dean of Chichester
Freckleton, T
"Fredsons" of Dunluce Street
Freeth, Christine
Friends of Williamson's Tunnels
Frost, Carole
Fullard, Joyce
Gabriel, L W

Gallagher, Susan
Gallimore, Peter & Ann
Gambles, David
Gardner, Mr Joseph
Garrity, Michael
Gavin, Joseph
Gee, David
Gee, William Henry
George, Muriel J
George, William
Gersten, Florence E
Gibb, Eric
Gibb, Raymond
Gillberry, Colonel George K
Gillman, Diane and David
Gilmore, Anne and Tom
Gilmore, John
Gilson, Mellina
Glasgow, Gordon Henry Harper
Godfrey, Mr and Mrs E
Goodman, Dr Mervyn
Goodwin, Peter
Gooseman, Bill
Goth, David
Gowans, Barbara
Grace, Frank
Graham, Maureen
Gray, Joseph Thomas
Greenland, Alfred
Greenway, Russell
Greenwood, E F
Greer, James
Grey, Doreen E
Griffiths, D M
Griffiths, Dominic
Griffiths, Mrs J A
Grifiths, Joe
Grundy, Patricia
Guinan, L
Gurney, M J
Hadfield, Rev. G F
Hainsworth, Mrs V
Hainsworth, William 1901

Hall, Peter A
Hamilton, J G & A C
Hanrahan, Mrs M A
Hanson, Pauline & Peter
Hardcastle, Enid
Harding, Mrs Dorothy, nee Young
Harper, Jean
Harper, John S
Harrison, Barbara C
Harrison, G J
Hawkins, Lyn
Heath, Marg & Graham
Heaton, James Mulgrave
Heaton, Mr R A
Hedley, Doreen & Bill
Henderson, Mr John
Henley-Smith, Pam
Hennessy, Gilian
Henshaw, David
Heyes, B
Hibbert, Jim & Eileen
Higham, Alexandra
Higham, Mr E
Highfield, John
Hill, A J
Hindhaugh, Nena
Hines, Margaret
Hirst, Catherine A
Hirst, Catherine Audrey
Hiscox, Rosemary L
Hobbins, Ruth
Hobbins, Val & Dave
Hodges, Frank
Hodgetts, Lilian
Hodson, Barbara J
Hogg, James, N.Z.
Hogg, John
Hollingsworth, Edith
Holloway, Mr Kevin
Holme, Anthony
Holmes, Leonard T
Holmes, Robert James
Holmes, Teresa

Holt, Lucy
Hope Valley CP School
Hopkins, John
Horn, Hilary
Howard, Michael Thomas
Howard, Rosemary
Howarth, Eric
Howe, Geoff
Howel, Marion
Hughes, Daniel E
Hughes, Edward
Hughes, Emrys
Hughes, George & Margaret
Hughes, George C
Hughes, Idwal
Hughes, Jennifer
Hughes, Mary Kathleen
Hughes, Phil
Hughes, Professor Quentin
Hughes, Richard
Hull, Anthony
Hulse, Enid
Hulse, John
Hulse, Joyce
Hunt, Mrs Margaret
Hunt, Robert
Hunton, Maureen
Hurst, David
Hurst, Mrs Pauline
Husband, L J M
Hussey, Anthony
Hussey, Elsie
Hussey, John
Hutcheon, George
Hyland, Peter
Iles, Chris
Ireland, Leslie
Ireland, Raymond & Margaret
Irving, Cllr Dave
Isam, Henry(Harry)
Isherwood, K H C
Ivison, Eliza
Jackson, Ann & Brian

Jackson, Derrick T L
Jackson, H
Jackson, V A
James, Edward & Sylvia
Jamieson, Gordon
Jamieson, Robert W
Jenkins, Barbara
Jennion, Arthur
Jerabek, Fred
Johnson, Barbara A
Johnson, Patricia J
Johnston, Donald
Johnston, Eileen
Joinson, Frank
Jolly, Lisa
Jones, A E
Jones, Adrian
Jones, D M
Jones, David H
Jones, Dr June
Jones, Ellen
Jones, Glyn F.R.P.S.
Jones, Joan
Jones, Mr Frederick Alan
Jones, Pam & Peter
Jones, Peter G
Jones, Philip James
Jones, Richard H
Jones, Stephen
Jones, Trevor
Jones-Wilde, Margaret
Kattou, Linda
Keane, Catherine
Kearns, Joan Ann
Keenan, Mr Stephen
Kehlenbeck, Frank
Keig, Sydney
Kelly, Frank
Kelly, Ivy
Kelly, John
Kelly, Mrs Avril
Kelly, Mrs T M
Kelly, Patrick

Kemjika, Mabel
Kennedy, Celia
Kennedy, Ron
Kensington CP Infant School
Keogh, Gordon
Kidd, Professor Bill
King, Andrew William
King, Miss Sara Elizabeth
King, Neville
King, Paul J
Kinvig, Sheila
Kirkham, M F
Kirkpatrick, E A & A
Kirwan, Elaine
Kirwan, T
Knowsley Library Service
Lamden, Mr R J
Lancaster, Cllr Bob
Lancaster-Smith, Marjorie
Lang, Elizabeth
Lappin, Mr Philip Joseph
Le Breton, Bill
Leach, Dave
Lebroc, June
Lee, Edward
Lee, Elsie
Leech, H
Leonard, Peter
Lever, Alan
Levin, Ann & David
Levin, Mrs Betty
Levitt, Michael, Riva, Amber & Yonatan
Leyland, Cathy
Leyland, Keith
Liggett, Paul
Lindsay, Bet & Sid
Lister Junior School
Lister, William
Liston, Andrew John
Little Family
Littlemore, Mrs P
Littlemore, Philip J
Liverpool World Heritage Site Bid

Livingston, Ray
Lloyd, G V
Lloyd, Heather M
Lloyd, V
London, Philip
Loughlin, James
Loughran, Sue
Lovering, Roy
Lowe, John
Lumsden, Audrey M
Lunt, Peter John
Lyons, Anne
Lyons, Ernest
Maddocks, Kathleen
Maginn, Monty Blue
Mahoney, Mrs Ethel
Makin, Mr J D
Maloney, Peter John
Manion, Philip
Manley, Albert
Margaret McFarlane/ Hesketh
Maritime Archives and Library(NMGM)
Markwick, Dorothy
Marriette, Margaret
Marsden, Stuart
Martin, Ailna B
Martindale, George Holme
Mason, Harriet Elizabeth
Matthews, Alan S
Maybry, Mary
Mayo, Lucy
Mc Kevitt, P J
McArdle, Edward Terence
McCann, Jo
McCarthy, Jean
McCourt, William
McCrea, A J
McDermott, Robert E
McDonald, Jacqueline
McDonough, Brian
McDuff, Kenneth
McEvoy, John
McGhee, Mr R

McGill, Mr William
McGuinness, Jo-Ann
McIntyre, Mrs N
McKenna, Mr Neil
McKenzie, I S
McKeown, John
McLachlan, Stan
McLoughlin, Joseph
McMahon, M
McMinn, Pat & Ian
McMorine, Alexander F B
McNulty, David
McParlin, Mrs Patricia
McShane, Mrs Pat
Meeson, Jean M
Meldrum, Rose
Mercer, George F
Mercer, Kenneth G
Merricks, Philip N
Merriman, W
Messenger, A
Metcalf, David Peter
Metcalf, Peter
Miller, Dorothy
Millett, Alan
Milling, Leonard
Millington, Chris M
Millington, N
Milne, Mr R
Milton, John L
Minards, Mark
Mochan, E
Molyneux-Johnson, R A
Moore, Ann & James
Moore, Colin
Moore, J F
Moore, John & Venita
Moore, Mrs Gene
Moores, Mrs W D
Moorhead, Claire Natasha
Moran, Ann Rattigan
Moran, Jim
Moran, Joyce

Moran, Kevin
Morley, Phil
Morrell, Heather & Cara
Morris, Ian
Morton, Joan
Mothershaw, Di
Muirhead, Mr K
Muraski, Mrs P
Murgatroyd, Tom
Murley, Leonard
Murphy, John H
Murphy, Linda
Murray, Brenda
Nelson, David
Netherway, Robert
Nevitt, Barbara
Newbold, David P
Newbold, Ron
Newell, A R
Newett, Julie
Ng, Dee & Vincent
Noonan, Edward
Northway Primary & Nursery School
Notre Dame Catholic College
Nowell, Diane
O'Brien, Peter A
O'Brien, Peter N
O'Connor, Freddy
O'Donovan, Margaret Mary
O'Farrell, Bernard
O'Hara, Roger & Lily
Oliver, S G
O'Neil, Jim
O'Reilly, F
Organ, E E
Our Lady of Reconciliation Primary School
Owen, Teresa
Owens, G R
Pallett, Mary
Park, George
Park, James
Park, Peter
Park, Robert

Parker, Daphne (nee Mahon)
Parker, Paul
Parrott, Kay & Tim
Parry, Mr George
Paterson. Don S
Patten, Mr Anthony
Patterson, Brenda
Patterson, Stuart W & Norma
Peace, Martin
Pearce, Andrew
Peers, Lewis
Penman, Dave
Perrins, John N
Perry, S
Petris, Simon Evaris
Phillips, Andrew James
Phillips, Harold
Pierpoint, R Brian
Pimbblet, Edward
Pinto, Dr A
Plant, Gordon(Beau)
Platt, Peter
Pleasant Street School
Polson, Jack & Joan
Poole, Norman
Pooley, Robert J
Pope, Pauline
Porter, Ken & Ruby
Porter, Mr G
Power, Tony
Price, B & T
Price, Barbara & Edward
Price, Jim
Pritchard, Steve
Pritchard, Walter
Procter, Margaret
Pugh, William Frank
Pugh, William Henry
Purcell, Margaret
Pye, Mr C J
Pyper, Dennis
Quade, Anne
Quinn, Michael

Radley, Gordon
Rafferty, Mrs L
Rainford, Suzan & Alan
Rattigan, Tom (in memory of)
Rawes, Jean
Rawlinson, K F
Readdy, Mrs N M
Redman, Don
Reeves, John
Regan, Vincent
Reid, Frank
Reid, Janette & Ian
Reid, Kiron
Reilly, Carol A
Renshaw, Sue
Reynolds, Arthur
Reynolds, Thomas
Rice, David
Richards, Mrs L E
Richardson, Andrew
Richings, Eve
Riley, Martin Robson
Rimmer, Doris
Rimmer, G M
Rimmer, Henry
Roberts, Ann
Roberts, John H L
Roberts, Joyce
Roberts, Margaret
Roberts, Mr & Mrs G O
Roberts, Paul
Roberts, Winifred E
Robertson, Mr Alec
Robinson, Eileen
Robinson, Miss E J
Robinson, Robert
Roche, Joseph
Rockliff, Sheila Roberta
Rogans, B B
Rogers, Mr & Mrs
Rose, Samuel
Rossi, Lynne
Rowan, F J

Rowan, Joyce
Rowson, Dr Freda M
Royle, J A
Ryder-Jones, Angela & Peter
Sanders, Edward
Sargeant, Peter H
Sarsfield, Ian M
Sarsfield, Rodney C
Schulman, Jacque-Lynne
Scott, J L
Seeckts, Roberts Cecil
Sewell, Peter
Sewruk, Frances Fielding
Sharples, C
Sharrock, S G
Shearson, Donna Marie
Shirley & Jimmy
Shirley, Anthony
Shorefields School
Shuttleworth, Thos. H
Simmonds, Debbie
Simpson, George
Simpson, Rod
Sinclair, Roy
Singleton, Richard
Sixsmith, C S H
Slack, Irene
Slack, V E
Slater, Margaret F
Slater, Mrs Anne
Small, John & Penny
Smart, James A
Smith, Alex
Smith, Charles H
Smith, Dorothy M
Smith, Joan Geddes
Smith, Mrs Muriel
Smith, Pamela F
Smith, Robert J
Smith, Robert K
Smith, Scott
Smith, William John
Smyth, John

Southern, Keith
Spike, Ken
Spruce, Jean
St Cleopas Primary School
St Finbar's Catholic Primary School
St Francis Xavier's College
St George's Hall
St Malachy's Catholic Primary School
St Margaret's (Anfield) C of E Junior School
St Margaret's Church of England High School
St Mary's West Derby JMI
St.Austin's School
Stacey, Sheila
Starkey, Daniel F J
Steel, G Anne
Steel, Paul
Stephens, Pete
Stock, William
Stoker Family
Stoker, Patricia & Terry
Stonall. Miss Cynthia
Stone, Jean
Stowe, Mr & Mrs P J
Strauss, Valerie
Stubbs, John & Pat
Sudley Infant School
Sullivan, Alan
Sunners, D C
Sunners, Sheila
Tanner, Carol & Wilson, Simon
Taxi Neil
Taylor, Dr Iain C
Taylor, Harry
Taylor, Janice
Taylor, John
Taylor, June
Taylor, Kenneth G
Taylor, Margaret
Taylor, Ms Mary Iris
Taylor, Paula
Taylor, Robert E
Taylor, Val
Teasdale, Anthony

Thomas, Barbara
Thompson, Madeline
Thompson, S N
Thomson, May & Donald
Threlfall, Alan
Thwaite, Roy
Tibbles, Anthony
Tiernan, John & Diane
Tinkler, Ken
Tinkler, Kenneth
Todd, D W
Tufnell, Gordon F
Turner Family
Turner, Peter, & Family
Tweedie, Philip
Tyndall, Edward
Upton, Gilbert
Vaughan, J E
Ventin, Andrew
Walsh, Margaret
Walsh, Michael Anthony
Walsh, Philip
Walton on the Hill History Group
Wareing, Philip
Warren, Joan
Waterworth, Alan W, Esq., JP, Lord-Lieutenant of Merseyside
Watson, Bill
Watson, J A
Watson, Mrs Ivy
Watterson, David
Webb, Neville & Eileen
Westbury, Mr & Mrs R W
Westgaph, Laurence
Whelehan, Mary
White, Alan E
White, June M
Whitfield, Matthew
Whittle, Joseph
Wilcott, Thomas
Wilcox, Laura Amy
Wilde, K
Wilkinson, Dave
Wilkinson, Pat

Willan, W K
Williams, B
Williams, J D, MRSC
Williams, Jacqueline B
Williams, Jim
Williamson Tunnels Heritage Centre
Wilson, Paul
Winstanley, Frederick
Wishart, James
Wolfenden, John L
Wood, Kathleen
Wood, Morgan C
Woodcock, Nora
Woods, John W
Woodward, P T
Woosey, B J
Woosey, Elizabeth
Workman, Janice Elizabeth
Worthington, Bill
Wray, Moira
Wright, Mr Anthony
Wright, Mrs A J
Wynne, P T
Yates, Mrs Sylvia
Young, Mrs E
Young, Walter